D0495209

THE TIMES

COMPACT
HISTORY
OF THE
WORLD

THE TIMES

COMPACT

HISTORY

OF THE

WORLD

Edited by

Geoffrey Parker

TIMES BOOKS
London

Fifth Edition
First published in 2008 by

TIMES BOOKS

An imprint of HarperCollins Publishers
77-85 Fulham Palace Road
Hammersmith
London W6 8JB

The Collins website address is www.collins.co.uk

First published by Times Books (as *The Times
Compact Atlas of World History*) 1995
Second edition 1997
Third edition 2001
Updated and reprinted 2002
Fourth Edition 2005
Fifth edition 2008

Copyright © Times Books 1995, 1997, 2001, 2002,
2005, 2006, 2008

The Times is a registered trademark of Times
Newspapers Limited, a subsidiary of News
International plc

All rights reserved. No part of this publication
may be reproduced, stored in a retrieval system,
or transmitted in any form or by any means,
electronic, mechanical, photocopying or otherwise
without the prior written permission of the
publisher and copyright holder.

Printed and bound in Hong Kong

British Library Cataloguing in Publication Data
A catalogue record for this book is available from
the British Library

ISBN 978-0-00-726731-6

EDITOR

GEOFFREY PARKER
*Distinguished University
Professor and Andreas
Dorpalen Professor of History
The Ohio State University
Fellow of the British Academy*

Editorial Consultants

Chris Scarre
*McDonald Institute
University of Cambridge*

Richard Overy
*Professor in History
University of Exeter
Fellow of the British Academy*

Editorial Direction

Thomas Cussans
Philip Parker

Cartographic Direction and Design

Martin Brown

Cartographers

Cosmographics, Watford
Bartholomew Mapping Services,
Glasgow

Designer

Colin Brown

Place-names Consultant, Index

Pat Geelan

For Fifth Edition

Editorial direction

Louise Stanley

Design/cartographic revisions

Susie Bell

Research

Helena Nicholls

Contents

PART THREE

The Rise of
the West

PART FOUR

The Modern World

Introduction

This volume, like *The Times Complete History of the World*, which has sold over 2.25 million copies in 17 languages worldwide since its first publication in 1978, attempts to cover the whole story of humankind from its origins, when our ancestors first emerged from the tropical forests of Africa, to the complex, highly articulated world in which we now live.

It differs, however, from the original *History of the World* in three important ways. First, as its name makes clear, it presents the data in a more compact form. Although it includes 80 spreads each contains fewer, simpler maps and (proportionately) more text. Second, every map has been reviewed in order to highlight the salient trends and facts it features. Third, the topics selected for treatment include far more material from the modern period: 24 spreads concentrate on the period since 1914 and no fewer than 17 of them cover the world since 1945.

Nevertheless, although the present volume incorporates new material and differs in several ways from its predecessor, it rests upon the same principles. Above all, it tries to break away from a concentration on Europe and to offer instead a view of history that is worldwide in conception and presentation and which does justice, without prejudice or favour, to the achievements of all peoples, in all ages and in all quarters of the globe. It thus remains true to the vision of the late Geoffrey Barraclough, who planned and edited the *History*:

'When we say this is an atlas of world history, we mean that it is not simply a series of national histories loosely strung together. In other words, it is concerned less with particular events in the history of particular countries than with broad movements – for example the spread of the great world religions spanning whole continents... In singling out topics for inclusion we have adhered to the principle of selecting what was important then rather than what seems important now.'

The essence of history, as Geoffrey Barraclough realized, is change and movement over time; and the historian's principal mission is therefore to discern the static from the dynamic, the aberration from the trend, and the contingent from the constant. So instead of presenting a series of individual snapshots, The *The Times Compact History of the World* emphasizes change, expansion and contraction. It aims to convey a sense of the past as a continuing process and thus to provide a fresh perspective on today's world which will meet the requirements and interests of present-day readers in all parts of the globe.

This new edition incorporates several distinctive features. First, we have updated all the later spreads – both maps and text – and added new spreads to cover developments down to October 2007. Second, other maps have been revised and provided with physical bases. Third the volume includes over 80 images and numerous new tables. Finally, we have corrected errors brought to our attention by readers.

GEOFFREY PARKER
October 2007

ONE

The Ancient World

About 6000 years ago, in a few areas of particularly intensive agriculture, the dispersed villages of Neolithic peoples gave way to more complex societies. These were the first civilizations, and their emergence marks the start of a new phase of world history. They arose, apparently independently, in four widely dispersed areas (the early civilizations of America emerged considerably later): the lower Tigris and Euphrates valleys; the valley of the Nile; the Indus valley around Harappa and Mohenjo-Daro; and the Yellow River around An-yang. The characteristic feature of them all was the city, which now became an increasingly dominant social form, gradually encroaching on the surrounding countryside, until today urban civilization has become the criterion of social progress. But the city possessed other important connotations: a complex division of labour; literacy and a literate class (usually the priesthood); monumental public buildings; political and religious hierarchies; a kingship descended from the gods.

Statue of the pharaoh Ramesses II
Great Temple of Abu Simbel, c. 1257 BC

INTERNET LINKS

www.becominghuman.org
Online documentary on
human evolution

Human origins

**1 Human origins
and colonization of
the world**

**dates of first human
occupation**

5 million to
1.8 million years ago

1.8 million years ago

1.5 million years ago

500,000 years ago

100,000 years ago

50,000 to
5000 years ago

5000 years ago to
AD 1492

fossil sites

○ more than 4 million
years old

◐ Australopithecines

◐ early *Homo
ergaster / rudolfensis*

◐ Asian *Homo erectus*

◐ *Homo
heidelbergensis /
African archaic
Homo sapiens*

○ Neanderthals

◐ late *Homo erectus*

● *Homo sapiens
sapiens*

The earliest known hominine fossils come from the Afar region of Ethiopia and are 4.5 million years old. Between three and four million years ago, skeletal and fossilized footprints of *Australopithecus afarensis* indicate a serviceable if not fully bipedal gait, hands still partly adapted for specialized tree climbing and a brain approximately one-third the size of ours. This species is the probable ancestor both of the robustly built Australopithecines ('southern apes'), all with large teeth and herbivorous diets, and of our genus *Homo* ('man'). These closely related but nonetheless distinct species not only lived at the same time but side by side in the same habitats.

About three million years ago, *Homo* began to undergo important evolutionary trends, acquiring a larger brain and full bipedalism. As larger brains need better diets to sustain them, the increase in brain size must have been accompanied by a move towards an energy-rich diet including animal proteins. And indeed the earliest-known stone tools, found in Gona, Ethiopia, suggest that 2.5 million years ago meat was a central part of hominines' diet. The sharpened stones were used to cut flesh and pound marrow-rich bones from carcasses either scavenged or hunted and then defended against other carnivores. Burnt bones found in southern Africa indicate that by 1.5 million years ago hominines had learned to cook their food, a development which would have aided digestion by breaking down animal proteins before eating.

This pattern of development was the basis for the colonization by *Homo erectus* of areas outside sub-Saharan Africa around 1.8 million years ago. Then, a million years ago *Homo heidelbergensis* migrated into North Africa and the Near East, reaching northern Europe about 500,000 years ago. Both *erectus* and *heidelbergensis* probably shared a common African ancestor,

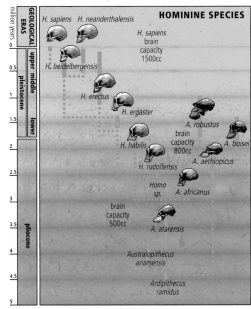

A hand-axe from Olduvai Gorge, Tanzania. Handaxes, which are more efficient butchery tools than stone flakes, began to appear around 1.5 million years ago. This probably coincided with an increase in active hunting – as opposed to scavenging – for meat.

Homo ergaster, best known from the Nariokotome skeleton. All three had brains of about 1,000 cubic centimetres and an adaptable stone technology: the weight and careful shaping of the edges of their distinctive handaxes, whether pointed or oval, made them effective butchery tools.

Stone technology in itself did not play a part in the evolutionary pressures that led to larger brains. The importance of *Homo*'s larger brain had less to do with the food quest than with allowing hominines to remember, to manipulate, to support and to organize others in more complex ways. This in turn allowed them to colonize harsher barrier habitats such as the Sahara at the margins of their homelands from where they could spread into more temperate areas beyond.

From about 500,000 years ago, this early burst of colonization came to a halt. There followed a period during which, through many dispersals of populations and much intermingling of genes, regional populations such as the Neanderthals developed, living side by side with other groups. But from 100,000 years ago, a second major dispersal began when anatomically modern people – *Homo sapiens sapiens* – emigrated from sub-Saharan Africa. By 50,000 years ago, Australia had been reached by boat; 33,000 years ago, the western Pacific islands were colonized; 15,000 years ago, the Americas were reached. Major expansion into the Arctic began about 4500 years as the continental ice sheets retreated. Finally, 2000 years ago, humans began to settle the deep Pacific islands from where they reached New Zealand around 1200 years ago, 1000 years before the island's discovery by Captain Cook.

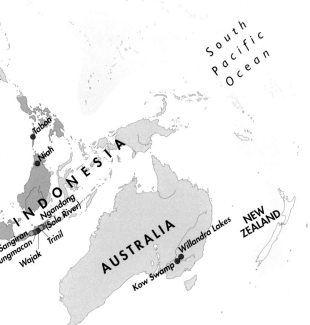

2 Hominine development

13

INTERNET LINKS

**www.bbc.co.uk/science/
cavemen/chronology**
The evolution of
modern man

c.200,000 BC
Emergence of anatomically-
modern humans

c.100,000 BC Migration
of *Homo sapiens sapiens*
northwards from Africa

c.50,000 BC Human
population begins to grow
again after period of
stagnation

c. 25,000 BC Extinction
of Neanderthals

c.10,000 BC End of last
Ice Age

The spread of modern humans

DNA studies have revealed that the first anatomical-ly modern humans (*Homo sapiens sapiens*) arose in Africa between 200,000 and 140,000 years ago. The earliest modern-looking human skulls yet found are about 130,000 years old and come from the Omo basin in Ethiopia and Klasies River Mouth in southern Africa. Around 100,000 years ago, these early populations began to migrate northwards out of Africa.

Archaeological and genetic evidence then point to a further rapid expansion of modern human populations and settlements about 50,000 years ago. There is evidence of lighter, multi-component weapons and of textiles and baskets. Camp sites became more orderly and included cold-weather dwellings and underground food stores. Trading networks also expanded dramatically and raw materials, particularly stone, which had previously been traded over distances of less than 50 miles, were now traded over many hundreds of miles.

Human colonisation of the Old World took place against the background of the Ice Ages. There have been eight Ice Ages in the last 800,000 years, alternating with warmer periods of about 10,000 years known as interglacials. During the Ice Ages, ice sheets advanced across the frozen wastes of the northern hemisphere and temperatures fell by up to 15 degrees centigrade. With so much of the earth's water locked into the ice sheets, sea levels fell,

opening up land bridges, but half the area between the tropics became desert as rainfall diminished. Animals withdrew to warmer latitudes during cold phases and humans, too, must have migrated with these changing climates, although they could also adapt to the cold through the mastery of fire, the invention of clothing, and new social and communication skills.

For many thousands of years, *Homo sapiens sapiens* shared the world with *Homo erectus* in East Asia and with Neanderthals in Europe and West Asia, both groups in many ways as sophisticated and successful in their mastery of their environments as *Homo sapiens sapiens*. The similarities between these contemporary hominine species are in most respects more striking than the differences. Nonetheless, the greater social sophistication of *Homo sapiens sapiens* proved decisive in allowing them to colonize a much wider range of habitats than any previous hominine.

By 12,000 years ago, the last Ice Age was drawing to a close. As temperatures rose, vegetation spread and animals re-colonized the cold northern wastes. With them went hunters and gatherers. Meanwhile, in South-West Asia, people had begun to move beyond their existing resources and to investigate new ways of producing food and manipulating plants and animals in the first experiments in farming.

**2 The spread of
Homo sapiens**

1 The Ice Age world, c. 10,000 BC

maximum extent of ice caps
mammoth steppe
savannah
tropical deserts
tropical forest refuges
forest steppe
grassland scrub
temperate desert
loess
ancient coastline
modern coastline
cave art or significant paleolithic site

Kanto Plain
Sokchang-ri
SIBERIA
Zhoukoudian Upper Cave
Salawusu
Tongliang
Malta
Buret
Shlenka
Shestakovo
Anyi
ASIA
SUNDA
Laharia-Dih
Kanto Plain
Sokchang-ri
Pacific Ocean
SUNDA
SAHUL
Nawamoyn
INDIA
Puritjarra
AUSTRALIA
Koonalda
Lake Mungo
Murray
Kutikina
Pushkari
Kostienki
Amvrosievka
Krakow Spadzista
EUROPE
NEAR EAST
Grotta dei Fanciulli
Kastritsa
Wadi Al-Hammeh
Lascaux
Kebara Cave
Wadi Jilat
Altamíra
Paglicci
Morin
Tamar Hat
Haua Fteah
Parpalló
Taforalt
Wadi Kubbaniya
Nile
Indian Ocean
Sahara
AFRICA
Ishango
Nasera
land-bridge
Arctic Ocean
Depression Cave
Sehonghong
Boomplaas
Nelson Bay Cave

A bison from the caves at Altamíra, near Santander in northern Spain. This 14,000-year-old masterpiece comes from the painted ceiling of a chamber covered with depictions of animals. The painters used more than one colour and exploited the natural contours of the ceiling to give a number of the creatures three-dimensional form. It remains among the most potent and vivid images created by the artists of the late Ice Age in Europe.

The origins of agriculture

INTERNET LINKS

www.bbc.co.uk/dna/h2g2/
a2054675
The Neolithic revolution –
how farming changed the
world

c.10,000 BC Foragers
using sites year-round

c.8000 BC Evidence of
domesticated cereals and
pulses in the Levant

c.6000 BC Evidence of
tree crop cultivation in
tropical Africa

c.7000 BC Evidence of
rice cultivation in China

c.4000 BC Agriculture
established across Europe

c.3000 BC Evidence of
maize cultivation in
Mesoamerica

The period 10,000 to 4000 BC witnessed three critical developments: the origins of settled life; the first farming; and the first cities. The origin of agriculture is often termed the 'Neolithic revolution', but archaeology reveals only gradual changes in techniques of food acquisition over thousands of years until present-day climatic conditions began to prevail, around 8000 BC.

Until then, humankind consisted of bands of hunters and gatherers who, although more numerous than ever before, pursued a lifestyle that differed little from that of their predecessors. In China and west Asia, however, new lifestyles began to develop, based on cultivation rather than collecting plant foods. Within the next 2,000 years substantial villages appeared in certain regions; and 5,000 years later there were towns and cities.

This decisive quickening in the pace of human development stemmed largely from the beginning of agriculture: the deliberate alteration of natural systems to promote the abundance of an exploited species or set of species. Many parts of the globe, especially those between latitude 10° South and 50° North, have contributed to the present-day repertory of domesticated plants and animals (map 1). Among the earliest and most important centres of cereal cultivation were South-West Asia, where the wild ancestors of wheat and barley grew; China and South-East Asia, where millet and rice thrived; and Mesoamerica, which developed maize as a staple crop. In Africa, people in the lands south of the Sahara and in the high grasslands of North-East Africa domesticated a wide variety of native plant species. Generally, cereal cultivation characterized temperate regions while root or tree crop cultivation – potatoes, yams, bananas – predominated in tropical zones.

At the same time, useful local animal species were domesticated to provide meat, milk, hides or wool, and (except in the Americas, which lacked suitable animals) an important source of power for ploughing and other agricultural tasks. On the steppe-lands of central Eurasia, animal-keeping prevailed over plant cultivation, and the domestication of the horse facilitated a specialized life-style based on nomadic herding.

The exact origins of agriculture remain unknown, but once chosen, farming developed a momentum of its own: there was no easy turning back, and the very success of the new lifestyle induced other fundamental changes. The ensuing increase in food resources made possible a spectacular growth of human population between 8000 and 4000 BC. It also required cooperative effort, particularly after the introduc-

MESOAMERICA

Cereals	Pulses
Maize	Common bean
Teosinte	Runner bean
	Tepary bean

Fruits	Other Crops
Avocado	Chilli pepper
Tomato	Squashes

NORTHERN SOUTH AMERICA

Pulses	Root Crops
Common bean	Manioc
	Potato
Lima bean	Sweet Potato
	Yam

Fruits	Other Crops
Guava	Cashew
Pineapple	Chili pepper
Soursop	Cocoa
Sweetsop	Peanut
	Quinoa
	Squashes

MESOAME...

Ta...

ANDES

LOWLA...

Guinea pig

Llama

Alpaca

African rock art painting
From around 9000 BC to 3000 BC the climate in the Sahara was much more favourable than today. Rock art paintings depict a great variety of plants and animals such as elephant, lion and buffalo as well as, from about 6000 BC, domesticated cattle.

tion of irrigation led to the establishment of settled organized societies, at first in villages and later in towns and cities, and the development of new technologies, social systems and ideologies.

The transformation from hunting and gathering to agriculture, from a migratory to a sedentary life, was a decisive event in world history. Hunters and gatherers survived but, as farming spread, they retreated to the marginal world environments where agriculture could not secure a foothold (map 2). Both absolutely and relatively, their numbers declined until today their representatives survive only in hot deserts (the Kalahari and central Australia), in the dense rain forests of the Amazon basin, central Africa and South-East Asia, and in the frozen Arctic. Even there, traditional lifestyles – followed by mankind for millennia – now face the threat of extinction.

2 The decline of hunting and gathering

world distribution of hunter-gathering peoples

15,000 BC
world population: 10 million
% hunters: 100

AD 1500
world population: 350 million
% hunters: 1.0

1960
world population: 3 billion
% hunters: 0.001

1 The origins of domestic plants and animals to 4000 BC

the origins of domestic plants and animals to 4000 BC

NORTH AMERICA

Pacific Ocean

Atlantic Ocean

Reindeer

SOUTH WESTERN STEPPES

CENTRAL ASIA

CHINA

Pig

Horse

Bactrian Camel

Yak

Chicken

Cattle

Pig

Cattle

Sheep

Water Buffalo

Goat

INDUS

SOUTHWEST ASIA

SOUTHEAST ASIA

Ass

Zebu

Pig

SAHARA

Dromedary

NORTHERN TROPICAL AFRICA

CHINA AND SOUTHEAST ASIA

Cereals	Pulses	Root Crops
Asian rice	Mung bean	Taro
Common millet	Soybean	Yams
Foxtail millet		

Fruits	Other Crops
Apricot	Aubergine
Banana	Coconut
Citrus fruits	Sago palm
Mango	Tea
Peach	

SOUTHWEST AND CENTRAL ASIA

Cereals	Pulses	Root Crops
Barley	Broad bean	Carrot
Oats	Chickpea	Parsnip
Rye	Grasspea	Radish
Wheats	Lentil	
	Pea	

Fruits	Other Crops
Apple	Garlic
Date	Onion
Fig	Safflower
Grape	
Olive	
Pear	

NORTHERN TROPICAL AFRICA

Cereals	Pulses	Root Crops
African rice	Cowpea	Yams
Finger millet	Pigeon pea	
Pearl millet		
Sorghum		

Fruits	Other Crops
Tamarind	Coffee
Watermelon	Oil palm
	Sesame

The first farmers of Asia

INTERNET LINKS

www.etana.org/abzu —
A guide to information on
the web about the
ancient Near East

c.10,000 BC Earliest semi-permanent villages in West Asia

c.9000 BC First cereal cultivation in Syria

c.8000 BC First walled towns in West Asia

c.7500–3500 BC Neolithic period in China

c.7000 BC First rice cultivation in South Asia

c.6000 BC First rice cultivation in Yangtze delta, China

The first economies to be based on the husbandry of animal and plant staples came into being in South-West Asia. In the upland areas around the Zagros and Taurus mountains, and in Palestine, moister conditions led to the spread of large-seeded grasses – the ancestors of modern wheat and barley – which early hunters quickly appreciated for their nutrition and ease of storage. By 10,000 BC small villages of circular stone-walled huts developed, whose inhabitants lived from both the hunting and herding of gazelle and the harvesting of wild wheat. About 9000 BC, in northern Syria, some communities began to cultivate cereals outside their natural habitat while sheep were domesticated in Mesopotamia. By 7000 BC wheat and barley cultivation was established, as was the herding of goats, from Anatolia to the Zagros mountains, and this agricultural revolution spread shortly afterwards to Greece.

In the 7th and 6th millennia BC, developed Neolithic villages appeared over much of the landscape. Their economies depended on domesticated plants and animals, and on technological developments. Excavations at Çatal Hüyük, 32 acres in area, revealed extensive evidence of wealth (obsidian and semi-processed stones) and house fittings bore elaborate ornaments (including wall paintings and

the plastered skulls of wild cattle). Much of the lowland area, however, remained too dry for cultivation. Only the development of irrigation – by spreading water from the rivers that drained from the mountains – allowed settlements to extend to the Mesopotamian plain in the 6th and 5th millennia. Sedentary farming began in South Asia on the Kachi Plain of Pakistan around 7000 BC. The early settlers cultivated barley and wheat, domesticated sheep, cattle and goats, and buried their dead with elaborate grave goods. From 6000 BC onwards, mud-brick storehouses divided into small compartments served as the focal point for food, tools and trade goods.

Plants and animals were independently domesticated in many other parts of the world. In northern China the cultivation of millet, another cereal, began on the great loess plain around the Yellow River and its tributaries around 7000 BC. It remained the staple crop of the region for many centuries. Further south the principal cereal was rice, first cultivated in the Yangtze valley before 6000 BC (map 2). Villages acquired defensive walls, from 8000 BC in the Near East (the first fortified community being Jericho) and from around 3500 BC in China.

Terracotta figurine
Characteristic products of the earliest farming villages are small terracotta figurines of women, with emphasis on their sexual characteristics. This small cult statuette, only 6.5 inches high, came from Çatal Hüyük in south-central Turkey.

In addition, the ox-drawn plough began to be adapted throughout much of Eurasia, enlisting animal traction to increase the efficiency of farming.

The greater size and permanence of farming settlements stemmed from three major factors: firstly, the exceptional productivity of the principal cultivated species could feed large concentrations of people all year round – something hunting and gathering can never do; secondly, plant foods could survive storage over many months, allowing the community to stay in one place and live off the previous harvest while a new crop grows and ripens. Finally, farmers need to live near their fields, both to protect them against human and animal predators and to minimize the travel and transport involved in preparing the ground, in weeding, and in harvesting.

Hunters and gatherers keep their possessions to a minimum, since they must carry everything around; but sedentary communities can produce and accumulate a wide range of items, both utilitarian and for ritual and pleasure – pottery and tools, ornaments and display items. Village farming communities became larger and more differentiated, with specialist craftspeople producing fine ceramics and metalwork. As complexity increased, new forms of social organisation developed, leading around 3000 BC to the first cities.

2 Early Chinese agriculture

- area of loess soil
- redeposited loess
- early millet cultivation
- approximate northern limit of wild rice distribution
- early wet rice cultivation

Chinese settlement
- ▲ 6000–5000 BC
- ■ 6000–4000 BC
- ● 5000–2500 BC

KOREA

Pohai

Yellow River

Tz'u-shan

Ma-chia-ya

Ta-wen-k'ou

P'ei-li-kang

Yellow Sea

Pan p'o

Ho-mu-tu

Yangtze

C H I N A

Hsien-jen-tung

Taiwan

Feng-pi-t'ou

Chiang-hsi-an

South China Sea

1 The ancient Near East, 12,000–3100 BC

- natural habitat of wild emmer
- natural habitat of wild einkorn and emmer
- southern limit of rain-fed agriculture (300mm average annual rainfall)

ancient sites:
- ● epipalaeolithic, 12,000–9000 BC
- ▲ pre-pottery Neolithic, 9000–6500 BC
- ● pottery Neolithic, 6500–5500 BC
- ○ Chalcolithic
  - 'Ubaid period, 5500–4200 BC
  - Uruk period, 4200–3100 BC
- ☐ multi-period Neolithic-Chalcolithic sites

Black Sea

Caspian Sea

L.Van

L.Urmia

Degirmentepe
Cafer Hüyük
ntepe
Nevali Çori
Hallan Çemi
Çayönü
Chagar Bazar
Nemrik
Tepe Gawra
Zawi Chemi
Tell Abr
Sabi Abyad
Tell Brak
Qermez Dere
Arpachiyah
Mureybet
Yarim Tepe
Nineveh
Abu Hureyra
Hassuna
Jarmo
Bouqras
Umm Dabaghiyah
Balikh
Khabur
Tell es-Sawwan
Gubba
Abada
Choga Mami
Tepe Guran
Ganj Dareh
Zagros Mts
Diyala
Tell Uqair
Nippur
Tigris
Ali Kosh
Choga Mish
Susa
Choga Banut
Uruk
Oueili (Awayli)
Eridu
Ur
Euphrates
M E S O P O T A M I A

Halileh

Persian Gulf

Abu Khamis

Dosariyah

Al Markh

Ain Qannas

19

INTERNET LINKS

www.historiasiglo20.org/
egypt/mesopotamia.htm
Mesopotamia and Egypt

c.3500 BC Ceremonial complexes built as the centres of the earliest cities in Mesopotamia

c.3200 BC Earliest readable documents from Mesopotamia

c.3100 BC Palace complexes at Abydos in Egypt

c.2500 BC Growth of urbanism in the Indus valley

c.2350 BC First ceremonial centres at Troy in western Anatolia

c.1800 BC Beginning of Shang dynasty in China

The rise of civilization

The first civilizations arose in the alluvial basins of four major rivers which drain from the mountain fringes where agriculture began: the Tigris and Euphrates in Mesopotamia, the Nile in Egypt, the Indus in India, and the Yellow River in China. Each proved capable of supplying the high, regular yields needed to support large urban populations. Cities of thousands, and then tens of thousands, evolved. In Mesopotamia, cities already existed by 3500 BC. Egypt adopted urban civilization in about 3200 BC and the Harappan civilization arose in the Indus plain from about 2500 BC. Civilization in north China appears to have developed, again wholly or largely independently, around 1800 BC.

These societies shared many common features: the development of cities; writing; large public buildings; and the political apparatus of a state. The large agricultural surpluses produced by irrigation – some Mesopotamian communities harvested 60, 70 or even 80 grains for each grain sown – made it possible to employ a significant segment of society in activities other than farming, such as manufacture and trade. This in turn led to the emergence of a ruling class which accumulated wealth through the exploitation of labour and the imposition of taxes. In Mesopotamia the ruler was also the chief priest and the temple centre provided a vital element of the political system, its monumental structure

1 The rise of civilization

fertile land

centres of urban civilization

areas of pastoral nomadism

forming a visual reminder to all citizens of the power that governed their daily life. The centralized control found in these societies fostered a special legal system, a standing army, a permanent bureaucracy, and the division of society into distinct classes. The state also supported scribes, who were usually trained and employed within the temples and palaces. The earliest writing was used as a means of keeping track of commodities, wages and taxes; but it soon served other purposes: to preserve religious traditions, which thereby became sacred books; to register social customs, which thereby became codes of law; and to record myths, which thereby developed into history and literature.

Since, apart from agricultural produce, the alluvial plains lacked most other natural resources, an extensive trading activity exchanged luxury goods and raw materials from other areas with the textiles and other manufactured goods of the cities and thus helped to develop other trading centres in a great arc from the eastern Mediterranean to the Indus valley and in China. The cities therefore exercised an influence out of all proportion to their comparatively small geographical extent. True, not all areas were affected: Australia, Africa, Europe and large parts of Asia had no cities; the first civilizations of the Americas did not emerge until about 1500 BC (and, when they did, owed nothing to ideas introduced from outside). Nevertheless the growth of the first urban centres, with their technology, literacy, and class divisions began a new phase in the development of human society.

The Royal standard of Ur
from the largest of the royal tombs at Ur. It has panels on each side depicting the activities of the king in peace and war. The war side shows helmeted infantry, four-wheeled battle wagons pulled by asses or onagers, and prisoners being presented to the king.

MONGOLIA
hunting fishing and gathering replaced by mounted nomadic pastoralism from the west

AMUR VALLEY
sedentary village communities supported by salmon fishing and millet farming

NOMADS

Balkhash

Atlai Mts

L.Baikal

Amur

Ob

Yenisey

Takla Maka

Gobi Desert

T I B E T

Kaocheng

Singtai

Lo-yang
Anyang
Chengchow

Erh-li-t'ou

Yellow Sea

C H I N A

•Rupar

•Alamgirpur

angan

Brahmaputra

Panlungchen•

Ganges

GANGETIC PLAIN
colonization of flood plain by rice-farming villages

Wucheng •

I N D I A

DECCAN
temporary hunting camps and cattle-herding pens replaced by farming villages

B a y o f B e n g a l

INDO CHINA
rice farming villages with domestic animals and bronze tool technology

South China Sea

90°

30

INTERNET LINKS

www.ancientegypt.co.uk
The British Museum's
ancient Egypt website

3000–500 BC
West Asia and Egypt

The earliest of all known civilizations, Sumer, rested upon some 12 city-states in southern Mesopotamia, the largest of them covering about 100 hectares, defended by a wall, and housing perhaps 30,000 people. At first, pre-eminence passed from one city to another, but towards the end of the 3rd millennium powerful leaders established hegemony over ever-wider areas. The first was Sargon (c. 2296-2240 BC), who created a new political centre at Agade (also known as Akkad) before conquering the cities of southern Mesopotamia and claiming authority as far west as Byblos. Sargon's grandson Naram-Sin (2213-2176 BC) enlarged the empire further, but within a generation it disappeared as subject cities asserted their independence. The rise of Agade had long-lasting effects on the region, with Akkadian (whose variants included Babylonian and Assyrian) replacing Sumerian as the main language of Mesopotamia.

Around 2000 BC, a new empire arose around Ur, its hegemony stretching from the Persian Gulf to Nineveh, but Ur also fell after about a century, and a kaleidoscope of shifting alliances brought new cities to prominence, most notably Mari and Babylon on the Euphrates. Under its powerful king Hammurabi (1728-1686 BC), Babylon created another empire that covered the whole of southern Mesopotamia; but, once more, it did not long survive the death of its founder (map 1).

Even before Sargon unified Mesopotamia, Egypt

came under the sway of a single ruler. The harnessing of the Nile's annual floods to irrigate the fields on its banks made possible a civilization that lasted for over 25 centuries. Around 3000 BC an Upper Egyptian ruler conquered the Nile delta and established a new capital at Memphis, which for almost 2000 years served as the administrative centre for a densely

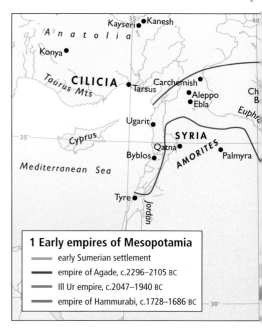

1 Early empires of Mesopotamia

early Sumerian settlement
empire of Agade, c.2296–2105 BC
III Ur empire, c.2047–1940 BC
empire of Hammurabi, c.1728–1686 BC

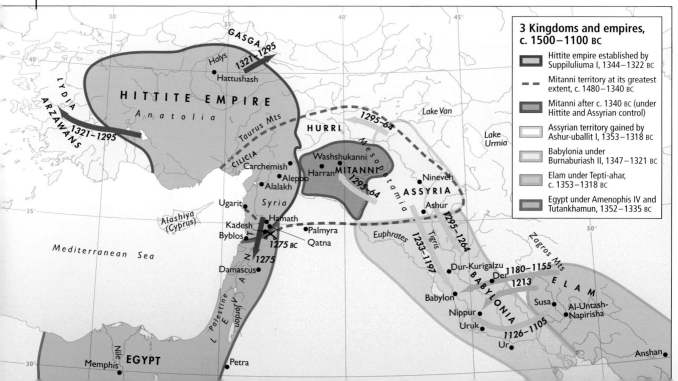

**3 Kingdoms and empires,
c. 1500–1100 BC**

Hittite empire established by
Suppiluliuma I, 1344–1322 BC

Mitanni territory at its greatest
extent, c. 1480–1340 BC

Mitanni after c. 1340 BC (under
Hittite and Assyrian control)

Assyrian territory gained by
Ashur-uballit I, 1353–1318 BC

Babylonia under
Burnaburiash II, 1347–1321 BC

Elam under Tepti-ahar,
c. 1353–1318 BC

Egypt under Amenophis IV and
Tutankhamun, 1352–1335 BC

populated region of some 15,000 square miles running from the first cataract at Aswan to the Mediterranean coast (map 2). At about the same time, writing in hieroglyphic script commenced. During the 'Old Kingdom' period (2685-2180 BC) the rulers of Egypt built a series of massive pyramid-tombs along the desert edge opposite Memphis which emphasised their power and prestige. Then, after a century of invasion and anarchy, the Egyptian state entered a second period of cultural achievement under the able rulers of the Middle Kingdom (2040-1783 BC); and another era of expansion under the XVIIIth and XIXth dynasties (1570-1200 BC). At home they undertook vast building projects, like the rock-cut temple at Abu Simbel created by Ramesses II (1290-1224 BC); abroad they advanced through Palestine into Syria and created an empire that extended almost to the Euphrates.

The continuity of Ancient Egyptian language, religion and culture stood in marked contrast to developments in Mesopotamia. The two civilizations also differed in other respects. First, because of the annual Nile flood, Egypt did not depend to the same extent on irrigation canals and dams; second, although it possessed some cities, they lacked the geographical concentration found in southern Mesopotamia, so that Egypt was more a territorial unit than an agglomeration of city-states. Third, and most important, Egypt rarely suffered foreign invasion. Admittedly the Hyksos, an Asiatic people, overran most of the country in the 18th century BC, but a new native dynasty expelled them c.1570 BC and then pursued the invaders northwards to the upper Euphrates. Egypt's Asiatic empire lasted until about 1200 BC when the 'Sea Peoples', marauders from the Aegean and Asia Minor, attacked all the major powers of the East Mediterranean and initiated a 'Dark Age', concerning which very few historical sources survive, until about 900 BC and the emergence of Assyria.

Babylon and Assyria weathered the storm of the 12th and 11th centuries with greatly reduced territory, and the 10th century saw the beginnings of an Assyrian recovery. In the following century Ashurnasirpal II (883-859 BC) sent his armies north and west and used the wealth they gained to build a spectacular new palace at Nimrud. Even greater gains were made by Tiglath-pileser III (744-727 BC) and Sargon II (721-705 BC) who annexed Babylonia and conquered the Phoenician cities on the Mediterranean coast. Egyptian weakness allowed Esarhaddon (680-669 BC) and Ashurbanipal (668-627 BC) to capture Memphis and Thebes, although the Assyrians did not attempt to formalize their control over Egypt.

To the Old Testament prophets, the Assyrians appeared invincible; yet their control over Babylonia was never secure: the Babylonian king Nabopolassar (626-605 BC) rebelled and, aided by the Medes, sacked the major Assyrian cities including Ashur and Nineveh. The Babylonians then inherited the Assyrian empire, but they too had to fight to keep it. In 605 BC the Egyptians attempted to annex Syria, but were defeated at Carchemish and Hamath. Nebuchadnezzar (604-562 BC) consolidated Babylonian rule, but his successors were unable to maintain their gains and Babylon fell to the Persians in 539 BC.

2 Old Kingdom Egypt, c. 2685–2180 BC

- town or city, c.3250–2000 BC
- royal tomb, c.3250–2650 BC
- pyramid, c.2650–2000 BC
- fertile land

A Limestone stela, now in the Louvre, of Naram-Sin of Agade (2213-2176 BC) depicting his victory over the Lullubu of the Zagros mountains. Naram-Sin led many successful campaigns in his reign, leaving rock-reliefs commemorating his achievements near Diyarbakir in Turkey and in the Zagros.

c.15,000 BC Humans
cross Bering land bridge
from Asia into North
America

c.3600 BC Evidence of
maize cultivation in
Mesoamerica

c.1150 BC Beginnings of
Olmec civilization in Mexico

c.1749 BC Foundation of
Zapotec capital at Monte
Albán, in Mexico

c.AD 100 Rise of
Teotihuacán

c. AD 600 Apogee of
Maya civilization; Huari and
Tiahuanaco expansion
begins

c.AD 700 Teotihuacán
destroyed

c.AD 850 Collapse of
Maya civilization

TO AD 1000

The Americas

The Americas were colonized from Asia late in the last Ice Age, when lowered sea levels turned the Bering Strait into dry land. The subsequent melting of the ice cut off the continent from Eurasia (page 14). It is one of the remarkable facts of human history that despite their geographical separation, development in Old and New Worlds followed much the same path: the adoption of agriculture; the creation of cities and empires; the invention of writing. These two geographical zones continued on parallel paths until the New World was invaded by Europeans after 1492 (page 86). The New World civilizations were highly inventive in their own right, and in some ways in advance of their western counterparts. They produced – quite independent of the Old World – magnificent art, remarkable mathematical and astronomical skills, and monumental architecture.

The inhabitants of Mesoamerica and the central Andes began to experiment with plant cultivation around 7000 BC and farming soon allowed a rapid increase in population. By 800 BC the Olmec on the Gulf of Mexico, the Zapotec at Monte Albán, and the people of Chavín in Peru had developed complex societies with populations that numbered tens of thousands, boasting a hierarchy of social classes, an efficient civil service, a professional priesthood, and specialists in all kinds of tasks, from manufacturing to commerce and government.

Around and between these civilizations, other communities remained at the chiefdom level. Maize, beans and squash cultivation spread from Mexico to north America, and their arrival initiated a period of rapid development. In Ohio and Illinois, between 300 BC and AD 550, Hopewell chiefs built elaborate burial mounds and maintained trade contacts from Florida to the Rockies. Most American chiefdoms were agricultural, based on plant cultivation, but along the north-west coast rich fishing grounds and an abundance of whales and seals supported large villages and a complex ceremonial life by hunting, fishing and gathering alone. Towards the extremities of the continent, however, harsh conditions precluded farming, settlement remained sparse, and nomadic lifestyles persisted (map 1).

The sudden rise of Teotihuacán about AD 100 eclipsed earlier developments in Mesoamerica. Laid out in a precise grid plan and covering 8 square miles (20 km²), its population grew eventually to some 200,000. The nature of the city's economy remains uncertain but the centre, with two mighty pyramids, was planned for rites that included human sacrifice. Whether or not in association with trade, the Teotihuacanos' influence spread widely. They colonized some neighbouring districts and possibly sponsored new towns further afield.

At the same time, the powerful lowland kingdoms of the Maya flourished. Their capitals were

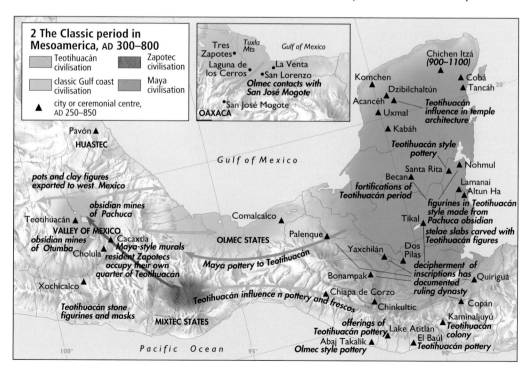

2 The Classic period in Mesoamerica, AD 300–800

- Teotihuacán civilisation
- classic Gulf coast civilisation
- Zapotec civilisation
- Maya civilisation
- ▲ city or ceremonial centre, AD 250–850

pyramid-studded ceremonial centres with extensive suburbs. Voluminous inscriptions in a distinctive hieroglyphic script reveal a sophisticated concern with astronomy and astrology: their experts calculated the exact length of the solar year and the lunar month, and predicted eclipses. However, whether on account of the chronic wars that their carved stones also recorded, or of popular discontent, or of environmental degradation by excessive population – or of all three factors – most of the towns were abandoned between 790 and about 860. Many districts revived in what is known as the 'Post-Classic' period, but the Maya never regained their grandeur (map 2).

A separate group of interrelated civilizations grew up in the central Andes, supported by spectacular irrigation systems in the lowlands and by ingenious terraced fields in the highlands. The Andean peoples developed sophisticated skills in working gold, silver and copper, and used these metals for tools as well as for jewellery. The coast of the central Andes is best known for the graphic pottery of the Moche, dating from AD 100 to 600, which reveals much about the daily life and religion of his makers.

Although its vast distances and harsh topography made this region difficult to unify, the centuries between AD 600 and 1000 saw the rise of a truly imperial power based on Huari in the Peruvian Andes. Many elements of Huari religion and art originated at Tiahuanaco, further south, but were quickly adopted by Huari and then spread by force to many parts of the coast and highlands. For a short time Huari was the capital of a state embracing most of Peru, but around AD 800 the city was sacked and abandoned for ever. The fragile unity soon collapsed and not until the Inca conquests of the 15th and 16th centuries would the central Andes be reunified under a single government (page 72).

The king of Yaxchilán (on the left above) prepares for battle against another Maya kingdom in AD 724. The hieroglyphs above the figures record that one of his wives (on the right above) helped him prepare.

1 Peoples of the Americas, 300 BC to AD 1300

- farming peoples
- chiefdoms
- civilized states
- hunters and gatherers
- site first occupied before AD 600
- site mainly occupied after AD 600

INTERNET LINKS

www.bradshaw
foundation.com
Ancient rock art,
archaeology, anthropology
and migration

c.50,000 BC Settlement
of Australia from southeast
Asia

c. 6000 BC Earliest
cereal cultivation in Africa

c. 4000–3000 BC
Desiccation of Sahara
begins; population moves
south and east

c. 2000 BC Settlement of
Melanesia begins

c.1300 BC Settlement
of Fiji

c.900 BC Kingdom of
Meroe established

c.550 BC Iron use begins
in sub-Saharan Africa;
southwards expansion of
Bantu speakers

c.AD 750 Settlers reach
New Zealand

TO AD 1500
Prehistoric Africa and Australasia

Both Australia and Sub-Saharan Africa have been largely isolated from the rest of the Old World for the last 10,000 years, the former by sea, the latter by desert. Although the inhabitants of North Africa began the transition from hunting and gathering to farming around 8000 BC, the desiccation of the Sahara after about 4000 BC cut off Africa south of the Equator for centuries.

In Australia, the aborigines mostly remained hunters and gatherers adapted to living in a large range of environments from tropical forest to harsh desert. They enjoyed a rich symbolic life, as evidenced by the marking of their sacred places with rock art from at least 25,000 years ago. The colonization of the Melanesian islands occurred considerably later, when settlers from New Guinea, associated with the distinctive Lapita pottery, reached Fiji around 1300 BC and then made their way into Polynesia via Tonga and Samoa, reaching the Marquesas islands in about 150 BC (map 1). From there they spread north to Hawaii (c. AD 400)

and south-west via the Cook islands to New Zealand between AD 750 and 1300. When the Europeans arrived in the 18th century, at least 750,000 aborigines inhabited Australia and up to 150,000 Maoris lived in New Zealand

The geographical isolation of southern Africa was never complete. In the east settlers spread down the Rift Valley from Ethiopia during the first millennium BC, while trans-Saharan trade increased in importance after the introduction of the camel from Asia, around 100 BC. Iron came into use in parts of sub-Saharan Africa after 750 BC. Aided by the new technology, Bantu-speaking farmers and cattle-herders began to colonize southern Africa in the early centuries AD. By the 13th century powerful Bantu chiefdoms had emerged, such as that centred on Great Zimbabwe, and on cattle-raising communities. These engaged in long-distance trade, long before the Portuguese arrived off both the south-east and south-west coasts of the continent at the close of the 15th century

Rock art became common in Australia 25,000 years ago. This more recent painting shows the two 'Lightning Brothers', ancestral spirits of the Wardaman Aboriginal people from northwestern Australia.

M e d i t e r r a n e a n   S e a

Atlantic
Ocean

Utica
Capeletti
Carthage
Mogador
Atlas Mountains
PHOENICIA
Cyrene
Leptis
(Homs)
Naucratis
Saïs
Greek colonies from 700 BC
Merimde
4200 BC
Memphis
Fayum
4300 BC
EGYPT
Thebes
Zemmour
Meniet
6000-5000 BC
Uan Muhaggiag
Adrar Tiouiyne
Immidir
Adrar Bous
3000 BC
Hoggar
Massif
Tassili
Massif
Tichitt
Arlit
Tibesti
Massif
Jebel
Uweinat
Iron
NUBIA
KINGDOM
OF MEROE
900 BC-AD 400
Napata
Nuri
KUSH
Meroe 500 BC
Adulis
Aksum
KINGDOM
OF AKSUM
AD 100-1000

Adrar
KINGDOM
OF GHANA
1st millennium AD
iron
2000 BC
Karkarchinkat
Air
Gao
Ennedi
Kadero
Shaheinab
3200 BC
Jebel Moya

Jenne-jeno
proto-urban settlement
by 1st century AD
Niger
Daima
Iron-working
widespread north of
equatorial forest
by c. 500 BC
S u d a n i c   B e l t
Ethiopian
Highlands

Ntereso
1400 BC
Kintampo
1500 BC
Taruga
Nok
Ife
Atwetwebooso
Igbo Ukwu
shrines
AD 800-900
Gulf of Guinea
500 BC
iron and cattle

2 Africa: the Stone Age to the Iron Age

possible spread of
cultivation to lower Congo
1st millennium BC
Batalimo
Congo forests
penetrated by
pottery-using
peoples late in
1st millennium BC
Funa River 270 BC
Congo
iron and cattle
Ileret
east African 'pastoral
neolithic' sites
Urewe
Katuruka
5th century BC
Narosura
Lake
Victoria
Elmenteita
Manda & Shanga
Crescent Is.
Kwale
ports involved in
overseas trade
by AD 800
Sanga
Kalambo
Lake
Tanganyika
late 1st millennium AD
cemetery
Sandawe
Kilwa
Lubusi
Kamnama
Kapwirimbwe
iron and cattle
iron and cattle
AD 200
Lake
Nyasa
Nkope
Salumano
Kalundu
Zambezi
Namib Desert
Ziwa
Gokomere
Great
Zimbabwe
Mabveni
Malapati
AD 800
Madagascar
Austronesian
settlement
Snake Rock
Falls Rock
Mirabib
Kalahari
Desert
Silver Leaves
AD 1100
Broederstroom
Lydenburg
Phalaborwa
Equus
Witkrans
Doornfontein
Blinkklipkop
Limerock
Dikbosch
Blackburn
Tortoise
Cave
Eland's Bay
Diepkloof
Steenberg
Kasteelberg
Hawston
Die Kelders
Nelson Bay
Byneskranskop
domestic sheep
herded by 1st century BC

**1 Initial settlement
of Polynesia and
island Micronesia**

rock art styles:
ʒ   paranamittee
    engravings
⊕   complex figurative
⊼   simple figurative

the Lapita potters:
── Lapita pottery area
●   sites with Lapita
    pottery
── other contemporary
    Melanesian pottery
    traditions
➔   settlement of
    Eastern Polynesia,
    150 BC–AD 1000

Hawaiian
Islands
c. AD 400
Fanning
Island
Line Islands
Marquesas
Islands
c. 150 BC
alu
slands)
Tokelau
Islands
Samoa
O   Fiji
L   Y   N   E   S   I   A
Tonga
Tahiti
to Easter I.
c. AD 400
Cook
Islands
c. AD 950
Kermadec Is.
to Pitcairn I.
c. AD 1000
North Island
c. AD 750
NEW
ALAND
Island
S o u t h   P a c i f i c
O c e a n

●   site of cattle domestication
▲   early agricultural site
▽   sites of southern African
    Stone Age herders
── approximate extent of iron
    -using farmers, AD 200–1100
●   important metal workers'
    sites
➔   possible arrival of iron
    technology
●   Greek colonies
●   Phoenician or Punic colonies

▲   fishing harpoon site
    area of Saharan rock painting,
    c. 6000–1000 BC
    areas of rock painting in
    southern and eastern Africa
── approximate extent of cattle
    herders, 6000–500 BC

27

INTERNET LINKS

www.metmuseum.org/toah/
ht/04/sse/ht04sse.htm
Timeline of South-East Asian
art history

3000 BC Rice cultivation begins in Southeast Asia

c.2500 BC Beginning of Harappan culture in the Indus valley

c.1750 BC Abandonment of major Indus valley cities

c.1000 BC Bronze-working begins in Southeast Asia

c.486 BC Birth of Buddha

c.232 BC Death of Mauryan Emperor Asoka

3rd century AD Earliest Sanskrit writing in Southeast Asia

AD 335 King Samudragupta ascends throne

TO AD 500
South and South East Asia

The first great Indian civilization emerged in the Indus valley in the 3rd millennium with complex urban societies at Harappa and Mohenjo-Daro, which developed a pictographic writing system (as yet not definitively deciphered) and traded as far afield as Mesopotamia (map 1). Around 1500 BC, for reasons that remain obscure, the major Indus valley cities suddenly collapsed

When the picture becomes clear once again the population of northern India had been transformed, with a Hindu religion, a Sanskrit literature, a caste system and (by about 800 BC) iron working, which enabled the spread of farming communities eastward into the rich plain of the Ganges. By 600 BC at least 16 political units had grown up along the Ganges, the subcontinent's new centre of gravity. By 400 BC war had reduced the states to four, and no doubt the resulting social tensions helped to spread new ethical and religious systems, for in the 6th century Gautama (Buddha), founder of Asia's most pervasive religion, was born in one of these states (see

page 34), while in another Mahavira formulated the teaching of Jainism.

A further turning point came in 320 BC when Chandragupta Maurya seized the state of Magadha on the lower Ganges, and occupied large parts of central India, and in 305 BC annexed the province of Trans-Indus from the successors of Alexander the Great (see page 32). Chandragupta's grandson Ashoka (273-232 BC) expanded this Mauryan empire southwards, bringing the greater part of the sub-continent under his rule and inscribing edicts on pillars and rock-faces all over India as a permanent reminder of his power (map 2). Ashoka's death introduced a troubled period, punctuated by invasions of both Greeks and nomads who founded states in the north-west, such as the Kushan empire, where Hellenistic and Indian influences mingled. Further south, the Satavahanas of the Deccan ruled a state that straddled the peninsula by AD 150. Then, in the 4th century, the Gupta dynasty, created an empire which by AD 400 extended from the Indus to the bay

1 The Indus civilizations of Harappa and Mohenjo-Daro, c. 2500–1750 BC

○ pre-Harappan settlements

● principal sites of Harappan civilization

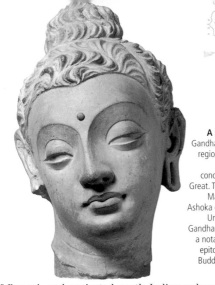

A head of Buddha from Gandhara *(left)*. The Gandhara region, in present-day north-western Pakistan was conquered by Alexander the Great. The region passed to the Maurya empire and under Ashoka converted to Buddhism. Under the Kushan empire, Gandhara became the centre of a notable school of sculpture, epitomised by images of the Buddha, with marked Greco-Roman influences.

of Bengal, and projected north Indian values and religions far beyond (map 3).

The barbarian invasions of the 5th century AD (see page 40) caused the collapse of Gupta power, but it was precisely during this period that Hindu and Buddhist influences began to spread to South-East Asia. The cultivation of rice in this area, beginning as early as 3000 BC, allowed the development of prosperous farming villages. Bronze came into use after about 1000 BC, reflected in distinctive bronze Dong Son drums, and iron followed after about 500 BC (map 4). By AD 300 trading links with India had burgeoned, and Buddhist images appeared by AD 500, notably in Burma, Cambodia, and Java. By AD 700 the construction of Hindu temples in the same three areas had begun.

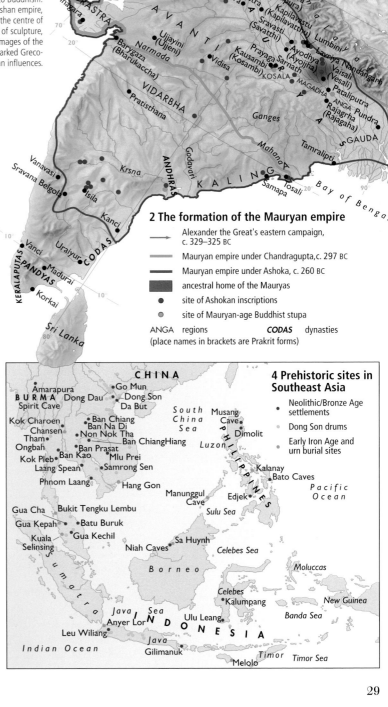

2 The formation of the Mauryan empire

→ Alexander the Great's eastern campaign, c. 329–325 BC

━ Mauryan empire under Chandragupta, c. 297 BC

━ Mauryan empire under Ashoka, c. 260 BC

▨ ancestral home of the Mauryas

● site of Ashokan inscriptions

● site of Mauryan-age Buddhist stupa

ANGA regions ***CODAS*** dynasties
(place names in brackets are Prakrit forms)

3 The Gupta-Vakataka imperial formation, AD 300–550

▨ Gupta core area
▨ Vakataka core area
━ maximum extent of Gupta empire
━ limit of areas at some time under Vakataka rule

4 Prehistoric sites in Southeast Asia

● Neolithic/Bronze Age settlements
● Dong Son drums
● Early Iron Age and urn burial sites

INTERNET LINKS

http://projectsx.dartmouth.
edu/history/bronze_age/
The prehistoric archaeology
of the Aegean

6500–1000 BC

Early Europe

c.6500 BC First agricultural settlement in Europe

c.4500 BC Beginning of copper production in the Balkans

c.4000 BC Farming spreads to Britain and Scandinavia

c.2000 BC Minoan culture develops on Crete

c.1400 BC Mycenaean invasion of Crete

c.1250 BC Mycenaean campaign against Troy

c.1200 BC Abandonment of Mycenaean palaces

Farming spread from West Asia to Europe about 6500 BC, beginning with the Balkans. Agriculture in these regions involved wheat and barley, sheep and goats, just as in western Asia; but as farming spread beyond into more temperate zones, major adjustments became necessary. New, more robust types of cereal developed, and cattle and pigs became the dominant livestock. By about 5500 BC agricultural communities had developed along the Danube valley, and their descendants spread northwest from there until they reached the Paris basin around 4750 BC. After a brief pause, the final phase saw the spread of farming to the northern fringes of Europe, including Scandinavia and the British Isles, where existing hunter-gatherer communities adopted it by about 4000 BC (map 1).

There has been much debate about whether the spread of agriculture was due to the expansion of colonizing populations from the southeast or to the adoption of the new way of life by existing foragers. Current evidence from archaeology and the analysis of the DNA of modern populations suggests that there was a colonizing element, probably associated with the expansion through the Balkans and the loess lands of central Europe, but that in most of Europe the dominant process was the adoption of agriculture and its material attributes by existing populations, perhaps in part because of the prestige of the new way of life.

Meanwhile, beginning in the Balkans, copper-working spread after c. 4500 BC and by 2500 BC it had become common to alloy the copper with tin to produce bronze. The need for these two raw materials stimulated the development of extensive trade networks, which also conveyed other materials, such as amber from the Baltic. Amber is found as far afield as Mycenae in southern Greece, where graves filled with sumptuous funerary offerings of gold and jewellery appeared from 1600 BC.

Mycenae was not the earliest European state: that honour belongs to the island of Crete where from about 2000 BC 'Minoan' culture, based on palaces decorated with colourful frescoes and equipped with sanitary and drainage systems, developed. Bureaucracy and trade flourished, and a script known as Linear A developed around 1600 BC. Two centuries later, however, the Mycenaeans (named after the fortress of Mycenae in the eastern Peloponnese) took control of Crete and became the principal military and eco-

nomic power in the Aegean (see map 2). They adapted the Minoan culture, including its script which they modified (to a form known as Linear B, an early version of Greek) and used to administer their own lands. Mycenaean Greece was divided among a number of independent leaders, each of whom ruled a small kingdom, in much the same way as Greece in the Classical period was divided into city-states (see page 32). The legend of the Trojan War, recorded centuries later in Homer's *Iliad*, is thought to recall a Mycenaean campaign of c. 1250 BC against the city of Troy, strategically situated at the entrance to the Dardanelles, and controlling access to the trade of the Black Sea. But this success, if indeed it occurred, must have been the final fling of the Mycenean warlords because by 1200 BC their palaces lay in ruins, overthrown perhaps by rebellion or by outside attack, and a 'Dark Age' which left very few records ensued all over Greece for the next four centuries.

Snake handler from Knossos
This faience statuette, dating from c.1700 BC, possibly represents a household goddess. Little is known about Minoan divinities, but most appear to be female.

1 The spread of agricultural settlement

→ main routes of agrarian expansion

dates of agricultural settlement
(based on tree-ring corrected radiocarbon dating)

by 7000 BC
7000–6000 BC
6000–5000 BC
5000–3000 BC
3000–2000 BC

bowl cultures early farming groups

• Hembury site of excavated farming village

SPAIN modern state names

INTERNET LINKS

www.museum.upenn.edu/
Greek_World/Index.html
The ancient Greek world

750–300 BC

The Greek world

- **c. 750 BC** First Greek colonizing expeditions

- **7th-6th centuries BC** Emergence of tyrants in many Greek states

- **500 BC** Reforms of Cleisthenes establish Athenian democracy

- **478-404 BC** Athens dominates Aegean through Delian League

- **431-404 BC** The Peloponnesian War

- **447 BC** Parthenon begun in Athens

- **399 BC** Socrates tried and executed at Athens

- **338 BC** Battle of Chaeronea: Philip II of Macedon gains control of Greece

- **336-323 BC** Alexander the Great of Macedon conquers the former Persian empire

The Acropolis (below). Acting as the defensive strong point for Athens since the Mycenaean period, the acropolis was also an important religious sanctuary. Its most famous temple was the Parthenon, begun in 447 BC.

The Greek heartland is an area of islands and plains divided by mountains. After the collapse of the Mycenaean palace system, the *polis* or city-state emerged and soon became the dominant form of political organization in the Mediterranean world.

The 8th century BC was a period of great transformations in Greece. It saw the appearance of the first monumental public buildings, changes in burial practices and new artistic styles. At the same time, literacy re-emerged, with a new alphabet. Though contact with the wider world had not totally disappeared in previous centuries, it now increased dramatically, above all on the island of Euboea, perhaps as the result of Phoenician exploration and settlement.

From the middle of the century, following in the wake of the Phoenicians, groups of Greeks created settlements around the Mediterranean, first in Italy and Sicily, but by the middle of the 6th century also in north Africa and, to the east, along the Black Sea coast. These included many cities that have remained famous to the present, such as Marseilles and Naples (see map 1). In the central Mediterranean, the Greeks came into conflict with the Carthaginians, who for many centuries disputed control of Sicily with them.

In Asia Minor, however, the Greeks came up against the Persian empire, which first sought to annex the city-states of the Aegean coast and in 490 and 480-479 BC invaded Greece itself. The Persians met with defeat and the next 50 years marked the great age of Greek culture: the tragic drama of Aeschylus, Sophocles and Euripedes; the comedy of Aristophanes; the histories of Herodotus and Thucydides; the splendour of the Parthenon; the sculptures of Phidias. Athens also built up a formidable fleet and used it to create an Aegean empire which the cities of the Peloponnese, led by Sparta, saw as a threat. In 431 BC, Sparta declared war on

3 The campaigns of Alexander

→ Alexander, 334–23 BC → Nearchus, 325–24 BC

2 The Peloponnesian War, 431–404 BC

Legend:
- Athens and members of the Delian League
- ally of Athens
- Sparta and allies
- neutral states
- ● allies of Athens in Magna Graecia
- ● allies of Sparta in Magna Graecia
- → Athenian campaigns
- → Spartan campaigns
- ✕ Athenian victory
- ✕ Spartan victory

Athens. The Peloponnesian war lasted 27 years and, despite victories on both sides, Athens fatally overstrained her resources with a disastrous expedition against Syracuse in Sicily (415-13 BC) and was finally defeated in 404 BC. Her empire fragmented (map 2).

The 4th century saw more jockeying for power, as Persia sought to intervene in Greek affairs, until the well-trained Macedonian army of King Philip II (359-336 BC) first subdued the city-states and then united them under his leadership for an attack on Persia. Philip's remarkable son Alexander (336-323 BC) invaded Asia Minor with an army of 35,000 men, both Greeks and Macedonians, in 334 BC; moved on to annex Egypt (332 BC) and the Persian empire (331 BC); and campaigned successfully in India and Central Asia (map 3). Alexander's death in 323 BC and the ensuing struggles between his leading generals created three major powers: Macedon, Egypt, and the Seleucid kingdom of western Asia.

Although politically the empire of Alexander the Great proved ephemeral, in other respects its consequences endured. Alexander and his successors founded some 70 cities, not merely as military strongholds but as cultural centres, and thus Greek culture and language spread throughout the entire region, as far as the borders of India.

1 Greek colonization in the Mediterranean world, 750–550 BC

Legend:
- Greek heartland in 750 BC
- ■ Greek parent community
- □ Greek oracular shrine
- ● Phoenician or Punic settlement
- ● Etruscan city
- ● 8th-century Greek colony
- ● 7th-century Greek colony
- ● 6th-century Greek colony
- ○ Philistine city

INTERNET LINKS

www.bbc.co.uk/religion/
religions —
Detailed resource on
world religions

C. 700 BC TO AD 600

World religions

Before the 1st millennium BC, polytheism was the dominant form of religious belief throughout Eurasia, with individual communities worshipping their own gods. As the empires of the ancient world emerged, a number of major religions, each characterized by a single doctrine and claims to universality, largely replaced these myriad cults, although elsewhere innumerable other creeds survived without making the transition to world religions.

All the great world religions originated in Asia, and three of them – Judaism, Christianity and Islam – developed in the same small region. Moreover, several were either established or radically reformulated at much the same time: the outstanding prophets and reformers of Hinduism, Buddhism, Judaism, Confucianism and Taoism all lived in the 6th century BC. Their appearance perhaps reflected a need in the rising empires for more universal creeds than local deities could provide, and their diffusion – particularly the spread of the great missionary religions, Buddhism and Christianity – played an important role in linking the different areas. The new religions also spread the values of those advanced cultures to people living beyond the frontiers.

All the world religions shared, to some degree, a belief in a single spiritual reality. Hinduism, the oldest of them, although it reveres

1 The diffusion of religions

- → dispersion of Jews to AD 500
- → spread of Christianity
- ▢ area converted to Christianity by AD 600
- → spread of Buddhism
- ---- first area of Buddhist missionary activity
- ·--· area of rise of Mahayana Buddhism
- ● Buddhist sites
- ▢ area of Hinduism
- ▢ area of Daoism and Confucianism
- ▢ area of Shintoism
- ▢ area of Zoroastria
- → spread of Mithrais
- ● Mithraic sites

A reclining Buddha from Polonnaruwa in Sri Lanka. The importance of Buddism grew after it was adopted by Mauryan emperor Ashoka and it spread throughout India. Missionary activity then brought Buddhist ideas to many places in south and east Asia. Buddhism reached Sri Lanka in the late third century BC.

numerous gods, emphasises the 'right way to live'; Buddhism, although it does not centre upon a god, instead stresses deliverance from suffering through the annihilation of desire. Originally a reformist movement within Hinduism, in its conservative, or Theravada form, Buddhism soon spread throughout India and on to Sri Lanka, Burma, Thailand and South-East Asia. It was the first and perhaps the greatest of all missionary religions, spreading to China by the 1st or 2nd century AD, Korea in the 4th century, and Japan in the 6th century.

Judaism spread mainly because of the persecution of the Jews by more formidable neighbours, beginning with their forcible removal to Babylon (586-538 BC). This led to a change in the emphasis of the faith from temple observance and ritual to morality and righteous living. Rebellion against Roman rule (64 BC) led to the destruction of the temple in Jerusalem (AD 70), and Jewish groups migrated until Judaism, too, became a worldwide religion. It was also associated with the origins of two other major creeds: Christianity (page 44) and Islam (page 50).

In East Asia, the 6th century saw the rise of the ethical system of Confucius (551-479 BC) and the mystical religion of the Tao, or 'the Way', associated with the shadowy figure of Lao-tzu. Zoroastrianism, the other great religion of the period, originated in Persia and saw life as a battleground between the forces of good and evil. It spread widely through the Roman world in the form of Mithraism, with shrines as far afield as northern Britain. Mithraism was ultimately suppressed in favour of Christianity while most Zoroastrian areas came under the control of Islam.

Most of the world religions spread along the trade routes, diffused by soldiers, administrators, merchants and ordinary travellers as well as by missionaries; and most tended to prosper under strong governments that brought peace. The development of larger, more centralized states and empires and the rise of these religions and codes thus went hand in hand, the new religions either becoming associated with or adopted by the great empires of the ancient world: Zoroastrianism with the Persian empire of Cyrus and Darius the Great; Buddhism with Ashoka's Indian empire; Confucianism and Taoism with China under the Chou. The world religions also provided the bonds that eventually linked areas of the world previously separate.

35

INTERNET LINKS

www.ghg.net/shetler/rome
Links to websites
on ancient Rome

264 BC–AD 565

Rome

Rome, a city-state governed by aristocratic families leading an army of peasant soldiers, came to control an empire that stretched from the Atlantic to the Euphrates and from the English Channel to the Sahara. But military success brought social disorder; rivalries between warlords led to civil war; and republican institutions became an autocracy.

In the 6th century BC Rome was just a small fortress-town in central Italy commanding both the lowest crossing point on the river Tiber and a salt route between the mountains and the sea. By exploiting quarrels with its neighbours, the Roman Republic emerged as the dominant power first in central Italy and then in the whole peninsula. By 264 BC Rome controlled the whole of Italy and challenged the other major power in the western Mediterranean: Carthage. After three savage wars Rome defeated Carthage to acquire Sicily (241 BC), Spain (206 BC) and North Africa (146 BC). At the same time, conflict with the Hellenistic kingdoms further east resulted in the conquest of Macedon, Greece and Western Anatolia. In this way, almost by accident, Rome became an imperial power with far-flung possessions.

Administration of these provinces overstrained the Roman constitution, which had not been designed to manage an overseas empire, and the Republic finally collapsed in a series of civil wars. The last of these brought to power Octavian, who established himself as *Princeps* ('first citizen'), accepted the title Augustus (in 27 BC), reshaped the constitution, and extended and strengthened the frontiers (map 1).

While maintaining undivided power in his own hands, Augustus allowed the Senate – the traditional government of Rome – to take a share in running the empire, with responsibility for several provinces. Thus, in theory, the Republican forms endured, and administration remained in civilian not military hands. Under his successors, Roman rule expanded further still, but the Senate lost most of its power. Nevertheless, strong central control

ensured peace for over two centuries and population expanded, trade flourished and cities grew. In the mid-3rd century AD, however, Germanic invasions in the west and Persian victories in the east brought the empire temporarily to its knees. A series of strong emperors between AD 268 and AD 284 restored a semblance of orderly government to the empire, but Diocletian (AD 284-305) realized that a single ruler could no longer hold the whole edifice together. He divided power between himself and a joint Augustus,

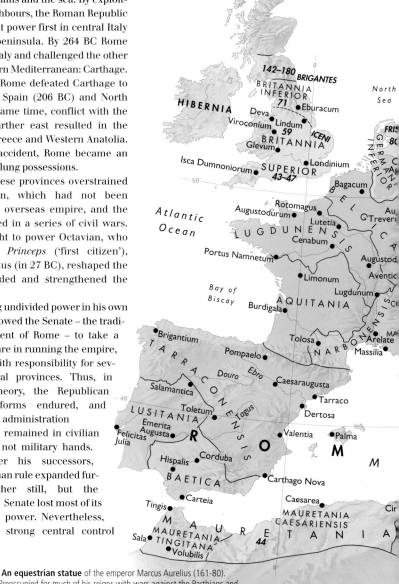

An equestrian statue of the emperor Marcus Aurelius (161-80). Preoccupied for much of his reigns with wars against the Parthians and the Germans (who in 170 invaded Italy), Marcus Aurelius maintained, but did not expand the Roman frontiers. He was the author of the *Meditations*, espousing stoicism as his philosophy in the face of adversity.

with two deputies (Caesars), and split the empire into four prefectures and twelve dioceses (map 2). By now the military had triumphed over the civilian, and a new basis had to be found for imperial authority. Under the influence of eastern ideas, the *Princeps* became *Dominus* (lord), an absolute ruler, at the head of a vast bureaucracy. Gradually the centre of Roman power shifted eastwards: Diocletian's successor Constantine (305–37) established a new capital at Byzantium (330), which he renamed Constantinople.

Although theoretically governed by joint rulers, the empire gradually broke into eastern and western halves, and when the western provinces crumbled before a new wave of Germanic invaders in the early 5th century, little help arrived from the east. Rome itself was sacked in 410 and 455, and the Ostrogoths created their own kingdom in Italy in 493. Justinian (AD 527–565) briefly recovered some of the western provinces but failed to reunite the empire.

Nevertheless, the Byzantine (East Roman) empire survived for another millennium, and many Roman traditions continued in the West. The Latin tongue, although developing into the derivative 'Romance' languages, long remained the language of churchmen and scientists; Roman Law forms the basis of most modern Western legal systems; many feats of Roman engineering genius survive to this day; and the Roman church lives on as a direct link with the past.

2 The Roman empire, AD 305–565

- – – – frontier of the Roman empire, AD 305
- ——— boundary of dioceses under Diocletian
- territory reconquered by Justinian, 533–54

Praetorian prefectures, c. 405:
- Praefectus Praetorio Galliarum
- Praefectus Praetorio Illyrici, Italiae, Africae
- Praefectus Praetorio per Illyricum
- Praefectus Praetorio per Orientem

1 The Roman empire, 31 BC–c. AD 250

- under administration of the Senate
- imperial provinces
- public provinces
- provinces added after AD 14, with date
- later subdivisions of provinces, with dates

INTERNET LINKS

www.metmuseum.org/toah/
hd/chem/hd_chem.htm
Comprehensive timeline of
Chinese rulers

TO AD 589

China: the first empires

c.1600–1030 BC The
Shang dynasty

c.1030-771 BC Chou
dynasty

c.475-221 BC Warring
States peiod

221 BC Shih Huang-ti
becomes first emperor of
China

202 BC–AD 9 Former
Han dynasty

AD25–220 Later Han
dynasty

AD 220 Last Han
emperor abdicates

220–589 Period of
political fragmentation

From the 16th to the 11th century BC China's first historical dynasty, the Shang, presided over a confederation of clans in the Yellow River valley. Around 1027 BC the Chou replaced them and extended their authority over the Yangtze valley as well, investing their supporters with fiefs to create a feudal hierarchy sustained by the services, food and clothes produced by peasant communities. Then in 771 BC western invaders sacked the Chou capital, and the feudatories seized the opportunity to break away. Over 100 belligerent political units sprang up. In the 5th century BC, however, bronze technology gave way to iron, animal power and irrigation transformed agriculture, increasing both food production and population, while warfare reduced the number of states. By 300 BC seven states still competed for hegemony; by 221 BC only one of them remained – Ch'in.

The Ch'in organized their subjects into groups which bore collective responsibility to maintain public order, and to provide manpower both for construction works (above all roads, canals and fortifications) and for the army (which was composed primarily of infantry). The defeated nobles suffered demotion and, instead of performing labour services to their lord, the peasants now paid taxes to the conqueror. A savage penal code, administered by a professional bureaucracy, enforced the new system.

In 221 BC Prince Cheng of Ch'in, took the title Shih Huang-ti (meaning 'first emperor'); ordered the construction of a national network of roads and canals, centered on his new capital at Hsieng-yang; rebuilt and strengthened the Great Wall; introduced a uniform coinage whose distinctive shape (circular with a square hole in the centre) remained standard until 1911; and took steps to standardize the written language throughout the empire. Small wonder that his dynasty gave 'China' its name.

The burdens imposed by the autocratic first emperor provoked civil war shortly after his death in 206 BC; but before long a new dynasty, the Han, reunited China. At first they worked through feudal principalities allocated to their family and supporters, but by 100 BC the fiefs had again come under strong central control. The Han also extended the Great Wall far to the north-west, undertook several military expeditions against the nomad Hsiung-nu in the north, invaded northern Vietnam and Korea, and for a brief period after 59 BC controlled the Tarim basin. They also eliminated the Min-Yüeh kingdoms of the south-east coast. A lively export trade, mainly in silk, began to Parthia and to the Roman empire.

Lake Balkhash

to Sogdiana
(K'ang-chu)

centre of Former
protectorate 59 BC–A

to Ferghana

Issyk Qul

Kashgar (Shu-le)

Takla Maka

Yarkand (Sha-ch'e)

Guma (P'i-shan)

to Bactria
(Ta-hsia)

Khotan (Ho-

Terracotta warriors from Sian (Xian). Discovered in 1974, close to the mausoleum of the first Ch'in emperor, thousands of terracotta warriors have since been excavated. Each figure was individually produced, and the varying uniforms, badges, weaponry and styles of armour provide information on the organization of the Ch'in army. By around 250 BC the Ch'in state was as large as all the other Chinese states put together. By 221 BC all the remaining states were absorbed by the Ch'in creating, for the first time, a unified China under Shih Huang-ti (the 'first emperor'). Although Ch'in rule collapsed in 206 BC, the Han dynasty inherited their unified kingdom.

1 The expansion of Han China

HSIUNGNU TRIBES

residence of the
Hsiungnu King

western extension to wall
built by Han emperors
117–100 BC

Li Ling's expedition 99 BC

Ho Ch'u-ping and Wei Ch'ing 119 BC

Li Kuang-li expedition 92 BC

Wei Ch'ing's expedition 128 BC

Karashahr
(Yen-ch'i)

田 Turfan
(Kao-ch'ang)

u-lei

Chiao-ho

Lo-lan

Lop Nor

Yü-men Kuan

Yang Kuan

田 Chuyen

Gobi Desert

-hsün

Tun-huang

Chiu
-ch'uan

CHIANG
TRIBES

brought under Chinese
administration 117–115 BC

arim Basin

Chang-yeh

Wu-wei

Yellow River

Great Wall rebuilt and strengthened
by Ch'in emperors 220–210 BC

administration 109–106 BC

KOREA

Yellow
Sea

Yellow River

Lo-yang

Mount Yi

Ch'ang-an

Sian

CH'IN EMPIRE
(221–207 BC)

1 The expansion of Han China

China, 207 BC

territory added under Former Han

maximum extent of Former Han empire

territory of Chinese protectorate of
Western Regions, c. 59 BC

journey of Chang Chien, envoy of
Han emperor, 138–126 BC

trade routes

田 administrative centre under Later Han
from AD 126

centre of Later Han protectorate,
AD 73–126

territory added under Later Han

new route opened by General
Pan Chao for Later Han

expeditions against Hsiungnu
(Huns)

(first explorations from 136 BC)
expeditions against Tien:
109 BC kingdom suppressed

86 BC ⎱ expeditions to far
82 BC ⎰ southwest

Yangtze

MIN-YÜEH

defeated 100 BC

KINGDOM OF NAN-YÜEH
(206–113 BC)

under Chinese
administration
after 111 BC

South
China
Sea

VIETNAM

A census in AD 2 revealed some 57 million people in the empire. Great cities abounded, the largest – Ch'ang-an, the capital – housing 250,000 people. The heart of the empire remained the Yellow River plain, where population densities in some areas approached 150 per square mile (see map 2). Shortly afterwards, however, court families and great feudatories increased their influence, while agrarian unrest mounted. Real power lay in the hands of the regional commanders and warlords and the last Han emperor abdicated in 220. The Han empire fragmented into three regional states and a century later the Hsiung-nu burst through the Great Wall and overran northern China (see page 40). China was to remain politically fragmented until AD 589.

Yellow River

2 The population of China, AD 2

very dense settlement,
approx. 150 per sq. mile

heavily settled,
approx. 100 per sq. mile

lightly settled,
approx. 30 per sq. mile

The transformation of the ancient world

INTERNET LINKS

www.friesian.com/
germania.htm
Successor states to Rome

316 Hsiung-nu sack ancient Chinese capital of Ch'ang-an

378 Visigoths defeat Romans at Adrianople

406 Vandals, Alans and Sueves breach the Roman frontier and invade Gaul

410 Visigoths under Alaric sack Rome

441 Hsien-pi invade north China

451 Huns – led by Attila – defeated by Romans at Châlons

476 Last western Roman emperor deposed

480 White Huns destroy Gupta empire of India

484 White Huns invade Persia and kill Sassanian emperor

By the 3rd century AD, a continuous web of large states stretched across the southern half of the continents of Europe and Asia. In the West, Rome controlled the whole Mediterranean world and much of Europe; in China, the Han ruled a state that equalled the Roman empire in population and extended from the Pacific to the Takla Makan desert in central Asia; in between lay the Persian empire. The co-existence of these great states brought to vast areas of the Old World internal peace and centralised government, conditions that made possible commercial and cultural interchange on an unprecedented scale.

But this 'imperial zone' formed only a narrow corridor, flanked to the north by the domain of nomadic tribes, expert horsemen who possessed in war a speed and striking power that their sedentary neighbours could rarely match. In

the 4th and 5th centuries AD, numerous nomad groups launched devastating attacks against all the major civilizations. A confederation known as the Hsiung-nu from Mongolia broke through the Great Wall of China in AD 304 and within a decade reached the Yellow River, sacking the ancient Han capital Ch'ang-an (AD 316). A succession of invaders from the steppes dominated northern China for the next three centuries.

1 The collapse of the ancient world

→ Hsiung-nu and Huns

→ Juan-juan (Avars)

→ Goths and Vandals

→ other peoples

▮ Roman Empire, c.AD 454

▮ Gupta Empire, c.AD 410

▮ Sassanian Empire, c.AD 261

▮ Han Empire, c.AD 100

ᴖᴖᴖ fortified frontiers

At the same time another nomadic people, the Huns, swept south-westwards through Asia, causing a chain reaction among the Germanic peoples along the Black Sea and the Danube. To escape them the Visigoths, perhaps 80,000 strong, forced their way into the Balkans and in AD 378 defeated a large Roman army outside Adrianople. Next, they moved into Italy and in AD 410 captured and sacked Rome itself. Meanwhile other Germanic tribes crossed the Rhine. The Vandals, the Alans and the Suevi invaded Gaul in AD 406 and plundered it for three years before passing on to Spain and north Africa. In their wake, the Franks, the Burgundians and the Alemanni also invaded Gaul, while the Picts from Scotland and marauders from the continent ravaged Britain. The empire's only success came in AD 451 when, with the aid of the Franks and Visigoths, a Roman army defeated and drove back the Huns, led by Attila, at the battle of Châlons.

In AD 480 another branch of the Huns invaded India and destroyed the Gupta empire (page 28) before attacking the Persian empire, where they defeated and killed its ruler in AD 484. Finally, around AD 550, warlike nomads from central Asia – the Avars – moved west and within a generation ravaged Gaul and the Balkans. They were followed by the Slavs and Bulgars, who also invaded the Balkans, and by the Lombards, who occupied northern Italy.

By AD 600 the great cities of Eurasia – Rome, Ch'ang-an, and countless others – were in serious decline. Yet the process, once seen as 'collapse', formed part of an ongoing transformation in which new power structures replaced the old. In many areas, traditional learning and skills were retained and adapted to changing conditions. In India and northern China, the invaders adopted native methods of government and co-operated with local elites, taking on their customs and culture as they did so. In Europe, too, the Roman tradition was modified rather than supplanted by the imposition of rulers of Germanic origin: the Franks in France; the Visigoths in Spain; the Ostrogoths in Italy. The deposition of the last Roman emperor in the west in AD 476 marked only a minor step in the transformation of the west from classical to medieval. The Latin tongue survived almost everywhere, while Christian monasteries and Islamic scholars transmitted knowledge of classical culture to future generations.

A helmet from the Anglo-Saxon ship burial at Sutton Hoo. Dating from around AD 650, the grave is testament to a period of transition in England between paganism and Christianity.

550 Juan-juan (Avars) drive westwards out of Mongolia by Blue (Celestial) Turks

Great Wall of China in AD 220

Hsien-pi invade north China by 440

north China reunified under Toba Wei

1st century AD Hsiung-nu broken by Han China and move westwards

Hsiung-nu renew attacks on China, sacking capital Loyang 311, Changan 316

expansion of Tibetans

480 White Huns destroy Gupta empire

TWO
The World Fragmented

After AD 500 the narrow chain of empires extending from Rome to China crumbled under attacks from nomads from the Asian steppes. Contacts between China and the West, between north Africa and Italy and between Byzantium and western Europe dwindled as each region fell back on its own resources and had to fend for itself.

In Eurasia, two phenomena dominated: the expansion of Islam after 632; and the emergence of the Mongol empire after 1206. Meanwhile, the Maya, Aztec and Inca civilizations appeared in America, the empires of Sri Vijaya and Majapahit grew in southeast Asia, and the empires of Ghana, Mali and Songhay developed in Africa. Europe, by comparison, remained backward until, in the second half of the 15th century, a series of path-breaking voyages of exploration laid the foundations for overseas expansion. Even then, however, Europe's achievements remained overshadowed and threatened by the expanding power of the Ottoman Turks for another century.

Death strangling a plague victim,
from the 14th-century Stiny Codex (Prague University)

INTERNET LINKS

www.earlychurch.org.uk
Extensive database on the
early church

TO 1500

The spread of Christianity

Christianity began as a Jewish splinter movement in Roman Palestine. Its founder, Jesus of Nazareth, claimed to be the Messiah, or Saviour, sent to prepare the Jews for 'the kingdom of God' but, after an initial, short-lived success, he was executed as a revolutionary (AD 29). Jewish orthodoxy rejected his message, but his followers turned instead to the conversion of non-Jews and by AD 200, despite repression and persecution, communities of Christians (as the followers of Jesus came to be called) flourished in several cities of the Roman empire (especially Antioch and Edessa). In AD 313 the Emperor Constantine granted the new faith toleration and in AD 325 at Nicaea presided over the first ecumenical council, representing the whole church, which defined beliefs for all Christians. A full ecclesiastical organization developed, with a hierarchy of bishops and a framework of patriarchates, provinces and dioceses throughout the empire (map 1).

The council of Chalcedon (451) attempted to enforce orthodoxy on the Christian world, but instead alienated the Monophysite (or Coptic) Christians of Egypt, Syria and Armenia, and the Nestorians who, expelled from Edessa, took refuge in Persia. Meanwhile the disintegration of the Roman empire in the West (page 36) undermined the position of the church. But salvation came from the periphery. The Coptic church of Egypt, with a strong monastic tradition, sent missionaries down the Nile from the 4th century, converting the peoples of Nubia and Ethiopia; while from the 7th century, the Nestorians of Persia expanded south into Arabia and east to China. In the west, the impetus for revival came from the monastic missionary church of Ireland, which evangelized first its Celtic neighbours in Britain and Brittany, and then in the 7th and 8th centuries the pagan tribes of continental Europe (map 2).

As the Muslim onslaught devastated the Christian Mediterranean (page 50), both Rome and Constantinople launched missions northwards among the Slavs. Russia opted for Orthodox Christianity, and in 988 the Russian prince Vladimir was baptized, while Poland (966) and Hungary (1001) chose Catholic Christianity. Although rivalry

between the two patriarchates resulted after 1054 in schism, the popes increased their authority by sponsoring Christian counter-offensives in Iberia, the Baltic and West Asia: the crusades (page 48). The attempt to restore Christianity to Palestine proved a costly failure, but the crusades made great advances elsewhere. Meanwhile, within Europe, monks and (from the 13th century) friars joined the expanding network of parish clergy in Christianizing the countryside and combating heresy. In 1387 Lithuania, the last remaining pagan state in Europe, converted to Catholicism, just as persecution by Timur and other rulers (page 60) extinguished the faith in Asia, the continent of its birth.

1 The early Christian churches

main areas of Christian growth, to AD 300

areas largely Christian by AD 600

● important Christian communities of the 1st century

● other important Christian centres, by AD 600

♀ the five patriarchates

✚ important bishops with dates of episcopate

◆ other important figures, with dates

2 Christianity in medieval Europe

- Roman-rite Christians, c. 1400
- Byzantine-rite Christians, c. 1400
- Monophysite Christians
- Islam
- ▬▬ extent of Catholic (Frankish) Christianity (c. 700)
- ▬ ▬ maximum extent of crusader states in the east in the 12th century
- ● important bishoprics
- (743) date of foundation of a bishopric or of conversion of a region to Christianity

Trondheim *(1029)*
FINLAND *(13th cent.)*
Bergen *(1070)*
Turku *(1220)*
Uppsala *(1164)*
Novgorod *(1135)*
Armagh
York
North Sea
Aarhus *(948)*
Riga *(1198)*
Polotsk *(1113)*
Moscow *(1326)*
Canterbury
Lund *(c. 950)*
Smolensk *(1128)*
LITHUANIA *(1387)*
Bremen *(788)*
Hamburg *(834)*
Gniezno *(1000)*
PRUSSIA *(14th cent.)*
Rouen
Magdeburg *(958)*
POLAND *(10th cent.)*
Paris
Rheims
Mainz *(743)*
Prague *(973)*
MORAVIA *(9th cent.)*
Cracow *(1004)*
Kiev *(988)*
Tours
Regensburg *(739)*
HUNGARY *(10th cent.)*
Salzburg *(798)*
Lyons
Gran *(1001)*
Avignon
SERBIA *(c. 870)*
Kherson
Santiago de Compostela *(c. 840)*
Saragossa *(1118)*
Rome
Black Sea
Lisbon *(1147)*
Toledo *(1085)*
Valencia *(1238)*
BULGARIA *(c. 870)*
Ochrida *(c. 870)*
Constantinople
GRANADA *(1492)*
Salonica

ICELAND *(1000)*

Mediterranean Sea

Antioch
Acre
Jerusalem
Alexandria

Sirmium
Singidunum
Black Sea
ARMENIA
Artashat
Serdica
+John Chrysostom (398–404)
+Nestorius (428–31)
Sinope
Neocaesarea
Sebastea
PERSIA
Philippi
Constantinople
Gangra
Ancyra
Caesarea
Melitene
+Basil (370–7/9)
Nisibis
Thessalonica
Nicomedia
Nicaea
Cappadociae
Samosata
Amida
Beroea
Cyzicus
Nyssa
Nazianzus
Edessa
+Ephrem (306–73)
Troas
Pergamum
Antioch
Iconium
Cyrrhus
Thyatira
Philadelphia
Lystra
Tarsus
Antioch
+Ignatius (d. c. 112)
Dura-Europos
Smyrna
Sardes
Hierapolis
Derbe
Gondeshapur
Athens
Ephesus **431**
Laodicea
Laodicea
Palmyra
Seleucia-Ctesiphon
Corinth
Patmos
Myra
Salamis
SYRIA
Damascus
Tyre
Pella
Caesarea
+Cyril (c. 350–86)
+Eusebius (d. c. 339)
Antioch
+Cyril (c. 350–86)
Diospolis-Lydda
Jerusalem
Gaza
Bethlehem
Pelusium
Ptolemais
Cyrene
Alexandria
Thmuis
EGYPT
◆Origen (c.185–254)
◆Arius (d. 336)
+Athanasius (328–73)
+Cyril (412–44)
Oxyrhynchus
Red Sea
Lycopolis
Chenoboskion

A stone slab of the Apostles Peter and Paul from the sepulchre of the child Amellus dating from after 313 (below). Following the conversion of Constantine, Christian art became more public and explicit representations of Christ and the saints were common. Portraits of Peter and Paul from Rome proudly allude to the connection of the two leading apostles with the city and its powerful bishops. In this example, they are depicted as Roman gentlemen of high social status, as the purple stripe of their togas attests.

PETRVS PAVLVS

INTERNET LINKS

www.wsu.edu/~dee/
CHEMPIRE/SUNG.HTM
Sung China

581–1279
China

581-617 China reunified under the Sui dynasty

618–907 The T'ang dynasty

960 Coup d'état of General Chao K'unag-yin, who becomes first Sung emperor

963–79 Sung reunite China

1126–7 Tatar Chin conquer northern China

1211–34 Mongols conquer northern China

1235–79 Mongols conquer southern China

After the barbarian invasions of the 4th and 5th centuries (page 38) the Sui dynasty (581-617) reunified China. They consolidated their empire through standardized institutions, a state-supported broad-based Buddhism, and the construction of a canal system linking the Yangtze with the Yellow River and the Lo-yang region. The T'ang dynasty (618-907) continued the process, creating a uniform administrative organization of prefectures, in which officials recruited through an examination system replaced the traditional aristocracy. The T'ang also extended their control to the Tarim basin and northern Korea: in the 660s, the Chinese empire reached its greatest extent and 88 Asiatic peoples recognised Chinese overlordship, adopting its culture, its written language and its political institutions (map 1).

In 751, however, at the Talas River, an Arab army defeated the Chinese, while a major rebellion rocked T'ang power in 755-62, causing many of the new conquests to be abandoned. Within the empire, power began to pass to the provinces until in 907, following a wave of peasant uprisings, China split into ten separate regional states. Although the Sung dynasty reunified the country between 960 and 979, they failed to regain the new territories. Nevertheless, Chinese economic growth continued. A massive movement of population into the fertile Yangtze valley and southern China produced large agricultural surpluses which stimulated trade and economic development. Between 750 and 1100, the population of the empire doubled; trade reached new heights; and a great concentration of industries arose around the capital, K'ai-feng, centre of the canal system and of the eastern road network.

2 Sung China, 960–1279

- ● provincial capitals
- —— canals
- —— principal roads
- —— boundary between Southern Sung and Chin after 1127

A foreign merchant. Most of the trade along the Silk Road – the trade routes linking China and West Asia – was handled by the Chinese and the nomadic peoples of central and western Asia. The T'ang generally regarded them with interested amusement, as is evident in this glazed pottery figure of a camel groom or trader with his exaggeratedly large nose.

powerful unified Turkish kingdom in 6th century, split into Eastern and Western groups c.585. Eastern Turks conquered by T'ang 630, but re-emerge from 681 and 699–715 are re-united with Western Turks. In 715 Western Turks break away: Eastern Turks finally destroyed 744

KIRGHIZ

Shih-Wei

AMUR

MALGAL

powerful kingdom on the T'ang model that included remnants of the Korean Koguryŏ ruling elite over Malgal tribespeople. Possibly the first Manchurian state. Independent from 698 and named Pohai from 712. Destroyed by Khitan 926.

TURKS to 744

UIGHURS
Uighurs replace Turks in the steppe 745–840; more stable, less anti-Chinese than Turks. Destroyed by Kirghiz

KHITAN (LIAO)
proto-Mongol people, raid T'ang border from 695, sometimes vassals of Turks. Set up own empire (Liao) in Manchuria in early 10th century

POHAI (PARHAE)

still occupied by Emishi aboriginal peoples

STAN

UNGARIA

Turfan

Hami

Gobi Desert

NINGSIA

T'ang occupation 668–676

Sea of Japan (East Sea)

m Basin

Yellow River

Pohai

SILLA

ng
–763

Tun-huang

to Tibet 763–843

KANSU

Ch'ang-an

Lo-yang

Yang-chou

JAPAN

Kyoto

Nara

unified kingdom c.600. Expansion after 650; under Chinese cultural influence until c.750 then Indian influence. Central control collapsed c.840

T'ANG

EMPIRE

OF

independent politically; increasing Chinese cultural influence from 6th century. In 7th century a strong centralized kingdom developed, based on T'ang institutions

ET

Ch'eng-tu

Silla allied with the T'ang and destroyed Paekche in 660 and Koguryŏ in 668. T'ang betrayed the alliance but Silla succeeded in expelling T'ang by 676

Yangtze

Ning-po

Brahmaputra

CHINA

NAN-CHAO
kingdom formed by federation of tribal groups organized on T'ang model

850–70

Canton

South China Sea

1 The Chinese world, 7th–8th centuries

under permanent T'ang civil administration

area of temporary occupation during 7th century

under T'ang military control

zone of Chinese cultural dominance

trade routes — Tibetan expansion

canals — advance of Islam

c. 800

Chiao-chou

ANNAM

PYU

Pagan

Sukhothai

Indianized Buddist kingdom invaded by Nan-chao in 8th and 9th centuries

Mekong

Hue

CHAMPA

KHMER

kingdom centred on Hue. Strong Indian influence

kingdom under strong Indian/Hindu influence

In 1126-7 the Chin, a powerful nomadic state north-east of the Great Wall, invaded and conquered all of northern China, with terrible devastation. The Sung now controlled only the centre and the south, but stood constantly on the defensive, maintaining huge armies and paying vast subsidies to their aggressive neighbours (map 2). Even after the Chin invasion, however, the Sung state remained immensely prosperous, since its southern territories proved far more productive than the old northern heartland of China.

Population continued to increase rapidly; trade and industry boomed; and the new capital, Hang-chou, became the world's largest city. This was also a period of great cultural achievement. The visual arts, literature, philosophy, science and technology all reached new heights; education became more widespread, aided by the dissemination of printing, which had been invented in T'ang times and now became commonplace. Merchants formed guilds and partnerships, setting up a complex commercial organization with banks, credit systems and paper money. The government was run by a mandarinate of career bureaucrats.

But their days were numbered. Between 1211 and 1234 the Mongols (page 60) had overrun the Chin empire, causing widespread devastation, and in the 1270s the forces of Kublai Khan – 'the most powerful man since Adam' according to a European visitor – annexed the entire Sung empire. For the first time, all of China lay under foreign rule.

INTERNET LINKS

www.metmuseum.org/explore/
byzantium/byzhome.html —
The Metropolitan Museum
of Art's Byzantium exhibition

610–1453

The Byzantine world

Almost from its inception, the Roman empire's centre of gravity moved to the east, first pulled by the lure of economic wealth in Egypt and western Asia; then pushed by the loss of the western provinces to Germanic invaders (page 36) and by the pressure of Sassanid Persia on its eastern frontier. Except during the reign of Justinian (page 37), the west was neglected and the Roman empire became an eastern, Greek-speaking state – normally known, from the reign of Heraclius (610-641), as Byzantium.

Heraclius ended the long contest with Persia victoriously, capturing Nineveh in 628, but almost at once Byzantium faced two even more redoubtable foes: Islam (page 50) and the Slavs. However, after the failure of two long Arab sieges of Byzantium (674-8 and 717-18), the empire launched a succession of vigorous counter-offensives. Basil II (976-1025) even managed to advance the imperial frontiers close to their earlier limits: the Arabs retreated into Palestine; the Russians met defeat at Silistra on the Danube; the Bulgars, who had advanced to within 60 miles of Constantinople, became imperial subjects; plans were laid to recover the former Byzantine territories in Italy. However, the constant campaigns imposed heavy financial strains, as well as profound and debilitating social change, and in spite of further phases of recovery, the frontiers steadily shrank (map 1).

The crucial development was the emergence, in the 11th century, of the Seljuk Turks (page 50), whose crushing victory over Byzantine forces at Manzikert in 1071 induced Emperor Alexius I (1081-1118) to call on the west for help, thus initiating the sequence of events that led to the First Crusade (1096-9). It proved

a disastrous move since the Franks were less concerned to aid Byzantium than to set up their own principalities in Palestine and Asia Minor; the Normans, already in control of Sicily and Byzantine Italy, coveted lands in Greece; and the Italian cities, led by Venice, strove to increase their share of Mediterranean trade. After a century of mounting tension, the soldiers of the Fourth Crusade in 1204 conquered and pillaged Constantinople, partitioned the Byzantine empire, and established Latin states all over the Balkans (map 2).

The Latin Empire proved short-lived – its Greek-speaking subjects resented it and a new dynasty, the Palaeologi, restored the Greek empire in 1261 – but the new Byzantine state was only a shadow of its former self and when, shortly afterwards, the Ottoman Turks established themselves first in Asia Minor and then advanced into Byzantium's European territories, its fate was sealed. The capital of the east Roman empire fell in 1453 (page 70).

Nevertheless, the history of Byzantium includes both greatness and lasting achievements. For centuries it transmitted Roman culture back to areas from which earlier invasions had largely effaced it. It also passed on its culture and its religion to the Balkan peoples and to Russia. 'Two Romes have fallen', a Russian monk wrote shortly after 1453, 'but the third is still standing and a fourth shall never be.' He referred to Moscow (page 56), now emerged as the heir to the Byzantine inheritance.

The emperor Constantine IV Pogonatus and his brothers hand privileges to the Ravenna church of Sant'Apollinare in Classe and to archbishop Mauro. During his reign Constantinople withstood a four year siege by Arab armies (674–8), although much of the Balkans was overrun by Slav tribes and the Bulgars.

Genoa
Fl

Corsica

Sardinia

Carali

Valentia

Balearic Islands

Carthago Nova

Carthage

AFRICA

1 Byzantine greatness and decline

Imperial frontiers

c. 628	c. 1143		
c. 1030	1328		

special areas:

Exarchate of Ravenna to Lombards, 751

Exarchate of Africa to Arabs from 670

Catapanate of Italy to Normans from 1071

temporary reconquests:

Africa, 685–710

Syria, 975–6

Sicily, 1038–43

Ani, 1054

Edessa, 1052

Rum, c. 1118

general territorial losses:

to Arabs, 636–641

to Arabs after 641

to Seljuk Turks from 1065

Sultanate of Rum from 1071

2 The West attacks Byzantium

- ·········▶ the Norman attack, 1084–5
- ·········▶ the Norman attack, 1147
- ──────▶ routes of the First Crusade, 1096–9
- ·········▶ the Norman attack, 1185
- ──────▶ route of the Fourth Crusade 1204
- ────── imperial frontier in 1180
- territory lost to other powers, 1180–1214
- despotate of Epirus (est. 1204)
- imperial territory in 1214
- Latin Empire in 1214
- Venetian territory in 1214
- other Greek states

**Upper map labels:**

CUMANS · CUMANS · Venice · DALMATIA · Adriatic Sea · SERBIA · Vidin · Danube · Ragusa · Serdica · BULGARIA · Mesembria · Black Sea · Sinope · EMPIRE OF TREBIZOND · Theodosiopolis · Manzikert · Philippopolis · Ochrida · Prilep · Vodena · Adrianople · Tzurulum · Constantinople · Nicomedia · Ancyra · Kastamuni · Sebastea · SELJUKS OF RUM · Dyrrhachium · Thessalonica · Cyzicus · Nicaea · EMPIRE OF NICAEA · Bari · Berrhoea · Adramyttium · Prusa · Dorylaeum · Halys · Caesarea · Tigris · Brundisium · Avlona · Castoria · Lemnos · Pergamum · Amorium · Philomelium · Samosata · Marash · Edessa · KINGDOM OF SICILY · Corfu · Larissa · Lesbos · Aegean Sea · Sardis · Smyrna · Chios · Meander · Iconium · Tyana · Carrhae · Nicopolis · Cephalonia · MOREA · Athens · Corinth · Chonae · Sozopolis · Attalia · Heraclea · Tarsus · Aleppo · Zacynthus · Modon · Cos · Rhodes · Cyprus · Antioch · Euphrates · Monemvasia · Crete · Homs · Mediterranean Sea · LEVANT · Tripoli

**Lower map labels:**

ISTRIA · Sava · ABASGIA · IBERIA · Tiflis · Bosporus · LAZICA · ALBANIA · Ani · enna · Iadera · MOESIA · Singidunum · Danube · Nicopolis · ✕ Silistra 971 · Chersonesus · Black Sea · Salonae · Odessus · Sinope · Trebizond · PONTUS · DUCHY OF SPOLETO · Ragusa · DACIA · Scupi · Serdica · Philippopolis · THRACE · Halys · Neocaesarea · Manzikert 1071 ✕ · L. Van · oles · DUCHY OF BENEVENTO · Dyrrhachium · Barium · NEW EPIRUS · MACEDONIA · Adrianople · Constantinople · Nicomedia · PAPHLAGONIA · Sebastea · Mosul · DUCHY OF NAPLES · Brundisium · Salonica · BITHYNIA · GALATIA · Caesarea · CAPPADOCIA · Samosata · Tigris · Edessa · Nineveh 628 ✕ · PERSIA · henian Sea · Tarentum · ANCIENT EPIRUS · Larissa · Cotiaeum · PISIDIA · Iconium · CILICIA · Beroea · Euphrates · icily · Messana · THESSALY · Smyrna · LYDIA · PHRYGIA · Ephesus · Miletus · PAMPHYLIA · ISAURIA · Tarsus · Antioch · Palmyra · Syracuse · Patras · Athens · Aegean Sea · Rhodes · Cyprus · to Byzantium 965 · Tripolis · Ionian Sea · Crete · to Byzantium 961 · Damascus · Bostra · Mediterranean Sea · Caesarea · PALESTINE · Jerusalem · Gaza · Petra · ARABIA · olis · Apollonia · Ptolemais · PENTAPOLIS · Alexandria · EGYPT · Damietta · Pelusium · Mareotis · Nile · Memphis · Arsenoe · Tabuk · OLITANIA

INTERNET LINKS

www.muslimheritage.com
Muslim history and culture
from AD 600

632–1517
The Islamic world

The rise and expansion of Islam ranks as perhaps the most significant development in world history between the fall of Rome and the European invasion of the Americas. Within a remarkably short time, a new world religion created a dynamic civilization which now embraces one-seventh of the global population: 600 million Muslims, spread from Morocco to Indonesia, and from Siberia to Zanzibar. 'Islam', which means 'submission to the will of God', was conveyed to humankind through the Koran, a volume of prescriptions on behaviour as well as belief, revealed by God to Mohammed his prophet, who was born in the religious and commercial centre of Mecca about 570. As Mohammed's followers grew in number, they aroused the hostility of the merchants of Mecca and in 622 the group withdrew to the neighbouring town of Medina (the *hijra*). But Mohammed returned to Mecca in triumph in 630, transforming it into the focal point for the new faith of Islam, and when he died in 632 his authority extended over the Hejaz and much of central and southern Arabia.

For the next century Islam expanded rapidly: Arab armies defeated Latin Christian, Byzantine, Persian, Indian and Chinese armies to spread the new faith from the Himalayas in the east to the Atlantic in the west (map 1). In 711 they crossed over the Straits of Gibraltar and conquered Spain. Until 656 political control over the empire remained with Mohammed's relatives, but then a split occurred, with some Muslims following Ali, the Prophet's cousin and son-in-law (the Shi'ites), and others – the majority – accepting the rule of the Umayyad dynasty from Mecca who claimed to represent the Sunna or traditions of the Prophet. The Umayyads ruled from Damascus in Syria between 661 and 750, followed by the rival Abbasid dynasty, who created a new capital at Baghdad in Mesopotamia and opened government to non-Arab Muslims (known as *mawali*).

Gradually, the Muslim world lost its political unity and split into a number of local dynastic entities, some Sunnite and others Shi'ite (map 2). In 1055, however, the centre of the Islamic world was strengthened when the Seljuk Turks established themselves in Baghdad and shortly thereafter drove the Christians from most of Anatolia (page 48). Despite invasions from the west in the 12th century (the Crusades: page 49) and from the east in the 13th (the Mongols: page 60), Islam retained its hold over West Asia, while missionaries and merchants carried the faith eastwards to Malaysia, Indonesia and the Philippines, and southwards both to the sub-Saharan states and the cities of the Swahili coast of Africa (page 58). For a millennium after the birth of Mohammed, Islam remained the western hemisphere's leading and most extensive civilization.

2 The Muslim world, 786–1260

- — Abbasid caliphate at greatest extent during rule of Haroun al-Rashid, 786–809
- areas recognizing Abbasid sovereignty, c. 1090
- disputed between Seljuks and Byzantine empire, c. 1070–c. 1180
- Zaidi Imams
- Almohads, c. 1160
- → lines of nomadic advance

The mosque at Córdoba with its ornate exterior decoration bears witness to the great wealth of Islamic Spain. The mosque was built by 'Abd ar Rahman I, a member of the ruling Umayyad family in Syria, who escaped their overthrow by the Abbasids to found a new Umayyad dynasty in Spain. Seizing power in 755, he made Córdoba his capital and resisted all attempts by the Abbasids to unseat him.

1 The spread of Islam

- growth under Mohammed
- growth under Abu Bakr, (632–4)
- growth under Omar, (634–44)
- growth under Othman (644–56) and Ali (656–61)
- expansion of Umayyad Caliphate, (661–750)
- expansion under the early Abbasids, (750–850)
- → routes of advance
- **638** date of Muslim conquest

www.bbc.co.uk/dna/h2g2/
A251542 —

Dynastic change in Francia;
from Merovingians to
Carolingians

INTERNET LINKS

486-843

Franks and Anglo-Saxons

Within a century of the Germanic invasions, settled kingdoms had grown up in western Europe, but not in Britain, where invaders from the continent met with resistance. During the 7th century, however, seven separate important kingdoms – which are traditionally known as the Heptarchy – emerged in England. Geographical obstacles seem to have prevented the states in the south-east (Sussex, Kent, Essex, East Anglia) from expanding, and leadership at first passed to Northumbria, whose progress benefitted from its early conversion to Christianity. Mercia led the opposition, sometimes in alliance with the 'Britons' on the periphery, and by the time of Offa (757-96) its pre-eminence was unquestionable: it controlled the four southeastern kingdoms, and even Wessex recognized Mercian overlordship.

On the continent, the Franks (whose original power base lay in what is now northern France, the Low Countries and the Rhineland) converted to Christianity under Clovis (481-511) and began to expand south and east. From their new capital at Paris, Clovis and his sons and grandsons defeated the Visigoths, conquered Burgundy and Provence, and extended their overlordship in Germany as far as the middle Danube.

Most of the new lands served to maintain the loyalty of the Frankish warriors, however, and when the conquests ceased in the mid-7th century the kings had to reward their followers and endow the Church by granting away their own estates and

revenues. In doing so they diminished their resources and, in time, power passed to the families which had benefitted from royal favour. Eventually Pippin of Herstal, from a leading Austrasian family, achieved prominence, and at Tertry (687) defeated his chief rivals.

Pippin and his son Charles Martel (from whom the dynasty took the name 'Carolingian') restored Frankish fortunes and inaugurated a second surge of territorial expansion (map 2). Charles Martel (714-41) defeated the Arabs at Tours in 732, halting their rapid incursion into western Europe, while his son Pippin the Short (d. 768) expelled them from southern France. In 751, with the sanction and support of the pope, Pippin made himself king of the Franks. His son Charles the Great or Charlemagne (768-814) conquered Lombardy (774) and established Frankish rule in much of Italy. He won great victories over the Frisians (784-5), Bavarians (788) and Saxons (finally subdued in 804); and created a march, or boundary province, across the Pyrenees

An image of Charlemagne from his tomb at Aachen. The tomb was endowed by Frederick Barbarossa in the 12th century. The masterpiece of gold enamels and gems shows that, for the later emperor, Charlemagne was a saint and a personal patron, able to confer political legitimacy.

52

between 795 and 812. In 800 the pope in Rome crowned him emperor of the west .

However, Frankish custom called for the royal domain to be partitioned. Charlemagne's father had divided it between his two sons – Charlemagne only inherited the whole when his brother died in 771 – and the new emperor likewise planned in 806 to partition his possessions among his three sons, a scheme frustrated only by the early death of two of them. This made it possible for the survivor, Louis the Pious (814-40), to inherit the whole empire. After his death, however, the treaty of Verdun (843) created three kingdoms: one in the east, one in the west, and a 'middle kingdom' which ran from the North Sea to Italy.

The Carolingians ruled through direct agents, rather than through Gallo-Roman bishops and counts as their predecessors had done; and throughout the 8th century these men generally remained loyal. After Charlemagne's death, however, their descendants tended to identify with the particular interests of their own localities, at the expense of the whole. Frankish hegemony in western Europe was thus disrupted by fragmentation just as it came under attack from the Vikings and Magyars.

1 Anglo-Saxon England, c. AD 800

Mercia and subordinate kingdoms under Offa (757–96)

allied with Mercia

British kingdoms

2 The empire of Charlemagne

Frankish realm 714

added to Frankish empire by 814

Frankish dependencies (with date of formation)

Frankish royal residences

archbishoprics

important monasteries

GASCONY 769 province with date of acquisition

INTERNET LINKS

www.britannia.com/history/
monarchs/mon6.html
Biography of Alfred the
Great

814–1250

Europe

Three separate groups of invaders in the 9th century shattered the relative stability achieved by Charlemagne in western Europe and by Offa of Mercia in England (page 52). The Saracens occupied the islands of the western Mediterranean and raided Italy and France; the Magyars of Hungary devastated northern Italy and Germany; the Vikings from Scandinavia not only plundered settlements around the European coast as far as the Mediterranean, but also created trade routes through Russia to Byzantium (page 56) and settled substantial parts of Britain, Ireland, northern France, Iceland and even Greenland.

The invasions disrupted royal authority and caused political fragmentation. In the Carolingian empire, the Frankish kings virtually capitulated to the Vikings, leaving defence to the local magnates who swiftly created their own power bases. In England, although determined resistance by Alfred the Great of Wessex (871-99) held the Danes at bay,

a second wave of Scandinavian invasions a century later proved irresistible. However in the eastern half of the Frankish empire, Otto I's defeat of the Magyars at the Lechfeld (955) proved a turning point, and Germany became the first country in Europe to recover from the invasions. This achievement assured its predominance in Europe for almost three centuries.

German rulers rarely sought to assert control over the west Frankish lands but, as heirs to the Carolingians, they claimed the imperial title and the right to rule over Italy and the lands of the former "middle kingdom" (page 53). In 962 Otto's coronation as emperor sealed the connection between Germany and Italy, and in 1034 his successors annexed Burgundy. However the emperors became increasingly dependent upon the wealth of Italy, and this embroiled Frederick I of Hohenstaufen (1152-90) with both the papacy and the populous fortified cities of the Lombard plain,

A carved wooden head from the Oseberg cart (c. 800) depicts a fearsome Viking warrior. Viking success was in large part achieved not through superior organization or tactical skill, but depended on their greater mobility. They were able to launch lightning attacks on undefended coastal settlements and penetrate far inland in shallow boats or on horseback.

which all saw Imperial power in Italy as a threat to their independence. The conquest of Sicily by Frederick's son Henry VI in 1194 made the Hohenstaufen the richest rulers in Europe; but the prospect of total encirclement once more alarmed the papacy and the Lombard towns, leading to a long and costly struggle with Henry's son Frederick II (1212-50). After his death, the Imperial position in Italy steadily deteriorated, and the last Hohenstaufen prince met defeat and death at the battle of Tagliacozzo in 1268.

Meanwhile, in Germany, the princes took advantage of their rulers' preoccupation with Italy both to consolidate their power and, on the eastern frontier, to direct a major expansion. The Slavs were driven out or enslaved, in favour of German settlers who, by 1250, had increased the German kingdom by about one-third and shifted its centre of gravity from the Rhine to the Elbe. The empire might no longer have been the strongest or richest polity in Europe, but it remained the largest.

2 The German empire to 1250

- eastward spread of German peasant settlement, 12th century
- German settlement, 1200–1250
- city with over 10,000 inhabitants
- member of Lombard Leagues of 1167 and 1226
- member of 1167 League only
- member of 1226 League only
- main royal routes
- German invasions, 1190–94
- Henry VI's Genoese and Pisan fleet, 1194
- main Hohenstaufen palaces and castles
- monasteries

The first Russian state: Kievan Russia

INTERNET LINKS

www.friesian.com/
russia.htm
Comprehensive guide to
Russian history

862 Vikings seize
Novgorod

882 Oleg unites Novgorod
and Kiev

941 Rus attack on
Constantinople

964-71 Campaigns of
Grand Prince Svyatoslav

c.987 Conversion of
Vladimir of Kiev to
Christianity

1093 Polovtsy sack Kiev

1237–8 Mongols attack
Vladimir-Suzdal

1240 Mongols sack Kiev

1240 Alexander of
Novgorod defeats Swedes
at the River Neva

Three factors shaped the early history of Russia: the eastward movement of Slav settlers; the impact of the Vikings (who were known to the Slavs as Varyagi or Varangians) from the north; and, most important of all, the division of the region into forests (in the north and centre) and treeless steppe (in the south). Before the arrival of the Vikings in the 9th century, the Slavs had begun to settle the central river basins, clearing the forests and living by agriculture, hunting, trapping and the fur trade, while nomadic tribes from Asia, such as the Pechenegs, occupied the grasslands of the south. At first the Slavs resisted the Varangians, but in 862 they called in 'Rurik the Viking' to protect them from Pecheneg raiders.

Since most of the rivers of Russia follow a north-south axis, great potential existed for trade between the Baltic and the Black Sea, and the Vikings sought to dominate and exploit these waterways and the territories adjoining them (map 2). Rurik therefore occupied Novgorod, and his followers soon pushed south to Smolensk and then down the Dnieper to Kiev (882). The principal trade route established by the Vikings ran from the Gulf of Finland up the river Neva, through Lake Ladoga to the river Volkhov, thence by portages to the Dnieper and on across the Black Sea to Byzantium.

Grand Prince Svyatoslav (962-72) campaigned to the south and east, greatly extending the frontiers of the Kievan state, which forged strong links with Byzantium, its chief trading partner; and from Byzantium it received the Christian faith during the reign of Vladimir Svyatoslav (980-1015). At the same time Kiev retained numerous connections with the West: one of Vladimir's granddaughters married the king of France, another the king of Hungary and a

A scene from Novgorod's victory over Suzdal in 1169. Novgorod was the capital of the Rus until Oleg moved his capital to Kiev in 882. In 1019 Iaroslav I granted Novgorod a charter of self-government, and thereafter the town elected its own prince. Grown rich on the trade in furs, Novgorod became pre-eminent in northern Russia. During the 12th century it came into conflict with the growing power of Vladimir-Suzdal to the south. However Novgorod defeated Vladimir-Suzdal in 1169 and 1216. It avoided the Mongol destruction and defeated the Germans and Swedes in 1240–2. A struggle for supremacy with Moscow in the 14th and 15th centuries saw the eclipse of Novgorod.

third the king of Norway. Half a century later, however, dynastic conflict and administrative inefficiency brought weakness and a new wave of Asiatic nomads, the Polovtsy, broke through the defences built by Svyatoslav and Vladimir. In 1093 they sacked Kiev itself.

A great northward exodus ensued to safer regions between the Oka and the Volga, where many new towns were founded (such as Vladimir, Suzdal, Rostov and Tver) and several new states developed – notably Vladimir-Suzdal, which included the fast growing commercial centre of Moscow (first mentioned in 1147), and Novgorod, which built up a fur-trading empire that reached to the Arctic and the Urals. Meanwhile, further south, Novgorod-Seversk, Vladimir-Volynsk and Galich broke away from Kievan rule (map 1).

Mongol invaders struck the final blow to the old order (page 60). In 1237-8, moving along the frozen rivers, they struck north and sacked the wealthy towns of Vladimir-Suzdal; in 1239-40 they advanced through southern Russia, systematically destroying settlements, including Kiev. Meanwhile Novgorod, although it escaped the Mongol onslaught as the onset of spring thawed the frozen rivers, faced repeated attacks by both Swedes and Germans in the Baltic region until Prince Alexander decisively defeated the former in 1240 on the river Neva (thus earning the title 'Nevsky') and the latter in 1242 on the ice of Lake Peipus. Despite these successes, however, even Novgorod had to recognize Mongol overlordship, exercised by the Golden Horde on the lower Volga, while the Lithuanian state expanded into the old Kievan heartland.

The Mongol invasion had other lasting economic, social and political effects. The destruction of so many towns decimated both trade and industry, while the elimination of the urban middle class smoothed the path of an autocracy which imitated its overlords in ruthless terror and extortion. The fall of Kiev destroyed the cultural centre of medieval Russia, with its rich Byzantine-based literature and art, while the Mongol forces, controlling the grasslands around the Caspian and the Black Sea, prevented almost all contact with Byzantium. Russia therefore inevitably developed a distinctive culture, society and political system of its own.

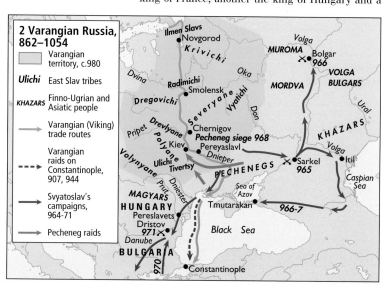

**2 Varangian Russia,
862–1054**

Varangian
territory, c.980

Ulichi East Slav tribes

KHAZARS Finno-Ugrian and
Asiatic people

→ Varangian (Viking)
trade routes

- - → Varangian
raids on
Constantinople,
907, 944

→ Svyatoslav's
campaigns,
964-71

→ Pecheneg raids

1 Kievan Russia, 964–1242

Kievan Russia, 1054
Yatvagi — tribes of the East Slavs
MARI — other peoples
movements of steppe nomads in the 11th century
campaigns of Svyatoslav, 964–71
waterway trade routes
defensive works built against nomads
Russian principalities, c.1200

INTERNET LINKS

www.fordham.edu/halsall/
africa/africasbook.html —
African history internet
sourcebook

900–1800

Trade and empire in Africa

By the end of the first millennium AD great changes had taken place in Africa. The rise of a culture based on iron-working (page 26) led to the appearance of extensive states and empires based on trade. In the south, Zimbabwe, with its monumental stone buildings, exported gold and copper via the port of Sofala; in the west, the Kongo state carried on an important trade. Further north, Arab traders developed the trans-Saharan trade routes and so assisted the growth of major sub-Saharan states. Although Ghana rose to prominence before the Islamic era, its successors, Mali and Songhay, owed much of their wealth and culture – described in glowing terms by Arab travellers – to the impact of Islam. So did the Kanem-Bornu empire around Lake Chad and the Hausa city-states. In the east Arab merchant colonies also spread down the Swahili coast as far as Kilwa and Sofala, bringing this part of Africa into an Indian Ocean trading complex. The staple exports in all cases were gold, ivory and slaves (map 1).

The arrival of the Portuguese in the 15th century at first made little impact on Africa. Their immediate object was to share directly in the gold trade, previously dominated by Muslim middlemen; the slave trade remained a secondary interest. However, with the development of labour-intensive sugar-plantations in the Americas (page 86), the slave trade attracted others. By the 18th century, nine European states maintained almost 50 fortified trading posts on the west coast, from Arguim to Lagos, to handle this burgeoning commerce, while the Portuguese continued to export slaves further south from Angola and Mozambique. Of some 15 million Africans shipped abroad by Europeans between 1450 and 1870, almost 90 per cent went to South America and the Caribbean, most of them during the 18th century. Muslim traders exported perhaps as many more again northward across the Sahara and from the Swahili coast. The effects on Africa of this appalling trade in human beings are impossible to quantify, not least because the loss of population was not evenly divided. Some states, such as Kongo and Lunda, suffered disproportionately, while others seem to have profited. Thus, after the destruction of the powerful Songhay empire by Moroccan troops in 1591, the forest states of Asante, Dahomey and Benin, having direct access to the Atlantic and thus to European slave-traders, increased in importance and political power (map 2).

1 The emergence of states, 1000–1500

- Islamic states or influence, 1000
- Christian states, 1000
- other states, 1000
- new states by 1300
- limit of Islamized areas, 1500
- Christian Ethiopia, 1500
- new states by 1500
- IFAT states that disappeared by 1500
- major gold producing region
- ■ Muslim settlement
- ◪ gold
- M musk
- ◡◡ slaves
- C copper
- ◸ bananas
- ◣ rice
- ◰ cattle
- ⊟ salt
- ⊘ millet
- 🐘 ivory

Apart from the Portuguese in Angola and Mozambique, and the fortified posts along the west coast, only the Dutch attempted to create a European colony in Africa before 1800: in the far south, around Cape Town. In the north-east, Islam continued to spread, but the Christian kingdom of Ethiopia still held its own. In the north, the Ottoman empire (page 70) maintained only nominal suzerainty over the states from Morocco to Egypt. In 1800, almost all of Africa thus remained independent of foreign control: a world unto itself, the 'dark continent'. However, precisely because of its autonomy, it would lack the ability to compete with the technological dynamism of the West in the 19th century (page 110).

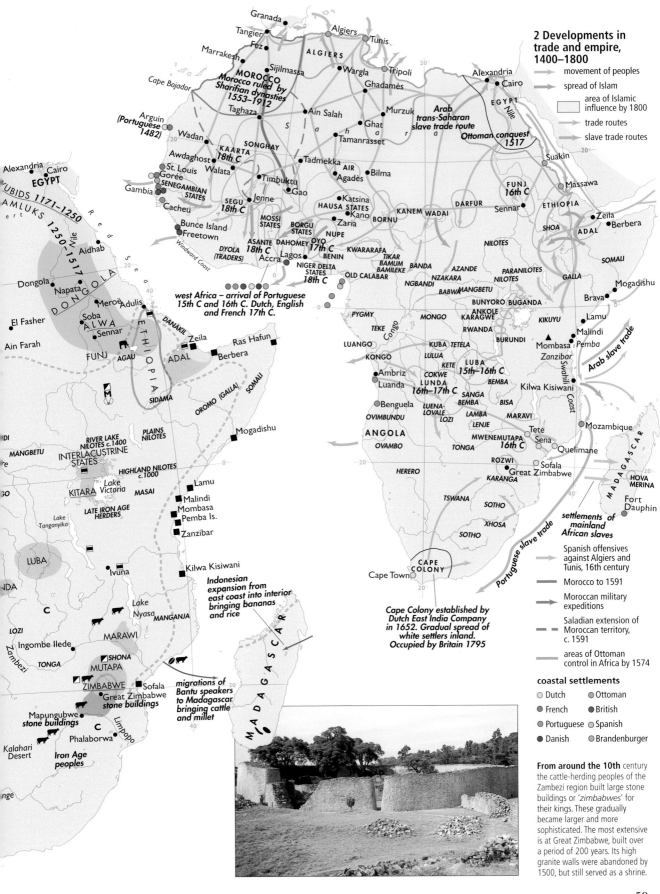

2 Developments in trade and empire, 1400–1800

→ movement of peoples
→ spread of Islam
area of Islamic influence by 1800
→ trade routes
→ slave trade routes

Granada
Tangier
Fez
Marrakesh
Sijilmassa
ALGIERS
Algiers
Tunis
Tripoli
Alexandria
Cairo

MOROCCO
Morocco ruled by Sharifian dynasties 1553–1912
Cape Bojador
Taghaza
Ain Salah
Ghadamès
Murzuk
Ghat
Tamanrasset
Bilma
Arab trans-Saharan slave trade route
Ottoman conquest 1517
EGYPT
Nile
Suakin

Arguin (Portuguese 1482)
Wadan
KAARTA 18th C
Awdaghost
Walata
SONGHAY
Tadmekka
AIR
Agadès
FUNJ 16th C
Massawa

St. Louis
Gorée
SENEGAMBIAN STATES
Gambia
Timbuktu
Gao
Katsina
Kano
BORNU
KANEM WADAI
DARFUR
Sennar
ETHIOPIA
Zeila
Berbera

Cacheu
SEGU 18th C
Jenne
MOSSI STATES
HAUSA STATES
Zaria
SHOA
ADAL

Bunce Island
Freetown
BORGU STATES
NUPE
OYO 17th C
BENIN
KWARARAFA
NILOTES
SOMALI

DYOLA (TRADERS)
ASANTE 18th C
DAHOMEY
Accra
Lagos
TIKAR
BAMUM
BAMILEKE
BANDA
AZANDE
PARANILOTES
NILOTES
GALLA
Mogadishu

NIGER DELTA STATES 18th C
OLD CALABAR
NZAKARA
NGBANDI
BABWA
MANGBETU
BUNYORO
BUGANDA
Brava

west Africa – arrival of Portuguese 15th C and 16th C. Dutch, English and French 17th C.
PYGMY
TEKE
MONGO
ANKOLE
KARAGWE
KIKUYU
Lamu
Malindi
Pemba

LUANGO
KONGO
Congo
KUBA
TETELA
RWANDA
BURUNDI
Mombasa
Zanzibar
Arab slave trade

Ambriz
Luanda
LULUA
KETE
COKWE
SANGA
BEMBA
LUBA 15th–16th C
Swahili Coast
Kilwa Kisiwani

Benguela
LUNDA 16th–17th C
LUENA-LOVALE
BISA
LAMBA
MARAVI
Mozambique

ANGOLA
OVIMBUNDU
LOZI
LENJE
MWENEMUTAPA 16th C
Tete
Sena
Quelimane

OVAMBO
TONGA
ROZWI
Sofala
Great Zimbabwe
HOVA MERINA
Fort Dauphin

HERERO
KARANGA
Great Zimbabwe

TSWANA
SOTHO
settlements of mainland African slaves

CAPE COLONY
Cape Town
XHOSA
SOTHO

→ Spanish offensives against Algiers and Tunis, 16th century
— Morocco to 1591
→ Moroccan military expeditions
- - - Saladian extension of Moroccan territory, c. 1591
— areas of Ottoman control in Africa by 1574

Portuguese slave trade

coastal settlements
○ Dutch ● Ottoman
○ French ● British
● Portuguese ○ Spanish
● Danish ○ Brandenburger

Alexandria
Cairo
EGYPT
AYUBIDS 1171–1250
MAMLUKS 1250–1517
Red Sea
Dongola
Napata
DONGOLA
Aidhab
El Fasher
Meroë
Adulis
Soba
ALWA
Sennar
DANAKIL
Zeila
Ras Hafun
Ain Farah
FUNJ
AGAU
ETHIOPIA
ADAL
Berbera
SIDAMA
OROMO (GALLA)
SOMALI
RIVER LAKE NILOTES c.1400
PLAINS NILOTES
Mogadishu
MANGBETU
INTERLACUSTRINE STATES
HIGHLAND NILOTES c.1000
KITARA
Lake Victoria
MASAI
Lamu
LATE IRON AGE HERDERS
Malindi
Mombasa
Pemba Is.
Lake Tanganyika
Zanzibar

Indonesian expansion from east coast into interior bringing bananas and rice

LUBA
Ivuna
Kilwa Kisiwani
Lake Nyasa
MANGANJA
LOZI
MARAWI
Ingombe Ilede
Zambezi
TONGA
SHONA
MUTAPA
ZIMBABWE
Sofala
Great Zimbabwe stone buildings

migrations of Bantu speakers to Madagascar bringing cattle and millet

Mapungubwe stone buildings
Phalaborwa
Limpopo
Kalahari Desert
Iron Age peoples

MADAGASCAR

Cape Colony established by Dutch East India Company in 1652. Gradual spread of white settlers inland. Occupied by Britain 1795

From around the 10th century the cattle-herding peoples of the Zambezi region built large stone buildings or 'zimbabwes' for their kings. These gradually became larger and more sophisticated. The most extensive is at Great Zimbabwe, built over a period of 200 years. Its high granite walls were abandoned by 1500, but still served as a shrine.

www.royalalbertamuseum.ca/
vexhibit/genghis/intro.htm
Virtual exhibition relating to
Genghis Khan

INTERNET LINKS

1206–1696
The Mongol empire

The Mongols, a nomadic people from the grasslands of Central Asia, staged a sudden and devastating irruption into world history in the first half of the 13th century (map 1). Theirs was not the first empire of the steppe, however. In the 7th century AD, in the wake of the upheavals that destroyed the ancient world (page 40), a confederation of Turkish tribes had managed to dominate the plains of Asia from the Great Wall of China to the Black Sea; but by 750 their rule had collapsed and the area disintegrated into feud and faction. Thus it remained for four centuries, when a charismatic leader, Temujin (1167-1227), gained recognition as supreme ruler and in 1206 took the title Genghis Khan, 'prince of all that lies between the Oceans'. Under his leadership the Mongols first invaded the Chin empire in north China and then turned against the Islamic states to the west. By the time of Genghis's death, his empire stretched from the Pacific Ocean to the Caspian Sea. His successors continued the tide of destructive conquests: Kievan Russia (1237-40); the Abbasid Caliphate (1256-60); Sung China (1271-9). Europe and Japan were also threatened: one Mongol army reached the gates of Vienna while another defeated a German-Polish army at Liegnitz in 1241; two amphibious expeditions unsuccessfully attacked Japan in 1274 and 1281.

However the vast empire lacked coherence and stability, and the Mongols failed to develop appropriate institutions. On hearing of the death of Genghis's successor Ogedei in 1241, the victorious commander of the Mongol forces in Europe withdrew eastwards with his army, in order to take part in choosing a successor. They never returned. Likewise in 1260, on

Mongol brutality in war did not end with Genghis Khan. In this late-16th century Mughal miniature *(right)*, the troops of Tamerlane are shown demolishing the fort of Mikrit in the Hindu Kush, and using the defenders' heads to erect a tower of skulls.

2 The conquests of Tamerlane, c. 1360–1405

1 The Mongol empire

- the Mongol empire by 1259
- → campaigns under Genghis Khan
- → campaigns of his successors
- ||||| Mongol incursions and limited Mongol control
- *OIROTS* Mongol tribes around 1220
- empire of Kublai Khan, 1260–94
- *CUMANS* other peoples

unsuccessful expedition to Java 1292–3

(Inset map labels)
THE GOLDEN HORDE
CHAGATAI KHANATE
Otrar
Tashkent
Samarkand capital of Tamerlane's empire
Kabul
Khotan
Kandahar
Lahore
Delhi
Indus
SULTANATE OF DELHI

---

hearing of the death of Ogedei's successor, the victorious commander of the Mongol forces in the Near East decided to return to the Mongol heartland, leaving only a skeleton force behind him. This soon became known in Cairo, and the Sultan of Egypt marched to the defence of Islam, still reeling from the sack of Baghdad, the capital of the Caliphs, two years before. At Ain Jalut on 3 September 1260 the Mongols suffered a defeat and withdrew to Persia.

The Mongol empire now fragmented. The title of Great Khan went to Kublai who, although never forgetting that he was the grandson of Genghis, spent most of his long reign (1260-94) seeking to reunify China and conquer Japan. The other Mongol states – the Golden Horde in the west; the Il-Khans in Persia; the Chagatai empire in the traditional Mongol heartland – went their own way.

Despite the widespread destruction of the Mongol onslaught, their temporary unification of Eurasia permitted the exchange of goods and ideas between the far east and the far west on an unprecedented scale.

For over a century the 'Silk Road' of ancient times revived: silver and gold from Europe and the Near East reached China while Chinese silks and porcelain circulated in Europe. But the Black Death (see page 66) and the rise of Timur, or Tamerlane, (1336-1405) changed all that, for he destroyed the Chagatai khanate, dislocated the Golden Horde, defeated the Ottoman empire at the battle of Ankara in 1402 (page 70), and initiated a policy of religious intolerance. However Timur died in 1405 before he had created the institutions and traditions required to ensure the survival of his vast empire (map 2). Instead, Mongol power in the west steadily lost ground to Russia (see page 84), and crumbled in China with the rise of the Ming dynasty (see page 94). Mongolia itself came under Chinese dominion in 1696.

1206 Foundation of the Delhi Sultanate

1335 Sultan Muhammad ibn Tughluq rules most of India

1398 Tamerlane invades India and sacks Delhi

1526 Battle of Panipat: Babur conquers Delhi sultanate and founds Mughal empire

1556–1605 Reign of Akbar: apogee of Mughal empire

1587–1629 Reign of Shah 'Abbas: apogee of Safavid state

1707 Death of Aurangzeb

1722 Last Safavid shah overthrown by Afghan rebels

1739 Nadir Shah invades India and sacks Delhi

1747 Nadir Shah assassinated: period of anarchy in Persia

1206–1747
The Muslim empires of India and Persi

Delhi, founded in the 8th century by a Rajput chief, remained the focus of north Indian politics and also the centre of Muslim culture from the 13th to the 19th century. It served as the capital of the six Muslim dynasties, all of Turkish or Afghan extraction, who sought (unsuccessfully) to extend their rule into the Deccan between 1206 and 1526; and, after the defeat of the last of the Sultans of Delhi at Panipat (1526) by Babur – a descendant of Timur (page 60) – it became the headquarters of his descendants, the Mughals.

Babur's grandson, Akbar (1556-1605), extended the frontiers of the empire to Bengal in the east, to Gujerat and the river Godavari in the south, and to Kashmir in the north. New territories were added under Akbar's grandson, Shahjahan (1627-56) and his son Aurangzeb (1656-1707), who annexed Bijapur and Golconda in the south, and Orissa in the east. However, these achievements depended absolutely upon the acquiescence of the 150 million or so Hindu peasant farmers and petty landlords who paid the taxes that supported the Mughals' 4 million warriors, and the court grandees who commanded them. It was a delicate balance, for if the peasants and landlords were overtaxed, they would revolt; and if the grandees were not rewarded with office and wealth they would desert the court. Around 1700 the Hindu Marathas began to ravage southern regions, while some Rajput states and the Sikhs rebelled. All this reduced tax yields, and after the death of Aurangzeb several frontier provinces split off from the empire (page 96).

Meanwhile, to the West, after 1500 the leader of a fanatical sect of Shi'a Muslims, Ismail Safavi, re-unified Persia – which had been in a state of chaos since Timur's invasions – and proclaimed himself Shah. However the Sunnite Ottomans under Selim I (page 70) invaded in 1514, defeated Ismail at the battle of Chaldiran and captured Tabriz, thus initiating a duel between the two powers that lasted for over a century. The conflict centred around the key cities of Mesopotamia, and Baghdad, Tiflis, Derbend and Basra changed hands repeatedly; but its intensity stemmed from the religious division within Islam between Sunnite and Shi'ite (page 50), which excited the same passions as the split between Protestant and Catholic Christians at the same time. Eventually Shah Abbas (1587-1629), with assistance from both Russia and the Christian West, managed to regain most of the lost territories; but the Turks recaptured much of Mesopotamia in the 1630s.

Both empires boasted a rich civilization. Akbar and Abbas each built luxurious new capital cities – at Fatehpur Sikri and Isfahan respectively – and attracted to their courts local and foreign writers, artists and craftsmen. Shahjahan built the magnificent Taj Mahal outside Delhi. Nevertheless, two developments threatened these achievements. On the one hand, as in all autocracies, government authority could suddenly collapse under a weak ruler. Thus in 1739 Nadir Shah, who had usurped the Persian throne three years previously, invaded India and sacked Delhi, leaving the Mughal empire fatally weakened; but in 1747 Nadir was assassinated and Persia too suffered a period of anarchy. On the other

Aral
Sea

Syr Darya

Urgench
Khiva
Tashkent
Khokand

UZBEK KHANATE

**KHANATE OF
KASHGAR**

Kashgar

Bukhara
Amu Darya
Merv
Samarkand

Balkh

Meshed
Nishapur
*1588–9
Safavid conquests*

P E R S I A

Herat *1506, 1588–9*

Kandahar

Kerman

Hindu Kush

Kabul
Mughal conquest 1504
Khyber Pass
Peshawar
Attock

KASHMIR

SIKHS

LAHORE

Lahore

Indus

T I B E T

Himalayas

Multan

MULTAN

*Panipat
1526*
Samana
Delhi
SATAMIS
DELHI
Mughal conquest 1504

Agra
JATS
OUDH

BALUCHISTAN

**(TATTA)
SIND**

AJMER

(RAJPUTANA)

Fatehpur Sikri
Biana
Ajmer
Hindaun
Gwalior

Lucknow

Ganges

RAJPUTS

Jodhpur

Allahabad
ALLAHABAD
Benares

Patna
BIHAR
Kasimbazar
Rajmahal
KUTCH

Brahmaputra

Dacca

BENGAL

Plassey

dar
bas
51
Ormuz
*(Portuguese
1515–1622)*

60°

Muscat *1551*

*Gulf of
Arabia*

Sarkhej
Ahmadabad
MALWA
Cambay
GUJERAT
Baroda
Narmada
Diu *1538*
(Portuguese)
Broach
KHANDESH
Surat
Asirgarh
Assaye

I N D I A

Nagpur

Pipli

*Bay of
Bengal*

D e c c a n

BERAR

ORISSA

Daulatabad
Ahmadnagar
AHMADNAGAR

70°

Godavari

Vizagapatam

Poona
Janjira
MARATHAS

Dabhoi
Satara
Golconda
Hyderabad
GOLCONDA

Rajapur
Kolhapur
Bijapur
Krishna

Vengurla

Goa
(Portuguese 1509)
BIJAPUR
Vijayanagar
Nizampatam
(Petapoli)
Nellore

Bhatkal
Chandragiri

Mangalore
Madras
Saint Thomé

MYSORE

Calicut
Mysore

Tanjore

10°

Madurai
Quilon
Kayal
Tuticorin
Ceylon

80°

Much of the early part of Akbar's reign was spent in the conquest of the Hindu Rajputs, who were to become important allies of the Mughals. In this typically sumptuous miniature of 1569, Surjan Hara, ruler of the fort of Ranthanbhur, submits to Akbar, offering him the keys to the fort and many gifts.

hand, the armed forces of various European states established themselves around the fringes of the empires. In the north, the Russians in the 1550s advanced to the mouth of the Volga (page 84), gaining access to the Caspian. In the south, the Portuguese created fortified bases around the Indian Ocean in the early 16th century, followed after 1600 by the Dutch, English and French. Although the number of Europeans in each enclave remained relatively small, they served corporate entities – the East India Companies – that never died. Whenever Mughal or Safavid control faltered, the Europeans stood poised to take advantage (page 96).

**1 The Safavid and
Mughal empires**

extent of Mughal empire

at Akbar's death, 1605

under Shahjahan, 1627–56

under Aurangzeb, c. 1700

extent of Safavid empire

at the death of Abbas the
Great, 1629

**Ottoman conquests from
Safavids**

conquests of Suleiman I,
1520–66

● conquest of town with date

from 1566–1639

TO 1511

South-East Asia

Situated at one of the world's main cross-roads, civilization developed early in South-East Asia: traces of 'Java man' date from the middle Pleistocene and remains of *homo sapiens* from c. 40,000 BC; rice cultivation in South China began about 6000 BC and bronze working in Thailand and Vietnam in 1500 BC or earlier (pages 12 and 18). Early trade routes linked India with ports along the coasts of Burma, Thailand, Cambodia and Vietnam; Hindu-Buddhist influences from India reached the area around the 2nd or 3rd century AD; and by the 5th century Buddhist images and votive tablets appeared, along with Sanskrit inscriptions. These influences never obliterated the unique character of South-East Asian civilization; instead, the next thousand years saw their assimilation to produce distinctive societies in the area. The culture of Java and southern Sumatra likewise became Indianized, but these areas also developed commercial and political links with China, which welcomed tribute missions from a growing number of states. From the 8th century temple complexes, each combining Hindu and Buddhist influences, evolved in four main areas: central Java (notably at Borobudur and Prambanan, from the 8th to 10th centuries), Cambodia (especially at Angkor, from the 9th to 13th centuries), Burma (Pagan, from the 11th to 13th centuries) and, associated with the Hindu-Buddhist

kingdom of Champa, along the coast of central Vietnam. Meanwhile Palembang (a centre of Sanskrit culture from perhaps as early as the 7th century) emerged as the capital of the maritime empire of Srivijaya, which for centuries controlled international trade passing through the straits of Malacca and Sunda, and across the Isthmus of Kra (map 1).

The great temple-states fell into decline after the 12th century. In Java, the area of Prambanan was superseded in importance by eastern Java, where three states developed in succession: Kediri (12th century), Singhasari (13th century) and finally Majapahit (late 13th-early 16th century). On the mainland, first Mongols and then Shans sacked Pagan in the 13th century, while Angkor fell to Thai attacks after 1369. Sukotai, the first of the lowland Thai cities, was itself in decline by the late 14th century. New political centres replaced the old temple cities: in Burma, Toungoo (1347), Ava (1364), and Pegu (1369), capital of a new Mon kingdom in the south; in Thailand, Chieng Mai (1296) and Ayutthaya (1350); in Cambodia, Phnom Penh and other cities along the Mekong; in Laos, Luang Prabang (1353). All were Theravada Buddhist in the Sinhalese tradition, with stupas rather than temples. Meanwhile, in Vietnam, after the failure of Chinese attempts at reconquest (despite invasions in 1075-7 and 1285-8) a

2 Cultural divisions South-East Asia, 1500
distribution of major religions:

- Theravada Buddhism
- Mahayana Buddhism mixed with Confucianism and Taoism
- Hindu-Buddhism
- Islamic states
- places sending tribute to China between 1370 and 1440

1 South-East Asia,
AD 300–1511

● towns with inscriptions
and monumental
religious buildings

⚓ trading ports,
no monumental buildings
known

🏛 temples with inscriptions

Halin
Ava
**KINGDOM
OF PAGAN**
11th–16th centuries
Pagan
kthano
Ksetra
Toungoo
**PYU
KINGDOM**
Pegu
Thaton

Luang
Prabang
LAO KINGDOMS

Chieng Mai

**KINGDOM
OF
SUKHOTHAI**

Sukhothai
Si Thep Phimai

VIETNAM
from 1471

Mi Son Tra Kieu
Dong Duong

Vijaya

CHAMPA PRINCIPALITIES
4th–15th centuries

Po Nagar (Nha Trang)

*South China
Sea*

Manila

Philippines

MON KINGDOMS
8th–17th centuries

Nakhon
Pathom
U-Thong
Ku Bua

Sukhothai

Ayutthaya
*Tonle Sap
(Great Lake)*
Angkor
Preah Khan

**KHMER
KINGDOM**
*7th–15th
centuries*
Phnom Penh

Po Klaung Gerai

**KINGDOM
OF
AYUTTHAYA**

Chaiya

Angkor Borei

Mekong

Oc Eo

Takuapa ⚓
Ko Kho Khao ⚓

Ligor

**JOLO
SULTANATE**
from 14th century

Celebes Sea

Aceh ⚓

Straits of Malacca

⚓ Malacca

Sumatra

Ternate ⚓
Tidore ⚓

**SULTANATES OF
TERNATE AND TIDORE**
from 14th century

Borneo

Celebes

SRI VIJAYA
7th–13th centuries

Sri Vijaya

Java Sea

**M A J A P A H I T
E M P I R E**
14th–16th centuries

Straits of Sunda

Dieng Plateau 🏛
Borobudur 🏛
Prambanan
**SALENDRA
KINGDOM**
8th–10th centuries

Trowulan
Singhasari
Kediri

Java

new kingdom, called
Dai Viet, emerged and
gradually absorbed
Champa (annexing its capital,
Vijaya, in 1471). Further south,
Srivijaya declined and a powerful new
Muslim state developed after 1400 at
Malacca, commanding the narrow straits
through which most east-west trade passed. By that
time the east Javanese empire of Majapahit was in
decline, and the west Javanese kingdom of Pajajaran
also collapsed before Muslim pressure from the northern coastal ports in the early 16th century.

Islam had began to influence northern Sumatra just
before 1300; now it spread further, often under
Malaccan influence, to the north Javanese trading ports,
the Spice Islands, Borneo and, in the 16th century, the
Philippines (map 2). When the Spaniards arrived,
Mindanao had already been converted and the spread
of Islam in Luzon was only halted by the Spaniards'
capture of the Muslim fort at Manila in 1571 and their
determined promotion of Christianity (page 80).

Meanwhile, in Vietnam, Confucian scholarship
strengthened, despite the failure of another attempt at
reconquest under the Ming; and all over South-East
Asia the series of voyages made by the Muslim admiral Cheng Ho in the early 15th century revived and
reinforced China's system of tributary relationships

(page 74). From the
1430s, however, China abandoned its interest
in the wider world and South-East Asia began
to assume its modern pattern of cultures and
polities which even the arrival of the
Europeans, starting with the
Portuguese capture of Malacca in
1511 (page 80) influenced
little until the 19th
century.

Prambanan was built in the
mid-9th century and was the
largest and most ambitious
temple complex ever constructed
in central Java. There are three
main temples dedicated to the
gods of the Trimurti: Shiva in the
centre; Vishnu on the north side;
and Brahma on the south.

Europe

INTERNET LINKS

http://historymedren.about.
com/library/weekly/
aapmaps1.htm
The spread of the Black
Death in Europe

The 14th century brought to an end the rise and consolidation of national monarchies in western Europe (page 54). Though growth in population and productivity was steady until the later 13th century, both began to decline thereafter. Part of the problem lay in a sudden climatic deterioration which terminated the agricultural boom that had prevailed since 1150: crop yields fell and marginal areas brought into cultivation were abandoned. In 1315-17 Europe experienced the first of many famines; and the weakening of human powers of resistance through inadequate nourishment may have accelerated the spread of the 'Black Death', or bubonic plague, which killed perhaps 20 million Europeans between 1346 and 1353, wiping out in some areas as much as a third of the population within two years (map 1).

However, the impact of the plague was not even. Some areas escaped altogether, and Eastern Europe seems to have suffered relatively little: Bohemia under Charles IV (1333-78), Poland under Casimir III (1339-70) and Hungary under Louis the Great (1342-82) all made rapid strides – aided in part by skillful exploitation of their natural resources, such as the silver mines of Kutna Hora in Bohemia. Above all, in the wake of the Mongol invasions (page 60) Lithuania expanded into the former heartland of Kievan Russia and united in 1386 with Poland to form the largest state in Eastern Europe (map 2).

1 Famine, plague and popular unrest

— main sea-trade routes

wine important commodities

extent of the spread of the Black Death

1346	end 1349
1347	1350
mid-1348	c. 1351
end 1348	c. 1353
mid-1349	little or no plague mortality

social unrest

areas of disturbance during Peasants' Revolt in England, 1381

● centre of urban revolt

rural uprisings

⊗ defeat of lower orders in battle

religious unrest

spread of Lollardy in England to death of Richard II, 1399

area of Hussite influence

■ Hussite centre

PORTUGAL
Santiago   Santan
iron   Léc
Lisbon   Tagus   wool
CASTIL
Tagus   Tole
cattle
Córdoba
Cádiz   Seville
Granada   dried fruits
Ceuta

40°

2 Eastern Europe, 1278–1389

growth of Lithuania, 1300-1377:

to 1300

under Gedymin, 1316–41

under Olgierd, 1345–77

under Jagiello and Witold from 1377

Poland-Lithuania after union of 1386

Habsburg lands

Bohemian lands

*Map labels:*
SWEDEN · Baltic Sea · LIVONIA · NOVGOROD · ORDER · HOLSTEIN · Königsberg · Polotsk · Vitebsk · SMOLENSK · Hamburg · Lübeck · POMERANIA · Danzig · POMERELIA · SAMOGITIA to Lithuania 1422 · Vilna · Vyazma · Smolensk · BRANDENBURG 1373 · TEUTONIC · Minsk · LUSATIA 1368 · Gniezno · Torún (Thorn) · Novogrudok · MEISSEN · Poznań · LITHUANIA · Bryansk · Breslau · POLAND · Lublin · Kursk · Prague · KINGDOM OF BOHEMIA · SILESIA 1368 · Sandomierz · Chernigov · Kutna Hora · Lwów (Lvov) · Kiev · UPPER PALATINATE 1359 · MORAVIA · Brünn · VOLHYNIA · Cracow · RUTHENIA · Halicz · to Poland 1366 · PODOLIA · KHANATE OF THE GOLDEN HORDE · AUSTRIA 1282 · Vienna · Pripet · Dnieper · STYRIA 1282 · Pest · MOLDAVIA · CARINTHIA 1335 · Graz · Carpathian Mts. · Hungarian suzerainty until 1365; independent until 1397; then under temporary Lithuanian control · CARNIOLA 1335 · Trieste · KINGDOM OF HUNGARY · Pécs · Danube · Venice · Fiume · SLAVONIA · CROATIA · Belgrade · WALLACHIA · Smederevo · under Hungary to 1369; Ottoman Tributary from 1389 · BOSNIA · Kosovo ✕ 1389 · REPUBLIC OF VENICE · Hungarian Rule 1328; independent from 1353 · SERBIAN EMPIRE under Stephen Dushan · BULGARIA · Durazzo · Üsküb (Skopje) · BYZANTINE EMPIRE

Unlike famine, plague affected every social class, and the psychological impact was profound. Until the mid-17th century, scarcely a decade passed without a recurrent outbreak. The disease, spread by infected fleas carried by rats, was particularly virulent, and few who caught it ever recovered. This illustration (left) from the Stiny Codex shows death strangling a plague victim.

But elsewhere the setback proved more serious. All the western states had overextended themselves financially, and the economic and demographic crisis exacerbated by the Black Death – combined with the tensions caused by the fragmentation of Italy and Germany after the end of Hohenstaufen rule in 1250 (page 55) or the Hundred Years' War between England and France – produced a series of popular uprisings in both cities and the countryside: the Jacquerie (1358) in France; the Peasants' Revolt (1381) in England; urban insurrections in Spain, Italy and the Low Countries. Few rebellions achieved their aims, but they all weakened state power even further.

1279–1644

China and Japan

The Mongol invasion of China caused immense destruction. During the conquest of the north (1211-34: page 60) much of the land went out of cultivation, many cities and industries perished, and countless people died or became slaves. The conquest of the south (1271-9) brought similar hardships, and Mongol rule proved harsh. Popular resentment erupted in a wave of popular uprisings after 1335, exacerbated by disastrous floods in coastal regions in the 1350s. One of the rebel leaders, Chu Yüan-chang, gradually overcame his rivals and in 1368 established a new dynasty, the Ming.

The Ming rebuilt irrigation and drainage works in great numbers, reforested on a grand scale, and moved vast numbers of people to repopulate the devastated north. New crops were introduced and the canal system extended to transport produce: by 1421 the 'Grand Canal' stretched from Hang-chou to just south of Peking and carried some 200,000 tons of grain northwards every year. Thanks to these measures, the Chinese population rose from some 60 million in 1393 (40 per cent fewer than a century before) to about 130 million by 1580. The great cities of the Yangtze delta became major industrial centres, particularly for textiles, while the southern ports fitted out the enormous fleets sent by Chu's son, the Yung-lo emperor (1402-24), to the South China Sea and the Indian Ocean (page 74).

The Ming entrusted control over the vast population to a gentry class of degree-holders, who had passed through the examination system and shared the values of the bureaucracy without actually holding office. But the system discouraged innovation and was overcentralized, with all major decisions dependent upon the emperor; and few of Yung-lo's successors possessed the dedication necessary for such heavy responsibilities. Nevertheless, the early Ming engaged in an aggressive foreign policy. They restored Korea to vassal status in 1392, occupied Annam from 1407 to 1427, and invaded Mongolia (map 1). However, after a northern campaign in 1449 resulted in the capture of the emperor, the Ming reverted to a defensive strategy, strengthening the Great Wall until it ran for almost 2,500 miles, and increasing the garrisons in the north and north-west. China remained relatively stable for another century, but in the 1430s the government banned all overseas trade by sea, except under close supervision. Not surprisingly, by 1500 smuggling had become commonplace in the south-eastern provinces and by 1550 heavily-armed bands of smugglers and pirates infested the seas around China and terrorized the coastal regions from their bases in Japan.

Central authority in Japan had collapsed in the 1330s and the country became plagued by local and provincial wars – almost continuously in the century after 1467. By about 1560, some nine leading families had formed alliances that covered most of the country, and competed openly for supreme power (map 2). In 1568 Nobunaga, leader of the Oda clan, captured Kyoto, the imperial capital, and by the time he was assassinated in 1582 by a jealous rival he had forced almost all the other lords to accept his orders. Within a decade, his ablest general Toyotomi Hideyoshi had completely reunified Japan, reorganizing the tax system and redistributing land to provide sufficient funds for his ambitious policies – including the invasion of Korea in the 1590s. After his death in 1598 another of Nobunaga's generals, Tokugawa Ieyasu, assumed power and in 1603 established the dynasty of shoguns who ruled Japan until the 19th century (page 88).

The Tokugawa put an end to the pirate problem, thus easing the pressure on the Chinese coast; but at just this time a new threat arose in the north-east, where the Manchu gradually expanded their power into the areas immediately to the north of the Great Wall and (in 1637) into Korea. Ming authority now

2 Civil War in Japan, 1467–1590

spheres of influence of the most powerful Daimyo clans

—— boundaries of Daimyo domains

Sea of Japan (East Sea)

Uesugi

Takeda

Hojo

Oda

Imagawa

Kyoto

Nara

Mori

Sogabe

Otomo

Shimazu

Pacific Ocean

Sha

Li-chiang

Ta-li

T'eng-yüeh

Meng-hua

BURMA

YUNNAN

Mekong

SIAM

1 Ming China

Legend:
- ▬▬ major post roads
- — minor roads
- ⊓⊔⊓ Great Wall
- ═══ Grand Canal
- ◼ national capital
- ◉ provincial capitals
- ◻ the nine frontier defence areas
- ○ prefectures and regional military commissioners
- ◼ guard units
- ➡ Japanese pirate invasions before 16th century
- ➡ Japanese invasions after 1550
- ➡ expedition of General Ch'iu Fu against the Mongols, 1409

expeditions of Yung-lo against the Mongols:
- 1st 1410
- 2nd 1414
- 3rd 1422
- 4th 1424

The 'Willow Palisade' surrounding area of Chinese settlement in Liao-tung.

Ming counter-attacks to defend Korea, 1592, 1597–8

Japanese invasions of Korea under Toyotomi Hideyoshi, 1592–8

collapsed. After 1627 a wave of rebellions broke out in the wake of repeated crop failures in the north-west, and much of central and northern China soon came under rebel sway. In 1644, one of the rebel leaders captured Peking and the last Ming emperor committed suicide. Almost immediately the Manchus intervened, seized Peking, and began the conquest of China (page 94).

Chu Yüan-chang (1328–98), founder of the Ming dynasty. In 1368 he proclaimed himself the founder of a new imperial dynasty, taking the title Hung-wu, meaning 'mightily martial'.

69

INTERNET LINKS
www.wsu.edu/~dee/
OTTOMAN/17TH.HTM —
The Ottoman empire in the
17th century

1300–1699
The Ottoman empire

The overthrow of the Abbasid Caliphate by the Mongols in 1256-60 (page 60) left the Muslim world in disarray for half a century. One of the centres of recovery lay in north-west Anatolia where, around 1300, a Turkish leader named Osman founded a state which became the core of the future Ottoman empire (map 1). The damage to the structure of the Byzantine empire caused by the Fourth Crusade in 1204 (page 48) facilitated the Ottomans' rapid advance in the 14th century. By 1354 the Turks had crossed the Dardanelles to Gallipoli, and their victories at Kosovo (1389) and Nicopolis (1396) left them masters of the Balkans. The invasion of Timur (page 61) and his destruction of the Turkish army at Ankara (1402) gave the hard-pressed Byzantine empire some respite, but the renewal of expansion under Murad II (1413-51) and Mohammed II (1451-81) sealed its fate. In 1453 Constantinople fell, and Mohammed went on to extend control over Moldavia, the Crimea and Trebizond, thereby turning the Black Sea into an Ottoman lake.

Selim I (1512-20) defeated the new Safavid rulers of Persia (page 62) and conquered the Mamlukes, and his son Suleiman the Magnificent (1520-66) annexed much of Hungary and besieged Vienna (1529), making the Ottoman empire one of the world's largest powers. It now extended over one million square miles, with some 14 million inhabitants; and its capital, Istanbul, had become the largest city in Europe with 500,000 inhabitants. Suleiman's son, Selim II managed to add Cyprus (1570-1) and Tunis (1574), although his fleet of galleys met with defeat at the hands of a Christian coalition at Lepanto (1571). However the wars of his successors against Persia (1578-90 and 1607-39) and against the Austrian Habsburgs (1593-1606) resulted in the loss of the Caucasus to the former and of annual tribute for Hungary from the latter.

The end of expansion, coupled with rapid price inflation (from 1584), a rising population and a static economy provoked a spate of popular and military uprisings between 1596 and 1610 in the Anatolian heartland of the empire (map 2). Nevertheless, Mesopotamia was regained from Persia in the 1630s and Crete conquered from the Venetians in the 1660s; and in 1683 a great army laid siege once more to Vienna. But it failed, and a Christian counter-attack drove the Turks out of Hungary by 1699 – although the Turks still remained a formidable power, controlling the entire Arab world east of Libya and most of the Balkans until the 19th century.

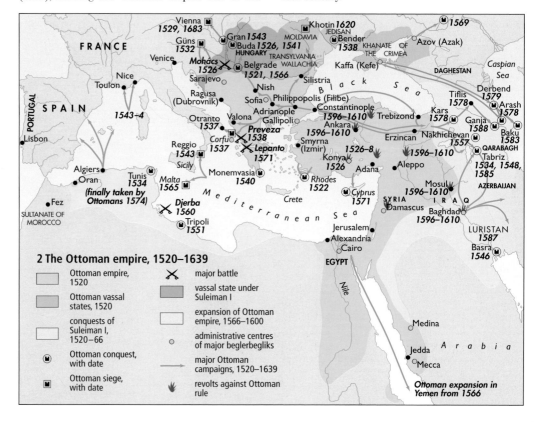

2 The Ottoman empire, 1520–1639

- Ottoman empire, 1520
- Ottoman vassal states, 1520
- conquests of Suleiman I, 1520–66
- ◉ Ottoman conquest, with date
- ▣ Ottoman siege, with date
- ✕ major battle
- vassal state under Suleiman I
- expansion of Ottoman empire, 1566–1600
- ○ administrative centres of major beglerbegliks
- → major Ottoman campaigns, 1520–1639
- ψ revolts against Ottoman rule

TEUTONIC ORDER

LITHUANIA

POLAND

RUSSIA

HOLY ROMAN EMPIRE

Moscow

Cracow

Vienna (Beç)
Buda

Danube

Carpathian Mountains

Suceava
Yaş (Jassy)

Dniester

Kiev
Dnieper

Cossack settlements

BOGDAN (MOLDAVIA) 1455

Sava
Zagreb

HUNGARY

TRANSYLVANIA

BUJAK

Akkerman (1484)

KHANATE OF THE CRIMEA (vassal 1475)

Don

Azov

VENETIAN REPUBLIC

BOSNIA
Jajce 1463 1528
Bosna Saray (Sarajevo)
HERZEGOVINA (1463–83)

Belgrade
Semendire 1444

EFLÂK (WALLACHIA) 1396
Yergögü (Giurgiu)
Bükres (Bucharest)

Danube

Kilia

DOBRUJA

Bakhchesaray (Bahçesaray)

Sea of Azov

Kerç

Kefe (Caffa)

ÇERKES (CIRCASSIA)

SERBIA 1389
Vidin

Dubrovnik
REPUBLIC OF DUBROVNIK (Ottoman vassal 1430–1804)

Kosovo 1389
Nish
Sofia

Filibe (Philippopolis) 1393

Edirne (Adrianople) 1361

Varna

Black Sea

Caucasus Mountains

Elbasan

BULGARIA

Manastir (Bitoli)

Constantinople 1453

Kastamonu

Sinop

ÇANDAR (KASTAMONU) 1393 1461

Samsun

Trabzon (Trebizond) 1461

Tiflis

Otranto temporary Ottoman occupation 1480

Yenisehir (Larissa)
Corfu

Selanik (Salonica) 1430

Gelibolu (Gallipoli) 1354

Bursa 1326

KARASI 1345
Söğüt 1265
Eskisehir 1289

Ankara 1402

ANATOLIA

Amasya

EMPIRE OF TREBIZOND

Cephalonia
Zante

Aegean Sea

SARUHAN 1390 1405

Izmir (Smyrna) to Genoa

GERMIYAN 1380 1428

SIVAS 1398

Sivas

Otluk-Beli 1473

Erzurum

MOREA 1460

Negroponte (Euboea) 1470

Athens

Naxos

AYDIN 1390 1426

HAMID 1381–90 1426

Konya

KARAMAN 1390 1468

Kayseri

KARAKOYUNLU

Modon
Ottoman 1500

KNIGHTS OF ST JOHN

MENTEŞE 1390 1426

TEKE 1391 1427

DHU'L-QADR 1398 1515

AKKOYUNLU

Lake Van

Çaldıran 1514

Crete

Rhodes

Adana

Marj Dabiq 1516

Aleppo 1516

Diyarbakir

Tabriz 1514

Lake Urmia

Cyprus (Venetian 1489, Ottoman tributary 1517)

Raqqa

Mosul

SAFAVID EMPIRE (from 1501)

Tripoli

MAMLUK EMPIRE

Beirut
Damascus 1516

Euphrates

Tigris

Jerusalem

1 The rise of the Ottoman empire, 1301–1520

- probable extent of Ottoman state, c. 1300
- conquests of Osman, c. 1300–26
- conquests of Orkhan, 1326–62
- conquests of Murad I, 1362–89
- TEKE 1390 absorbed Emirates with date of first absorption
- conquests of Bayezid, 1389–1402
- ✕ major battles
- 1398 dates of Ottoman control
- Venetian territories, 1510
- ◉ successive centres of Ottoman state, with dates of conquest
- reduced frontiers of Ottoman state after Tamerlane's invasion and civil war of 1403–13
- Emirates restored by Tamerlane, 1402
- 1427 final reincorporation into Ottoman empire
- boundary of Ottoman state at the accession of Mehmed II, 1451
- vassal states, 1512
- Ottoman empire, 1512
- western frontiers of Safavid state, c. 1512 including tributary states
- Ottoman sphere of influence, c. 1520

The fall of Constantinople, in 1453, came as no surprise to observers in the east. Sultan Mehmet II had managed to close the Bosphorus by building castles at its narrowest point; the city was now cut off from western naval assistance and from its traditional sources of food and supply. When the final siege began, on 6 April, there were only some 7000 Christian defenders facing and Ottoman army of more than 80,000. On 29 May a final assault took the city within a few hours.

71

TO 1533
Precolumbian America

Two major civilizations confronted the Spaniards when they arrived on the American mainland in the early 16th century: the Aztec Empire in Mexico, with a subject population of perhaps 12 million, and the Inca empire in Peru, ruling some 6 million. The rest of the continent remained sparsely inhabited – perhaps 1 million people lived north of the Rio Grande with another million in the rest of South America – divided among more than a thousand small tribal societies with distinct languages. Few regions, particularly in the north, had reached the stage of settled agriculture, despite some contacts in the north-east with Europeans around the year 1000 (map 1).

The Aztec and Inca Empires differed markedly in character, and no evidence exists of any contact between them. Like the Toltecs, who between 968 and about 1170 controlled much of the valley of Mexico from their capital at Tula, the Aztecs came from the north. In 1325 they arrived in the valley and settled on a group of islands in the swampy margins of Lake Texcoco, where they built their capital, Tenochtitlán (site of Mexico City). Serving at first as mercenary warriors for neighbouring towns, by 1428 they had overthrown them all and, led by a priest-king and an hereditary warrior aristocracy, embarked upon an ambitious programme of conquest. When the Spaniards arrived in 1519, the Aztecs controlled the greater part of Mexico and had entered Maya territory in Yucatán (map 2).

The Inca formed one of the numerous tribes of Quechua stock inhabiting the central Andes, but until the accession of Pachacuti Inca in 1438 they played only a minor role. Within 45 years, however, Pachacuti's conquests extended Inca control from Lake Titicaca to Huánaco in the north, while his son Topa pushed north into Ecuador and south to Chile, and from the Pacific coast to the Upper Amazon. This created an empire 200 miles wide and 2500 miles long, held together by an impressive system of highways, post-stations and relay runners (map 3).

The Incas created a genuine imperial system, with an hereditary dynasty of absolute, 'divine' Incas, a Quechua aristocracy, and a highly trained bureaucracy. All land was state-owned, with a complex system of irrigation. The ordinary Inca subject spent 9 months working for the state, but in return received protection from

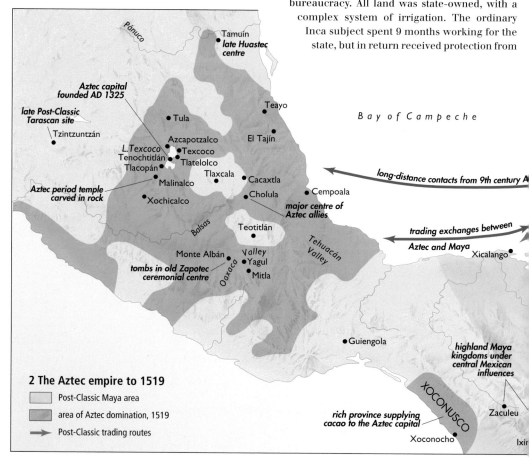

2 The Aztec empire to 1519

▢ Post-Classic Maya area

▢ area of Aztec domination, 1519

➤ Post-Classic trading routes

famine (through state-owned food stores) and support during sickness and old age. The Aztec Empire, on the other hand, exercised harsh military dominion over vassal peoples who enjoyed political autonomy provided they paid heavy tribute to Tenochtitlán in food, textiles and other goods – increasingly in humans for ritual sacrifice to the Aztec gods (up to 50,000 a year by 1510). These demands help to explain why so many people in the valley of Mexico welcomed the Spaniards, just as a recent succession dispute provided allies for the European invaders in Peru. Although both the Aztec and Inca polities expanded faster than any 15th-century state in Latin Christendom, neither empire proved as stable as it seemed. Mexico fell to a force spearheaded by under 2,000 Europeans in 1519-22, Peru to a band of less than 200 in 1531-3 (see page 86).

An Aztec or Mixtec sacrificial knife. The Aztecs believed that the continuation of human society required that the sun and earth be nourished with human blood and hearts. War was necessary to provide the sacrificial victims, whose hearts were removed with knives such as this. It is 12 inches long with an inlaid handle in the form of a warrior costumed as an eagle, or *quauhtli*, which was also a name for the sun.

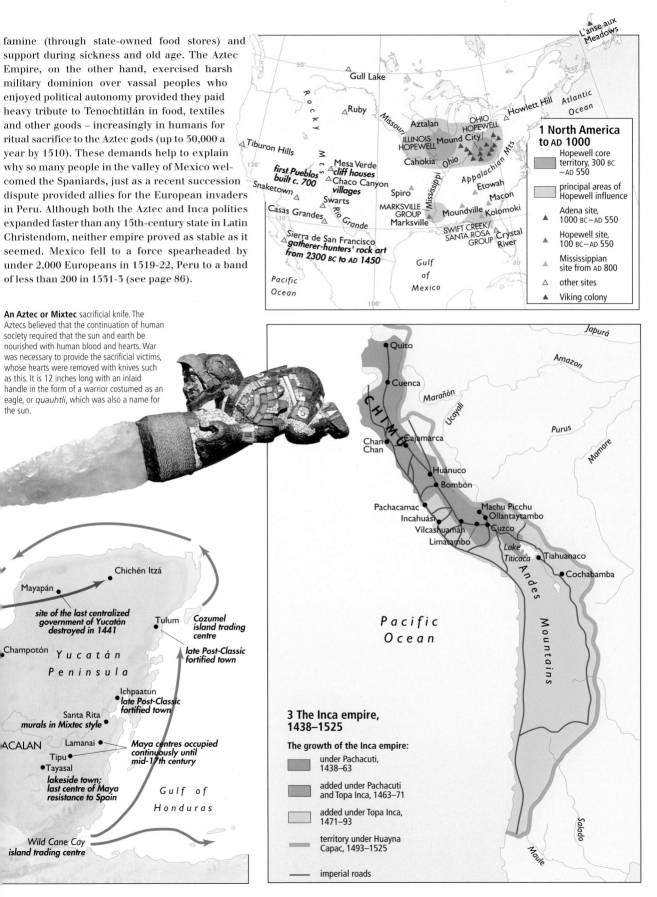

1 North America to AD 1000

- Hopewell core territory, 300 BC–AD 550
- principal areas of Hopewell influence
- ▲ Adena site, 1000 BC–AD 550
- ▲ Hopewell site, 100 BC–AD 550
- ▲ Mississippian site from AD 800
- △ other sites
- ▲ Viking colony

L'anse aux Meadows

Gull Lake
Ruby
Rocky Mts
Tiburon Hills
Missouri
Aztalan
OHIO HOPEWELL
ILLINOIS HOPEWELL
Mound City
Howlett Hill
Atlantic Ocean
Cahokia
Ohio
Appalachian Mts
Mesa Verde
cliff houses
Chaco Canyon
villages
first Pueblos built c. 700
Snaketown
Swarts
Spiro
Etowah
Macon
Casas Grandes
MARKSVILLE GROUP
Mississippi
Moundville
Kolomoki
Rio Grande
Marksville
SWIFT CREEK/ SANTA ROSA GROUP
Crystal River
Sierra de San Francisco
gatherer-hunters' rock art from 2300 BC to AD 1450
Gulf of Mexico
Pacific Ocean

3 The Inca empire, 1438–1525

The growth of the Inca empire:
- under Pachacuti, 1438–63
- added under Pachacuti and Topa Inca, 1463–71
- added under Topa Inca, 1471–93
- territory under Huayna Capac, 1493–1525
- imperial roads

Japurá
Quito
Amazon
Cuenca
Marañón
CHIMU
Ucayali
Purus
Chan Chan
Cajamarca
Mamore
Huánuco
Bombón
Pachacamac
Machu Picchu
Incahuasi
Ollantaytambo
Vilcashuamán
Cuzco
Limatambo
Lake Titicaca
Tiahuanaco
Cochabamba
Andes
Pacific Ocean
Mountains
Salado
Maule

Chichén Itzá
Mayapán
site of the last centralized government of Yucatán destroyed in 1441
Tulum
Cozumel island trading centre
Champotón
Yucatán Peninsula
late Post-Classic fortified town
Ichpaatun
late Post-Classic fortified town
Santa Rita
murals in Mixtec style
ACALAN
Lamanai
Maya centres occupied continuously until mid-17th century
Tipu
Tayasal
lakeside town; last centre of Maya resistance to Spain
Gulf of Honduras
Wild Cane Cay island trading centre

www.ucalgary.ca/applied_
history/tutor/eurvoya
15th- and 16th-century
European voyages of
exploration

INTERNET LINKS

1405–33 Chinese trading voyages under Cheng Ho

c.1450 Population of Ming China reaches 100 million

1492 Columbus reaches Americas

1493 First Spanish settlement in New World

1498 Vasco da Gama reaches India by sea

1500 Shah Ismail founds Safavid dynasty in Persia

1505 Portuguese establish trading posts in east Africa

c.1510 First African slaves shipped to Americas

c.1565 Potato introduced to Europe from South America

The world circa 1492

The central feature of world history since the 1490s has been the expansion of Europe and the spread of European civilization throughout the globe. Until then, the world had, on the whole, pressed in on Europe; thereafter the roles became reversed. In the 16th century, however, Europe continued to stand on the periphery of the civilized world, eclipsed by Ming China (the most powerful and advanced state of the period, with over 100 million inhabitants – equal to the whole of Europe) and by the rising Ottoman, Safavid and Mughal empires of the Middle East. Meanwhile Islam won converts in central and South-East Asia, and among the peoples of sub-Saharan Africa.

The total area occupied by the major civilizations, roughly co-terminous with the area of plough cultivation, nevertheless remained relatively small. Almost 80 per cent of the world's surface was inhabited either by food gatherers or herdsmen (as in Australia and most of Siberia, North America and much of Africa) or by hand cultivators (especially in South-East Asia, West Africa and Central and South America). But plough cultivators proved far more productive, and the relatively small area that had been brought under the plough probably supported between two-thirds and three-quarters of the global population (map 1).

Until the 1490s, worldwide racial segregation prevailed. Although Christians and Muslims from all over Eurasia made pilgrimages to their Holy Places in the Middle East, they seldom settled; and although merchants travelled widely across and around Asia, their numbers remained few. In the early 15th century a succession of Chinese voyages, commanded by the Muslim admiral Cheng Ho, secured tribute and extended recognition of the new Ming dynasty; but they led to no lasting interchange of population.

Until the 1490s, therefore, the Negroids remained concentrated in sub-Saharan Africa and a few Pacific islands; the Mongoloids in Asia and the Americas; the Caucasoids in Europe, North Africa, the Middle East and India; and the Australoids in Australia (map 2). By 1800, however, the pattern had fundamentally altered as the result of six intercontinental migrations: from Europe and Africa to the Americas; from northern Europe to Africa and (later) Australasia; from Russia into Siberia; from China to South-East Asia; and from India to Africa, South-East Asia and the Caribbean. By far the greatest change occurred in the Americas, where the native population declined dramatically in the

1 The economies of the world, c. AD 1500

non-agricultural economies

- generalized gathering, hunting and fishing
- specialized hunting

agricultural economies

- root crops dominant
- grain crops dominant
- nomadic pastoralism
  - ▵ dromedary   □ horse/reindeer   ○ cattle

— limit of plough cultivation

— Cheng-ho's voyages, 1405–33

century following the first contact with the Europeans – in some cases by 90 per cent – to be replaced by Europeans, Africans, and in some parts of Latin America by a mixed race of mestizos (map 2).

Nevertheless, the tempo of change must not be exaggerated. Although in America the Aztec and Inca empires collapsed suddenly in 1521 and 1533 respectively (page 72), elsewhere the political impact of Europe remained limited until the 18th century. China and Japan survived intact, and India kept the Europeans at arm's length for 250 years following the arrival of Vasco da Gama in 1498. There, as in Africa and South-East Asia, the European presence long remained confined largely to trading stations and fortresses along the coast.

A pepper harvest in Malabar. Pepper accounted for over 70 per cent by volume of the world spice trade in the 16th century. The most valuable variety, *piper nigrum*, shown here, was native to India and hard to transplant successfully. Demand from Europe and China spread it to selective parts of the East, but Portuguese efforts to introduce it in Africa and America in the 17th century met with little success.

2 The diffusion of races

Mongoloid   Caucasoid   Australoid   Negroid

before 1492

after 1492

The cultural influence of Europe was even more negligible: Christianity made little headway, except when imposed by the conquerors (as in the Americas and the Philippines), until it received the backing of western technology in the 19th century.

The comparative fragility of the Aztec and Inca civilizations in the Americas, and of the African kingdoms immediately south of the Sahara, despite their outstanding achievements, may be partially explained, first, by their geographical isolation and relative lack of external stimulus and, second, by their dependence on hand cultivation. After 1492, when all the continents came into direct contact with each other for the first time, many of these non-Eurasian civilizations proved unable to offer more than a feeble resistance to outside aggression. To be sure not until the 19th century, with the opening of the Suez Canal and the construction of the transcontinental railways in North America, Siberia and Africa, did areas that had previously been separate finally blend into a single world economy; but the first stages of global integration were completed in the three centuries following 1492.

THREE

The Rise of the West

Before 1500, civilization had been essentially land-centred, and contacts by sea relatively unimportant; thereafter direct sea contact linked the continents. This resulted not only in the growth of a global system of regions which hitherto had developed in isolation, but in a challenge to the traditional land-centred balance between the civilizations of Eurasia.

Nonetheless, the impact of European expansion should not be exaggerated. To many Europeans, the Ottoman, Mughal and Chinese empires exemplified civilized living. Industrialization put Europe ahead; but the fruits of that process – some of them poisonous – were only garnered in the 19th century. Until then, for all its thrusting novelty, Europe remained closer to its agrarian past than to its industrial future.

Between 1815 and 1914 Europe expanded and inaugurated the process of transformation throughout the world which dethroned agricultural society as it had existed for thousands of years, replacing it with an urban, industrialized, technocratic society.

Marble bust of Louis XIV
by Bernini, 1665

INTERNET LINKS

www.ers.north-ayrshire.
gov.uk/voyages.htm
Historical and contemporary
voyages of discovery

1480–1630
European exploration

In 1480 European shipping remained largely confined to the North Atlantic, the Baltic and the Mediterranean, while the West African coast had been explored cursorily, and only very recently by Europeans; Indian, Persian, and Arab vessels plied the northern Indian Ocean; Chinese and Indonesian junks sailed in the western Pacific, but rarely went beyond Japan, the Philippines and the Indonesian archipelago; and local craft navigated the Caribbean and the coasts of Peru and Ecuador. No shipping used the southern Indian Ocean, the South Atlantic, or the main basin of the Pacific. In the course of the next 150 years, however, European navigators opened all the seas, except in the regions of circumpolar ice and the South Pacific, to European ships. Initially, in the 15th century, two series of voyages sought a sea passage to southern Asia in the hope of initiating direct trade in spices. One series, mounted from Portugal, sailing by a south-eastern route and employing local navigators in the East, eventually reached their declared destinations: the entrance to the Indian Ocean (1488), Malabar (1498), Malacca (1509), and the Moluccas (1512-13). The other series, mounted from Spain and sailing west or south-west, proved less successful in its immediate purpose but more fruitful in incidental discovery: the Spaniards hit upon the West Indies (1492) and the Spanish Main (1498). Eventually they too reached South-East Asia (1521), but by a route too long and arduous for commercial use – for to reach the Pacific they had to circumnavigate an immense land-mass which, although it was initially thought to be a peninsula of Asia, by the 1520s had been recognized as a new world. They immediately began to settle the area (page 72). Taken together, the Spanish and Portuguese discoveries proved that all the oceans of the world, at least in the southern hemisphere, were connected.

For most of the 16th century, by the use and threat of force, the Iberian powers managed to prevent other Europeans from using the connecting passages, except for occasional raids. The third great series of voyages, therefore, mostly by English, French and Dutch navigators, searched for alternative routes to Asia in the northern hemisphere, in the west, northwest, and northeast. Although unsuccessful in their primary purpose, they revealed another continental land-mass with a continuous coast extending from the Caribbean to the Arctic, and opened the way for the European exploration and settlement of eastern North America (page 86).

VOYAGES INTENDED FOR SOUTH ASIA BY SOUTH-EAST ROUTE:

1/Dias 1487–8 (outward) discovered open waters of Cape Agulhas; entered Indian Ocean; reached Great Fish River.

2/Vasco da Gama 1497–8 (outward) made best use of Atlantic winds on way to Cape of Good Hope; reached India, guided by local pilot.

3/Cabral 1500 (outward) second Portuguese voyage to India; landed in Brazil, probably accidentally.

4/First Portuguese voyage to Malacca, 1509.

5/Abreu 1512–3 visited Moluccas.

6/First Portuguese visits to Macao, 1516.

VOYAGES INTENDED FOR CHINA AND SOUTH ASIA BY WEST OR SOUTHWEST ROUTE:

7/Da Mota, Zeimoto and Peixoto 1542–3 Portuguese reach Japan.

8/Columbus 1492–3 (outward and homeward) visited Bahama group, explored north coasts of Cuba and Hispaniola; found best return route.

9/Columbus 1493–4 (outward) explored south coast of Cuba; reported it as peninsula of mainland China.

10/Columbus 1498 (outward) explored Trinidad and Venezuela; recognized coast as mainland.

11/Columbus 1502–4 explored coast of Honduras, Nicaragua and the Isthmus.

12/Ojeda and Vespucci 1499–1500 (outward) reached Guiana coast, failed to round Cape São Roque, followed coast west to Cape de la Vela.

13/Coelho and Vespucci 1501 (outward) followed coast south from Cape São Agostinho to 35°S.

14/Solís 1515 entered River Plate estuary and investigated north bank.

15/Magellan and Elcano 1519-22 discovered Strait of Magellan, crossed Pacific, reached Moluccas via Philippines; first circumnavigation.

16/Saavedra 1527 discovered route from Mexico across Pacific to Moluccas.

17/Urdaneta 1565 found feasible return route Philippines to Mexico in 42°N. using west winds.

18/Schouten and Le Maire 1616 discovered route into Pacific via Le Maire Strait and Cape Horn.

VOYAGES INTENDED FOR ASIA BY NORTHWEST AND NORTHEAST ROUTE:

19/Cabot 1497 (outward) encountered Newfoundland, first sighted by Norsemen 11th C.

20/Corte-Real 1500 visited Greenland.

21/Verazzano 1524 traced east coast of North America from (probably) 34°N. to 47°N.; revealed continental character of North America.

22/Cartier 1534 and 1535 explored Strait of Belle Isle and St Lawrence as far as Montreal.

23/Willoughby and Chancellor 1553 rounded North Cape and reached Archangel.

24/Frobisher 1576 reached Frobisher Bay in Baffin Island, which he took for a 'strait'.

25/Davis 1587 explored west coast of Greenland to the edge of the ice in 72° N.

26/Barents 1596–7 discovered Bear Island and Spitsbergen; wintered in Novaya Zemlya.

27/Hudson 1610 sailed through Hudson Strait to the south extremity of Hudson Bay.

28/Button 1612 explored west coast of Hudson Bay, concluded Bay landlocked on the west.

29/Baffin and Bylot 1616 explored whole coast of Baffin Bay; concluded no navigable northwest. passage existed in that area.

1 Major European voyages of discovery, 1480–1630

→ voyages intended for Southern Asia by southeast route

→ voyages intended for China and south Asia by west or southwest route

→ voyages intended for Asia by northwest and northeast routes

⇨ approximate prevailing winds (shown for the first quarter of the year)

⇨ alternating monsoons

A 17th-century Spanish painting of Columbus's fleet *(below)*. Under the sponsorship of the Spanish monarchs Ferdinand and Isabella, Columbus made his first voyage across the Atlantic in 1492. Making landfall on Haiti, Columbus believed he had found a westward route to Asia. He made three further voyages to the Americas.

European overseas expansion

INTERNET LINKS

http://bell.lib.umn.edu/
Products/Products.html —
Trade products in the early-
modern period

1480 Portuguese find and
fortify Elmina

1507 Portuguese occupy
Mozambique

1510 Portuguese capture
Goa

1511 Portuguese capture
and occupy Malacca

1515 Portuguese occupy
Ormuz

1557 Portuguese
established at Macao

1600 English East India
Company incorporated

1602 Dutch East India
Company incorporated

1619 Dutch East India
Company established at
Batavia

1652 Dutch settlement at
Cape of Good Hope

By 1492, Portugal already possessed several archi-
pelagos in the Atlantic and the Gulf of Guinea, some
fortresses in Morocco, and a few trading stations in
West Africa (above all the castle at Elmina). In the
next half century she established some 50 forts and
trading posts around the shores of the Indian Ocean,
as well as coastal enclaves in Angola and Brazil.
Strategically, the most important bases were
Mozambique (1507), a port of call for fleets sailing to
India; Goa (1510), headquarters of Portuguese Asia;
Malacca (1511), a major market on the strait
connecting the Indian Ocean with the South China
Sea; and Ormuz (1515), a key entrepôt of the
international spice trade. East of Malacca the
position of the Portuguese was far more precarious
and their activities remained purely
commercial. A few bases, some
fortified, grew up in the Moluccas; a
clandestine settlement developed at
Macao on the Chinese mainland after
1557; and from 1580 Jesuit missionaries
held a lease on the Japanese port-city of
Nagasaki (map 1).

In Africa and Asia the Portuguese
generally sought to control trade rather
than production; and though they could
not eliminate the commerce of others in
the Indian Ocean, they forced many ships
to use harbours under their control, and
extorted tolls or duties from the rest. The
Spaniards in the Americas, by contrast,
embarked on a deliberate policy of conquest and colonization: from the 1490s in
the Caribbean islands; from the 1520s in
Mexico; from the 1530s in Peru; and
from the 1570s in the Philippines.

Few dared to challenge the Iberian
monopoly – apparently enhanced by the
union of Portugal and Spain in 1580 –
before the 17th century. However, the

2 Commercial expansion to the East,
c. 1600–1700

- places under Dutch control
- places under English control
- places under French control
- places under Portuguese control
- areas under Portuguese control

trade routes
→ Dutch
→ English
→ French
→ Portuguese

Manila to Acapulco
with silk

1 Spanish and Portuguese trade and settlement by c. 1600

→ principal Portuguese trade routes   → principal Spanish trade routes

areas under effective Portuguese control   areas under effective Spanish control

• Portuguese-controlled towns   • Spanish-controlled towns

■ seat of Audiencia (Spanish admintraive division)

MEXICO

Charcas

Havana to Seville via Azores

San Agostin

Havana

Santo

Domingo

Seville to Veracruz via Canary Is.

ombre de Dios via Canary Is.

North Atlantic Ocean

Azores

Lisbon

Seville

Canary Islands

Cape Verde Islands

mate position of Tordesillas ation line

Olinda

Recife

Elmina to W. Indies with slaves

Elmina to Bahia with slaves

Luanda to Bahia with slaves

Bahia to Luanda with tobacco and sugar

South Atlantic Ocean

ASIA

Sea of Japan

JAPAN

Nagasaki

Manila galleons with silk

Manila galleons with silver

CHINA

Canton

Macao

Luzon

Philippines

Manila

Cebu

South China Sea

Ternate

Molucca

Amboina

Spice Islands

Timor

Alexandria

Cairo

Red Sea

Ormuz

Diu

Hooghly

Arabian Sea

INDIA

Goa

Calicut

Cochin

Ceylon

Colombo

Maldives

Laccadive Islands

Malay Archipelago

Malacca

Borneo

Celebes

Sumatra

Java

AFRICA

Bab el Mandeb

Aden

Elmina

Guato

Gulf of Guinea

São Tomé

Malindi

Pemba

Kilwa

Mombasa

Zanzibar

Luanda

ANGOLA

Mozambique

Sofala

Madagascar

Réunion

Indian Ocean

Lisbon to Goa (alternative route, second half of year)

foundation of East India Companies by the Dutch, the English and (later) the French brought the Portuguese under increasing attack. Dutch forces first established independent bases in the East (above all at Batavia, the heavily fortified headquarters of the Dutch East India Company) and then between 1640 and 1660 wrested Malacca, Ceylon, most South Indian ports and the lucrative Japan trade from the Portuguese. In 1652 they also created a useful south African base on the route to the East at Cape Town. The English and French also established modest settlements in India, and developed a promising trade with China. Even the Spaniards undermined the Portuguese, exporting Chinese goods after 1572 through their colony in the Philippines (map 2). Elsewhere in Asia, however, Europeans during this period traded in competition with local merchants on terms laid down by local rulers, and their efforts constituted but a fraction of Asia's total commerce.

The murder of Atahuallpa *(right)* in November 1532 set the seal on Spain's conquest of the Inca empire. Although there were perhaps only 180 Europeans in Peru, most of them young men in their twenties, their brutal murder of the 'divine Inca' broke the resistance of the Peruvian peoples. This vigorous illustration of the deed comes from the *Royal Commentaries* published between 1609 and 1616 by Garcilaso de la Vega, the son of a conquistador and an Inca princess

CONQVISTA
CORTALE·LA·CAVESA·A
ATAGVALDA·INGA·VMATACVCHV

INTERNET LINKS

www.le.ac.uk/hi/bon/
resources/bourb/Socgov/
Part4.html
Society and government in
France 1624–1661

1440–1789

The expansion of France

In 1415 English troops invaded France and by 1429 had established suzerainty over almost half the kingdom. In the 1440s, however, with the aid of a powerful artillery train, Charles VII (1422-61) began a rapid reconquest which by 1453 had expelled the English from all but the port-city of Calais, and doubled the size of the royal domain. His successors annexed Burgundy (1477), Brittany (1491) and Bourbon (1527) by force, and inherited Anjou and Provence (1481). Several other semi-independent fiefs came to the crown at the accession of Louis XII (1498), Francis I (1515) and Henry IV (1589) (map 1).

After Henry's death in 1610, continuing religious division, costly foreign wars and aristocratic faction, culminating in the Fronde revolt (1648-53), brought France to the brink of dissolution again. However Henry's grandson Louis XIV (1643-1715) restored order and made France the dominant state of Europe. During the relatively peaceful years between 1659 and 1672 the king and his ministers struggled to develop the French economy (agriculture, manufacture and trade), to extend overseas possessions, and to expand the army and navy. They also developed commercial harbours and sponsored public works, such as the Languedoc Canal connecting the Atlantic and the Mediterranean. The richness of resources available to the French, including a population of perhaps 20 million (the largest of any 17th-century European state), undoubtedly played a part in these achievements; but so did the ceaseless efforts, directives, and resources emanating from the Court (map 2).

Despite France's gains at the peaces of Westphalia (1648) and the Pyrenees (1659), Louis still feared Habsburg encirclement (page 92). He sought both to secure territories that might plug the gaps in his frontier (in wars fought in 1667-8 and 1672-8 which brought the acquisition of territory from the Spanish Netherlands and of Franche-Comté), and to erect an 'iron frontier' of state-of-the-art fortresses, thickest on the ground in the north and east, to create a defence in depth that would prevent any enemy forces from penetrating to the heart of the realm as the English and the Habsburgs had done in the past. Perhaps his success in this endeavour made him too bold, for in 1700 he accepted the will of the childless Spanish Habsburg Carlos II which bequeathed to Louis's grandson Philip the entire Spanish empire – Spain, Spanish America, the South Netherlands and half of Italy – even though he knew this sudden concentration of territory in the hands of the Bourbon dynasty would provoke a general European war. After some initial French victories (1702-3), followed by a string of searing defeats (1704-9), the 'iron frontier' showed its worth and forced France's exhausted enemies to conclude the compromise peaces of Utrecht (1713) and Rastatt (1714), by which Philip retained Spain and Spanish

1 The reunification of France 1440–1589

- lands recognizing English suzerainty, 1429
- frontier of France, 1492
- Royal domain, c. 1475
- lands annexed from Burgundy, 1477
- lands of René of Anjou, annexed 1481
- lands of Duke of Brittany, annexed 1491
- lands brought to the crown by Louis XII, 1498
- lands brought to the crown by Francis I, 1515
- lands of Duke of Bourbon, annexed 1527
- lands brought to the crown by Henry IV, 1589
- other fiefs annexed, with date
- fiefs still independent at the end of the 16th century

Calais *1558*
ARTOIS *(lost 1493)*
ST POL *1477*
PICARDY
NORMANDY
BRITTANY
VALOIS
ALENÇON *1525*
PERCHE *1483*
MAINE
ORLÉANAIS
VENDÔME
NEMOURS *1503*
BLOIS
ANJOU
TOURAINE
POITOU
BERRY
NEVERS
BURGUNDY
LA MARCHE
BOURBON
CHAROLAIS *Habsburg possession from 1493*
ANGOULÊME
FOREZ
LIMOGES
PÉRIGORD
AUVERGNE
GUYENNE
DAUPHINÉ
ALBRET
ROUERGUE
GASCONY
ARMAGNAC
BÉARN
BIGORRE
ASTARAC
COMMINGES
LANGUEDOC
COMTAT VENAISSIN *papal state*
PROVENCE
RETHEL
Verdun *1552*
Metz *1552*
BAR *1552*
Toul *1552*

In the vast palace of Versailles, seen in the background behind Jean-Baptiste Tuby's bronze sculpture of Apollo rising from the waters *(right)*, Louis XIV directed the fortunes of France. The complex served as the king's court, the centre of his government and a source of inspiration – and envy – to monarchs throughout Europe.

America, while Savoy, Britain and the Austrian Habsburgs partitioned the rest (map 3).

Louis had thus secured the integrity of France's frontiers, and ended for ever the threat of Habsburg encirclement; but the ruinous cost of his wars created a legacy of financial disorder and internal discontent which served to hamstring his successors. Although Louis XV (1715-74) managed to incorporate Lorraine in 1766, and his successor Louis XVI (1774-93) assisted the successful rebellion of the American colonies against Great Britain (page 104), both monarchs sacrificed (as Louis XIV had done) France's overseas possessions and accumulated such monstrous public debts that, in 1789, the government summoned a representative assembly, the States-General, to solve the financial crisis. In doing so, it unleashed revolution (page 116).

2 Administrative units and defensive fortifications

— frontier of France 1713–14

— administrative units of Louis XIV's reign, the *généralités* (generalities)

⊙ seat of *intendants*, Louis XIV's royal commissioners

⊕ *parlement* (law courts)

ALSACE *pays d'état*

defence:

■ fortifications (the so-called *barrière* or *frontière de fer*)

▣ fortifications built by Vauban but ceded during the reign of Louis XIV

⚓ galley port

⚑ naval port

economic:

‡ commercial harbours

major manufactures:

▤ brandy
◇ cloth
▢ glass
⊟ iron
● madder dye
◺ paper
⌐ pottery
⌐ printing
▣ salt
◉ silk
◊ soap
⊠ tapestry and carpets
▼ wine

3 The War of the Spanish Succession, 1701–14

✕ Allied victory

✕ Bourbon (French) victory

✕ inconclusive

principal territorial changes

to Spanish House of Bourbon

to Great Britain

to Austria

to Savoy

to France

to Prussia

INTERNET LINKS

www.metmuseum.org/toah/
ht/08/eue/ht08eue.htm
Timeline of art history in
Eastern Europe and
Scandinavia, 1400–1600

1462-1815

Russian expansion in Europe and Asi

After the Mongol invasion of the 13th century (page 60), the lands which had formed part of Kievan Russia fragmented. Lithuania expanded in the west, while the east and south became subject to Mongol overlords, in whose service the principality of Muscovy rose to prominence. Ivan III (1462-1505) opened another phase of expansion: in 1478 he annexed the city republic of Novgorod and in 1480 proclaimed independence from the Mongols. In 1510 his son Vassily (1505-33) overran the republic of Pskov, bringing Muscovite control close to the Baltic; and his grandson Ivan IV (1533-84) conquered the Tatar states of Kazan (1552) and Astrakhan (1556), gaining control of the Volga down to the Caspian Sea (map 1). In addition, from the 1580s, the lucrative fur trade lured enterprising Russians deep into Siberia. Crossing the Urals, they followed the River Ob until they came within portage of the Yenisey, where they built and fortified Turukhansk (1607); thence they reached the Lena river system, where they built Yakutsk (1632), and finally the Pacific, where they built Okhotsk (1649) – some 6,000 miles (9,700km) east of Moscow (map 2).

However Ivan IV failed to realise his principal territorial ambition, the acquisition of Livonia and direct access to the Baltic, while his attempt to break the power of the traditional nobility by creating a 'private domain' (the *oprichnina*) around Moscow resulted in massive depopulation. Muscovy was also still not entirely safe from the Crimean Tatars, who sacked Moscow in 1571. Then succession disputes following the extinction of the old Muscovite ruling house (the 'Time of Troubles', 1598-1613) caused the loss of much territory to Poland and Sweden.

Recovery came only in the mid-17th century, when a successful war with Poland (1654-67) brought substantial gains, including Smolensk and the Ukraine. Meanwhile the settlement of Siberia continued: 23,000 Russians lived there by 1622, 105,000 by 1662 and 230,000 by 1709. However the Amur Basin, acquired in the 1650s, had to be ceded to China in 1689 (albeit in return for useful trading concessions: map 2) and attempts to force access to the Black Sea failed. Instead, Peter I ('the Great', 1682-1725) concentrated on achieving a 'window on the west', wresting Estonia and Livonia from Sweden in 1721, acquiring the ancient port of Riga and founding the new one of St Petersburg (1703). Peter's successors reverted to his policy of expansion on the Black Sea. Catherine II ('the Great', 1762-96) annexed the Tatar khanate of the Crimea. She also acquired large parts of Poland – although the cost of her campaigns, on top of the oppressive social system which required serfs to spend almost all their time labouring on their lords' lands, provoked a major peasant uprising under Emelyan Pugachev (1773-5). The period 1772 to 1815 saw the Russian land frontier expand 600 miles (970 km) at the expense of Poland. Finally, despite a French invasion which reached Moscow in 1812, the Congress of Vienna in 1815 confirmed Russia's acquisition of Finland, Poland, Bessarabia and Transcaucasia (page 116).

The population ruled from Moscow had grown, both by territorial acquisition and by natural increase, from some 10 million in 1600, to over 15 million in 1725 and to almost 43 million in 1812, and the empire – the largest in the world – now stretched over 11 of the world's 24 time-zones.

2 Russian expansion in Siberia, 1581–1800

- Russian territory in 1581
- territory added 1581–98
- territory added 1598–1618
- territory added 1618–89
- territory added in 1650s; returned to China 1689
- territory added 1689–1725
- territory added 1725–62
- territory added 1762–1800

● Bratsk forts and trading posts
1630 (with date of foundation)

1 From Muscovy to Russia, 1462–1815

boundary of all Russian territories in 1462

Lithuania, 1462

1783 date of foundation of new town

KALMYKS native peoples

the expansion of Muscovy:

Moscow territory at end of 13th century

1478 date of acquisition by Muscovy

acquisitions to 1462

acquisitions under Ivan III, 1462–1505

acquisitions during 16th century

acquisitions during 17th century

acquisitions during 18th century

acquisitions, 1801–15

territory ceded to Sweden 1617 and Poland-Lithuania, 1618

acquired from Poland-Lithuania, 1634

acquired from Poland-Lithuania, 1667

BARENTS SEA

PECHORA

Pechora

Mezen

Obdorsk 1595

Berezov 1593

YUGRA

1501

Archangel 1584

Kholmogory

Solvychegodsk

Ustyug

Solikamsk

1472

Kama

NOVGOROD TERRITORY

1478

Kargopol

Lake Onega

Onega

Lake Ladoga

1478

FINLAND 1809

1743

Åbo

Helsingfors

Aland Islands

Stockholm

SWEDEN

Vyborg 1721

Kronstadt 1704

St. Petersburg 1703

Gulf of Finland

Narva 1581

Revel

Reval

ESTONIA 1721

Novgorod

1478

1362–89

1393-1425

Vologda Soligalich

1364

Galich

Vyatka

1489

Perm 1724

Nizhniy Tagil 1724

Kungur

Yekaterinburg 1725

UDMURTY

SIBERIA

BALTIC SEA

Riga

LIVONIA 1510

Pskov

1772

1478

Velikiye Luki

1503

1389–1425

1514–21

1494

Tver

1302

Dmitrov

Vladimir

1451 1364

Nizhniy Novgorod

Kostroma

Yaroslavl

1364

1389–1425

1364

MARI

CHUVASHI

KHANATE OF KAZAN

Kazan

COURLAND

Memel

Königsberg

Danzig

LITHUANIA

Polotsk

Vitebsk

Smolensk 1514

Minsk

Kovno

Vilna

1353–59

Vyazma

Mozhaysk

1301

Moscow

Kolomna

1364

Murom

1393–45

Arzamas

1552

MESHCHERA

Simbirsk 1648

Ufa 1586

Volga

Vistula

Warsaw

1807

Grodno

Bialystok

1795

Brest-Litovsk

Pinsk

1793

Mogilev

1772

1634

1494

1425–62

Ryazan

Tula

1521

1393

MORDVA

Penza 1650

Syzran 1683

Samara 1586

Orenburg 1743

POLAND

Kalisz

1815

Lublin

Pripet

Gomel

1503

Chernigov

Novograd-Volynskiy

1503

1586

Kursk

1503

Bryansk

Orel 1564

Yelets 1586

Don

Belgorod 1593

Voronezh 1586

Tambov 1636

Saratov 1590

Ural

Lwów

1634

1667

Kiev

Pereyaslav

1793

UKRAINE

Kharkov 1654

Poltava 1709

Don

Donets

Kamyshin

NOGAI TATARS

Volga

KALMYKS

AUSTRO-HUNGARIAN EMPIRE

Debrecen

Kolozsvár

TRANSYLVANIA

Brassó

Vinnitsa

Kamenets

Bratslav

Yekaterinoslav (Kodak) 1786

Sech

1739

DON COSSACKS

Cherkassk

Tsaritsyn 1589

KHANATE OF ASTRAKHAN

Guryev 1645

1791

Kishinev

Ochakov

Nikolayev 1789

1783

Taganrog

Azov

1783

Astrakhan 1556

MOLDAVIA

BESSARABIA

Jassy

1774

Kherson 1774

Odessa 1794

Akkerman

KHANATE OF CRIMEA

KUBAN COSSACKS

KALMYKS

Stavropol

Kuma

WALLACHIA

Bucharest

Danube

Ruschuk

OTTOMAN EMPIRE

Sofia

Varna

1812

Yevpatoriya

Bakhchisaray

Sebastopol 1783

Karasubazan

Simferopol (Ak-Mechet) 1784

Feodosiya (Kaffa)

Kerch

Yekaterinodar 1792

Pyatigorsk

Terek

Vladikavkaz

1784

CASPIAN SEA

BLACK SEA

1810

Sukhum-Kale

1806

1804

Kutaisi

Poti

Tiflis

GEORGIA 1806

DAGHESTAN

Derbent

1806

Baku

Caucasus

Kura

AZERBAIJAN

1805

Erivan

1813

ceded temporarily by Persia, 1723–32

PERSIA

Russian woodcut showing a procession of merchants carrying furs at the court of the Holy Roman Emperor c. 1570. In the early 17th century the demand for luxury furs fuelled expansion eastwards into Siberia to tap its seemingly inexhaustible supply.

INTERNET LINKS

http://members.aol.com/
TeacherNet/Colonial.html
Extensive resources on
Colonial America

1500–1783

The Americas

The daring conquest of Mexico by Hernán Cortés in 1519-21 and of Peru by Francisco Pizarro in 1531-3 (page 73) laid the foundations of a huge Spanish colonial empire in the Americas. By 1535, when the crown established viceregal government in Mexico and Lima became the capital of Peru, all the major centres of indigenous population in the former Aztec and Inca empires lay in Spanish hands: an area four times the size, and containing eight times the population, of the country from which the conquerors had come. Although the frontiers of colonial settlement continued to advance – with new viceroyalties in New Granada (1739) and Rio de la Plata (1776) and new military governments in Texas (1718) and California (1767) – none of these later, sparsely inhabited conquests compared with Mexico and Peru in wealth and importance. Potosí

in Peru and Zacatecas in Mexico became the largest producers of silver in the world, and by 1560 silver formed America's principal export to Europe.

Elsewhere on the continent colonization proved slower. The Portuguese only settled the Atlantic coast of south America after 1549 for fear that the French might do so. By 1600, although coastal Brazil had become studded with profitable sugar plantations and mills, worked by slaves from Africa, the Brazilian interior remained the domain of native Indian tribes until the 1690s, when the discovery of enormous gold deposits in the interior provoked a new wave of colonization. In the north-west, Russian explorers and traders pressed on; but by 1819 only 19 settlements existed between the Aleutian islands and California (map 1).

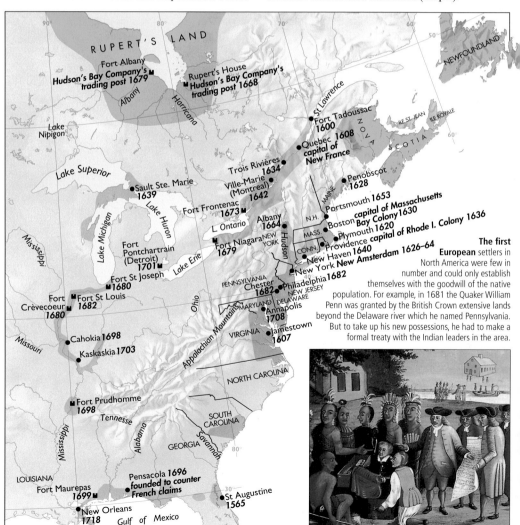

The first European settlers in North America were few in number and could only establish themselves with the goodwill of the native population. For example, in 1681 the Quaker William Penn was granted by the British Crown extensive lands beyond the Delaware river which he named Pennsylvania. But to take up his new possessions, he had to make a formal treaty with the Indian leaders in the area.

2 European settlement in North America

- early English settlements and claims
- early French settlements and claims
- early Spanish settlements

The Atlantic seaboard of north America, with its harsher climate and poor soil, also at first attracted few Europeans (who came mostly for fish and furs). Settlement only began with the foundation of Acadia (Nova Scotia) by the French in 1604, of Virginia (1607) and Massachusetts Bay (1620) by the English, and of New Amsterdam (later New York) by the Dutch (1624). Gradually, however, the Europeans pressed inland: the French advanced down the St Lawrence and (after 1682) the Mississippi, creating a chain of fortified posts all the way to the Gulf of Mexico and founding New Orleans in 1718; the English spread out around the rich fur-hunting grounds of Hudson Bay. Wars between the European states now regularly involved the Americas, with England gaining first the Dutch colonies along the Hudson (1664) and then French Canada (1763). By 1700, perhaps 250,000 Europeans lived in North America, but by 1820 that number had soared to 9 million (compared with just over 3 million in Spanish America).

The Spaniards in America relied from the first on Indian labour, both in ranching and mining, and readily intermarried; hence an extensive mestizo population developed, especially in Mexico and Peru. The British, however, who wanted land for farms and plantations, expelled or exterminated the native population: by 1820, only 600,000 lived in the English speaking areas (compared with 7.5 million in Spanish America). Instead, in Virginia, and then later in the Carolinas, where tobacco was introduced as a cash-crop, African slaves were imported to work on the plantations (like those of the sugar producers of Brazil and the Caribbean islands). By 1820, almost 2 million Africans lived in north America (compared with 800,000 in Spanish America).

Throughout the period, each mother country maintained a tight grip on its colonies. The colonists tolerated this as long as they felt insecure – whether from the threat of native uprisings or through the series of wars between the mother countries. Britain's resounding victory over France in 1763, however, brought total security to her American colonies, whose elites soon came to resent the continuing tax demands of the government in London. In 1776 they demanded their independence (page 98) and the colonies of Latin America followed suit after 1808. (page 112).

1511–1826
South-East Asia and Japan

1511 Portuguese capture Malacca

1543 Portuguese traders arrive in Japan

1603 Tokugawa Ieyasu become first Tokugawa shogun

1619 Batavia founded by Dutch; beginnings of Dutch colonial empire in the East Indies

1640 European traders (except the Dutch) expelled from Japan

1641 Dutch capture Malacca from Portuguese

1786 Penang acquired by English East India Company

1819 Singapore founded by Britain as free trade port

In 1603 the Japanese emperor conferred the title of Shogun (military leader) on Tokugawa Ieyasu, who had established control over the state re-unified in the 1590s (page 68). The Tokugawa dynasty exercised power until 1868, giving Japan a prolonged period of political stability. A complex system of government emerged in which the shoguns in Edo (modern Tokyo) dominated or regulated the 250 or so fiefs of the feudal lords, organized society in a hierarchy of classes, and enacted a comprehensive legal code. From 1612 they banned the Christian missionaries (active in many areas since the mid-16th century) and persecuted their adherents. They also forbade all Japanese to travel abroad; limited foreign contacts to the Dutch (who maintained a trading post at Nagasaki), the Chinese and the Koreans; and until 1853 successfully repulsed various attempts by the Russians, British, French and Americans to open trade (map 1). Yet despite this isolation, Tokugawa Japan prospered: trade and cities grew rapidly; the population rose from 20 to 30 million; high literacy rates prevailed; industry and credit spread widely. By the mid-19th century, Japan was far better prepared than any other part of Asia to meet the challenge of Western expansion (page 122).

Initially, however, Western traders showed far more interest in the spices of South-East Asia. The disintegration of the empires of Srivijaya and Majapahit (page 64) left behind scores of petty states with little cohesion, opening the way to Portuguese acquisition of Malacca (1511) and footholds in the Moluccas (page 80). Their presence at first changed little: in Asia they aimed to dominate the spice trade through a chain of fortified stations, linked by naval power, not to acquire territory. The arrival of the Dutch and then the English after 1595 (page 80) did not initially change this, for they too sought primarily to monopolize the spice trade, and even after the establishment of a fortress at Batavia (1619) the Dutch directed most of their territorial ambitions towards acquiring Portuguese and English bases, rather than to conquering native states. The only substantial European colony in the area remained the Philippines, where the Spanish authorities began to foster the cultivation of tobacco, sugar, hemp and other commercial products from the later 18th century (map 2).

The mainland monarchies of South-East Asia – Arakan, Burma, Siam, Cambodia, Luang Prabang and Annam – had little direct involvement in European trade, and concentrated instead on extending their power at the expense of their neighbours. Over the period as a whole, Annam (Vietnam) and Siam expanded at the expense of Luang Prabang (Laos) and Cambodia. Burma almost disintegrated after the Mons rebelled in 1740, set up a king of their own at Pegu, and in 1752 captured the Burmese capital of Ava. However a charismatic leader, Alaungpaya (1735-60), defeated the Mons and established Rangoon as the southern port of a reunited Burma (1755), while his successors invaded Siam (1767) and conquered Arakan (1785).

Two factors complicated state-building in the area: the constant pressure of the hill peoples of the interior (like the Mons), always eager to assert their independence, and the steadily increasing interference of the Europeans. A group of Iberian adventurers temporarily seized power

Daimyō **and their retinues** enter Edo castle to participate in one of the many courtly ceremonials *(right)*. Edo, now Tokyo, was originally a fishing village, near which a castle was built in 1456. It rapidly became a powerful centre and in 1590 Tokugawa Ieyasu selected Edo for his residence, building an elaborate castle which remained the seat of the shogunate for 260 years, although it became the capital only in the 19th century.

1 Japan in isolation

- provincial borders
- Five Highways
- extensions to the Five Highways
- secondary roads
- sea routes
- important castle towns

feudal territories:
- major Tokugawa domains
- American, Russian, British and other naval visits

C H I N A

to Japan

FORMOSA
Spanish colonies in
north Taiwan, 1626–37;
Dutch in southwest
Taiwan, 1624–61

Pacific Ocean

to Acapulco

Noga Hills
Mogaung Myitkyina
Imphal
IPUR
Tagaung Bhamo
YUN-NAN
BURMA
hwebo
Mandalay
Ava
Amarapura
SHAN
STATES
1785
1564
1707
KAREN NI
Magwe STATE
An Pass
Thayetmyo
Toungoo
Prome Lamphun
ungup Pegu
Pass
Bassein
Rangoon
om 1755
Syriam
to 1755
MONS
Tavoy
Mergui
Mergui
Archipelago
nan Is.

Canton
Macao
to Japan

TONGKING
Hanoi Bac Ninh
Haiphong
Chiang Saen
Luang Thanh Hoa
Prabang
Chiang Rai
Chiengmai
Vientiane Ha Tinh
Lampang Porte d'Annam
Sawankhalok
Sukhothai Hue
Lopi Buri Tourane *French from 1787*
Korat Champassak
Ayutthaya
Bangkok Stung Treng Binh Dinh
Thon Buri Angkor Qui Nhon
Sisophon
Battambang
Chanthaburi Kratie Nha Trang
CAMBODIA Kompong Cham
COCHIN
Phnom Penh CHINA
Gulf of Siam Bien Hoa
Kampot Saigon
Ha Tien Chau Cho Lon
Doc
Isthmus of Kra
Nakhon Si Thammarat
Phuket Trang
Songkhla
Pattani

Hainan

from
Canton
to all
major
S.E. Asian
ports

*South China
Sea*

Luzon

PHILIPPINES

Manila

from Acapulco

Sulu
Sea
Balambangan
Mindanao
Sulu Archipelago

Penang
British from 1786
MALAYA
dras
lcutta
Tiku
Fort de Kock
(Bukit Tinggi)
Padang
Painan
Djambi
Bangka
Palembang
Benkulen
Billiton
Sukadana
Bantam
Batavia
(Jakarta)
MATARAM
Jogjakarta Surabaya

Straits of Malacca

Malacca
*Portuguese 1511–1641
Dutch 1641–1826*
Singapore
British from 1819
Pontianak

Brunei

SARAWAK

Borneo

Manado

Tidore Halmahera

Strait of Macasser

Celebes

Bandjarmasin

Macassar

MOLUCCAS
(Spice Islands)

Buru Ceram
Amboina
Banda Is.

Banda Sea

Karimata Strait

Java Sea

Sunda Strait

*Indian
Ocean*

Bali Sumbawa
Lombok Flores
Sumba Timor

**2 The Europeans
in South-East Asia**

European possessions, 1826

British	Spanish
Dutch	Portuguese

trade routes:
developed by Dutch and
English East India Companies
developed by Arab and Gujerati traders
developed by the Dutch in the 17th cent
used by English shipping from 1786
used by the 'Manila Galleon'
local trade routes
⊙ principal trading centre

Vietnamese expansion
Vietnamese border, 1500
expansion to 1611
acquisitions from
Cambodia in early
18th century
Vietnamese expansion
in 19th century
kingdom of Luang
Prabang, 1707
area which broke away
under Vientiane in 1707
Burmese conquests
Siamese conquests

in Cambodia in the 1590s; the French briefly
garrisoned some Siamese strongholds in the 1680s;
both the French and English East India Companies
intervened in Burma in the 1750s. Meanwhile, the
Dutch began to extend their control over Java and the
Spice Islands, and at the same time the British established their base at Penang (1786) and a free trade
port at Singapore (1819) on the Malayan peninsula.

These acquisitions led to tension between the
two colonial powers, which only abated after a treaty
in 1824 obliged the British to withdraw from Sumatra

and the Dutch from Malacca. Secure in the east, the
British now turned on Burma and, after a short war
(1824-6), annexed Arakan, Assam and Tenasserim.
The future Dutch and British colonial empires in
South-East Asia were taking shape, but their control
remained loose and indirect. Only after the industrial
revolution, and the expanding demand for raw
materials at home, did the Europeans seriously
impinge upon the lives and fortunes of the peoples of
the region.

www.fordham.edu/halsall/
mod/modsbook02.html
The Reformation in Europe

INTERNET LINKS

1517–1650
The Reformation and Catholic Reformation

1517 Luther launches debate over church reform

1520 Luther burns papal bull of excommunication

1541-64 Calvin reforms the Genevan church

1563 End of the Council of Trent

1589 Independent Orthodox patriarchate established in Moscow

1596 Union of Brest establishes Greek Catholic (Uniate) church in Poland–Lithuania

1598 Edict of Nantes: religious peace in France (revoked 1685)

1648 Peace of Westphalia: religious peace in the Holy Roman empire

Of the 250,000 or so works printed in Europe between 1447 and 1600, about 75 per cent concerned religion. The Reformation and the Catholic response would have been impossible without printing presses like this one *(below)*, from the cover of a book printed in Frankfurt in the early 17th century.

The shattering of the unity of Latin Christendom altered the course of European history. The fall of Constantinople (page 48) allowed the Roman church to ignore the Orthodox areas; and, except in Bohemia and Moravia, heresy scarcely existed in the West. Complacent, the Papacy failed to deploy its immense wealth adequately, producing widespread pluralism and absenteeism; this, coupled with the materialism of the hierarchy, discredited the Western church in the eyes of many Christians. Some, like Erasmus of Rotterdam (1466-1536) and Thomas More (1478-1535), hoped for spiritual renewal within the church; but in Saxony Martin Luther (1483-1546) criticized clerical abuse and in 1520 called upon the German nobility to reform the church. Meanwhile, inspired by Huldreych Zwingli (1484-1531), the magistrates of the Swiss canton of Zürich renounced allegiance to Rome.

These successful protests sparked others. By 1560, seven out of every ten inhabitants of the Holy Roman Empire no longer accepted papal authority, and Protestantism (as the dissident creeds became known) also prevailed in Scandinavia, the Baltic lands, and England. Further defections from Rome came through the teaching of John Calvin (1509-64) in Geneva. Calvinism made rapid progress in France, Poland, Hungary and Scotland (where it became the official creed after 1560).

In addition, a number of more radical sects sprang up, called 'Anabaptists' by their enemies because of their belief that only adult baptism was valid. They rejected ritual, spiritual and temporal authority, and many social conventions in favour of Biblical simplicity. Many combined evangelism with social protest, and participated both in the major rising of the German peasantry in 1524-5 and in the radical government of the city of Münster in 1534-5. Both movements were brutally repressed and Anabaptism, where it survived, became a secret, separate creed.

Eventually the Catholic church reformed itself. The Council of Trent (three sessions 1545-63) condemned abuses, defined doctrine, and created a more effective and educated clergy; at the same time new religious orders (most notably the Jesuits, incorporated in 1540) targeted key areas for reconversion. By 1650 the Protestants had been expelled from Bavaria (1579), Austria (1597) and Bohemia (1628), and the number of Protestant churches in Poland had declined from 560 in 1572 to 240 in 1650. Spain eradicated its small Protestant minorities, and in 1609 expelled its substantial Moorish population. In the Holy Roman Empire, however, the Protestants fought back, provoking the savage religious conflict known as the Thirty Years' War (page 92).

1 Religious divisions in 1570

Roman Catholic · Orthodox · Greek Catholic (Uniate) · Lutheran · Calvinist · Anabaptist · Islam · Anglican · Hussite

NORWAY
(Danish)

SWEDEN

ICELAND
■1552

• Bergen

• Christiania
■1539

■1527

Åbo ■1528

Helsingfors

Stockholm •

Reval
■1524

ESTONIA

RUSSIA

COTLAND
0

• Edinburgh

North
Sea

LIVONIA

Pskov •

Riga ■1524

COURLAND

■1561

• York

• Aarhus

DENMARK

Copenhagen •

Malmö •

Baltic Sea

Dünaburg •

LITHUANIA

Vilna •

ster •

NGLAND
▲1534

• Oxford

• London

Amsterdam •

NETHERLANDS
2

Mons •

Brussels •

Cologne •

SLESVIG ■1542 ■1536

HOLSTEIN ■1542

Emden • ■1529

■1526
■1542

Lübeck ■1531

Hamburg ■1548 ■1549

Bremen ■1525

BRUNSWICK
LÜNEBURG ■1545

Hannover •

BRANDENBURG

■1539

Berlin ■1525

Magdeburg ■1525

Wittenberg ■1522

Danzig •

POMERANIA
■1534

Stettin •

Königsberg
■1523

PRUSSIA

■1525

Minsk •

Poznań •

Warsaw •

2

Rhine

Münster •

HESSE
■1524

NASSAU
■1528

DUCHY OF
SAXONY
■1539

Leipzig •

ELEC. OF
Dresden
SAXONY ■1525

Breslau ■1524

SILESIA

Oder

POLAND

• Rouen

Seine

• Rheims

• Paris

Frankfurt
■1530

PALATINATE
Metz ■1546
• ■1559

Nuremberg

■1528

Prague
■1524

BOHEMIA

Elbe

MORAVIA

Brünn •

Cracow •

Lwów •

Dniester

• Orléans

Loire

FRANCHE-
COMTÉ

Dijon •

WÜRTTEMBERG
Strassburg ■1534

■1524

Ulm ■1530

Munich •

Danube

2

Vienna •

AUSTRIA

Pozsony •

2

Eger •

Kassa •

Buda •

Debrecen •

MOLDAVIA

RANCE

Tours •

NEUCHÂTEL
■1530

BASLE
■1523

■1529
Berne •

Zurich
▲1524 APPENZELL

THURGAU
▲1524

SÄNKT GALLEN

Jassy •

• Limoges

26

VAUD
▲536

Geneva
▲536

SWISS
CONFEDERATION

▲1524
GLARUS
▲1525

GRAUBÜNDEN

Salzburg •

Graz •

HUNGARY

Kolozsvár •

TRANSYLVANIA

Szeged •

Brassó •

ouse •

SAVOY

Turin •

MONTFERRAT

MILAN

Milan •

MANTUA

Venice •

Verona •

Trieste •

VENETIAN

Zágráb •

Pécs •

Temesvár •

WALLACHIA

Bucharest •

Lyons •

PARMA

FERRARA
MODENA

Bologna •

Belgrade •

Danube

Ruschuk •

Nizza •

MONACO

MASSA
LUCCA

Florence •

SAN MARINO

DUCHY OF
URBINO

Zara •

Bosna
Saray •

OTTOMAN

Nish •

• Marseille

ORANGE
VENAISSIN

Avignon •

REP. OF GENOA

Genoa •

TUSCANY

Perugia •

PAPAL

Spalato •

Mostar •

MONTENEGRO

REPUBLIC OF
RAGUSA

EMPIRE

Sofia •

Philippopolis •

rcelona •

DORRA

STATO
DEI
PRESIDI

STATES
Rome ■

187

DUCHY
OF
CASTRO

PONTECORVO

BENEVENTO

Naples •

Bari •

Taranto •

Üsküb •

Adrianople •

SARDINIA

Cagliari •

10

NAPLES

SICILY

Palermo •

Messina •

Salonica •

Janina •

Athens •

20

3 delegates sent to last session
    of Council of Trent, (1562–3)

■ date of change from
    Catholicism to Lutheranism

▲ date of change to Calvinism,
    Zwinglianism or Anglicanism

INTERNET LINKS

www.antiquesatoz.com/
habsburg
Biographies of
the Habsburg dynasty

1519–1659

The Habsburg ascendancy in Europe

Charles V's election as Holy Roman Emperor in 1519 created a Habsburg hegemony in Europe. He already ruled lands in Austria, South Germany and the Netherlands, and the realms bequeathed by his maternal grandparents in Spain, Italy and North Africa. Each of these inheritances soon increased. In 1526 his brother Ferdinand succeeded to the crowns of Bohemia (which included Moravia, Silesia and Lusatia) and Hungary. In 1535 Charles himself acquired both Lombardy and Tunisia, and throughout his reign he added to his holdings in the Netherlands (map 1). Moreover, in America, his Castilian subjects toppled first the Aztec and then the Inca states (see page 80). Although the central European lands (and the Imperial title) passed to Ferdinand and his successors, Charles's son Philip II also ruled a formidable inheritance. He, too, managed to extend it – adding the Philippines by conquest after 1571, and Portugal with her overseas possessions by inheritance after 1580.

Such centralization did not prove popular, however. Apart from provoking the enmity of France, which felt encircled, Charles V faced rebellions from his subjects in Spain (1520-2) and Germany (1552-5), the former provoked by taxation,

the latter arising from religious dissent provoked by the Reformation (page 90). Philip II (1556-98) contended, in the Netherlands, with the longest-lasting revolt in modern European history (map 2). The various provinces inherited or acquired by Charles V became part of a single state only in 1548. Local customs, often guaranteed by charter against central government interference, nevertheless survived and Philip II's attempts to override them – both to raise taxes and to persecute heretics – provoked insurrection. A timely display of force stifled an uprising in 1566; but in 1572 the provinces of Holland and Zeeland sustained rebellion, helped by the threat of a French invasion which made difficult a concentration of Spanish forces, until the cost of opposing them compelled Philip to withdraw his troops in 1576-7. Although forces loyal to (and maintained by) Spain reconquered many areas in the 1580s, fighting went on with the northern rebels for more than 20 years. Only in 1609 did Spain finally conclude a 12-year truce with the largely Calvinist Dutch Republic.

The Netherlands' struggle resumed during Emperor Ferdinand II's war against his rebellious subjects in Bohemia and Austria (map 3). He routed them at the battle of White Mountain in 1620.

Spain's attempts to suppress the Dutch Revolt provoked much hostile propaganda. Here *(below)* the devil crowns the duke of Alba, who led Spain's efforts 1567-1573, while a Cardinal wields bellows to fill his head with Catholic zeal. Alba holds allegorical figures of the Dutch provinces on a chain, while his agents execute Counts Egmont and Hornes, defenders of Dutch liberties. (The execution itself took place in Brussels on 5 June 1568).

2 Dutch Revolt, 1572–1648

— Netherlands, 1548

---- rebel areas, December 1572

— furthest extent of Dutch revolt, July 1577

— rebel areas, December 1606

▨ Dutch conquests, 1621–48

☐ Dutch Republic, 1648

North Sea

GRONINGEN
FRIESLAND
DUTCH
Amsterdam
Deventer
ENGLAND
OVERIJSSEL
Zutphen
UTRECHT
HOLLAND
The Hague
GELDERLAND
REPUBLIC
Nijmegen
ZEELAND
HOLY
Sluis
Antwerp
ROMAN
Bruges
Axel
Dunkirk
Mechelen
Leuven
Maastricht
SPANISH
Brussels
Liège
EMPIRE
Ieper
Namur
NETHERLANDS

FRANCE

Encouraged by this success, with Spanish and Papal support Ferdinand turned in 1621 against the German Protestant states, especially the Calvinists. Despite aid from Britain, Denmark and the Dutch, they lost and in 1629 Ferdinand issued an 'Edict of Restitution' by which he reclaimed Church lands acquired by Protestant rulers. Swedish military aid turned the tables against the emperor, and saved the German Protestants from collapse: an army led by King Gustavus Adolphus routed the Imperialists at Breitenfeld (1631) and drove them from much of Germany. Spain intervened to restore Habsburg fortunes but its victory at Nördlingen (1634) provoked France to declare war first on Spain (1635) and then on the emperor (1636). The war spread to almost the whole continent.

After many more years of largely unsuccessful campaigning, at the peace of Westphalia (1648) the emperor was abandoned virtually all his powers in Germany, agreed to toleration for Protestants and Catholics, and promised not to assist his Spanish cousins in their war against the Dutch rebels; by the peace of Münster (1648) Spain formally recognized the independence of the Dutch Republic (and their possession of all territories conquered since 1621); and by the peace of the Pyrenees (1659), Spain ceded all areas gained by France on the frontiers of both Spain and the Netherlands. The religious and political frontiers of central Europe which were agreed by these treaties lasted unchanged for 100 years. The Habsburg bid for European hegemony had failed.

3 The Thirty Years' War, 1618–48

- → route of Gustavus Adolphus, 1630–2
- → route of the Spanish army, 1634
- ✕ Imperial (Catholic) victory
- ✕ Imperial (Catholic) defeat
- — Holy Roman Empire
- — affected by Edict of Restitution, 1629
- ■ date region became Lutheran
- ▲ date region became Calvinist

the religious position in 1640:
- Lutheran
- Calvinist
- Catholic
- regained by Roman Catholics

1 The Habsburg empire in Europe

- Aragonese inheritance of Charles V
- added by Charles V, with date
- Austrian inheritance of Charles V
- added by Ferdinand I, with date
- Castilian inheritance of Charles V
- Burgundian inheritance of Charles V
- added by Charles V with date
- states favourable to Charles V
- 'The Spanish Road' connecting Habsburg dominions
- ruled by Charles V as Holy Roman Emperor

China under the Ch'ing dynasty

A new era in Chinese history opened in 1644 when the Ming dynasty, beset for a century by pirate raids, civil wars, and northern invaders (see page 68), fell to the forces of a Manchurian dynasty which ruled the country until 1911. The Manchu, or Ch'ing, rulers met with resistance in southern China for half a century, but quickly established a working relationship with the gentry who staffed the Chinese bureaucracy and, with its support, began a successful policy of territorial expansion which continued until the mid-18th century (map 1).

At the same time population trebled from about 100 million in 1650 to 300 million in 1800 and reached 420 million by 1850, while vast quantities of tea, silk, cotton, lacquer and porcelain were exported (mostly to Europe). But the financial strain of the wars of expansion and the pressure of the growing population on land and food caused hardships that led to recurrent unrest and revolt, not only among the ethnic minorities who were harshly exploited by Chinese and Manchus alike, but also in the heartland itself, beginning with the 'White Lotus' rebellion, 1796-1805. China remained the world's largest and most populous state, but its economic difficulties and inadequate bureaucracy prevented effective resistance to the pressures of the Western powers who sought to open the Chinese market for the goods produced by their empires.

China's defeat in the Opium War (1839-42) resulted in the cession of Hong Kong to Britain and the opening of the first five Treaty Ports (their number steadily increased)

1 Chinese imperial expansion from c. 1620

Manchu expansion Phase 1: China
- Manchu homeland
- expansion before 1644
- expansion, 1644–59
- **1644** date of incorporation

tributary states:
- before 1644
- after 1644

- ⊗ seat of main Lamaistic patriarch
- ★ risings of non-Chinese people
- sectarian risings of Chinese
- ■ official centre of foreign commerce

Phase 2: New Territories
- **1724** New Territory with date of incorporation
- → military expeditions
- border of China under the Ch'ing dynasty, at its greatest extent

RUSSIAN EMPIRE

Lake Balkhash

TANNU TUVA

Russian protectorate 1912

Manchouli

Aigun   to Russia 1860

MARITIME PROVINCE

Harbin

occupied by Russia 1897–1905; Japanese influence after 1905

Suifenho

Hunchun

Vladivostok

ILI PROTECTORATE

to Russia 1871–81

MONGOLIA
tributary territory;
autonomous 1912

Changchun

Mukden

Yellow River
(Huang Ho)

Kalgan

Peking

Newchwang

Antung

Dairen

to Russia 1898
to Japan 1905

KOREA
to Japan 1910

Sea of Japan
(East Sea)

S I N K I A N G
tributary territory

Tientsin

Taiyüan

Port Arthur

Chefoo

Weihaiwei
to Britain 1898

Tsinan

Tsingtao
to Germany 1898

C H I N A

T I B E T
tributary territory;
autonomous 1912
under British influence

British protectorate 1817

Nanking

Chinkiang

Soochow

Wusung

Shanghai

Wuhu

Hangchow

Ningpo

Ichang

Yangtze

KOREA

J A P A N

NSH
IA

NEPAL   SIKKIM

BHUTAN

ASSAM
to Britain 1826

Chungking

Kiukiang

Yochow

Changsha

Wenchow

Santuao

Foochow

to Japan 1872

Ryukyus

**2 The dismemberment
of the Ch'ing empire,
1842–1911**

— boundary of Ch'ing
empire in 1850

— states formerly
tributary to China

— area affected by Taiping
rebellion, 1850–64

Kunming

Tengyueh

Mengtze
Manhao

New Territories
to Britain 1898

Nanning

Lungchow

Canton

Macao
to Portugal
1557

Kowloon to Britain 1898

Hong Kong
to Britain 1842

Amoy

Taiwan
to Japan 1895

Tamsui

BURMA
to Britain
1886

TONGKING

Haiphong

Pakhoi

Kwangchowwan
to France 1898

Kiungchow

LAOS
to France
1893

FRENCH
INDO
CHINA
1884

SIAM

Hainan

**colonial
possessions:**

**spheres of
influence:**

Russian

British

Japanese

French

German

In the Sino-Japanese war of
1894–5 the carefully modernized
Western-style Japanese army
disastrously routed the ill-led
Chinese forces.

railways:

– – – Russian   · · · · · French

– – – British   ╟─┼─╢ German

——— Japanese   ┼─┼─┼ Chinese

Treaty ports and towns:

◒ 1842 Treaty of Nanking

⊗ 1858 Treaty of Tientsin

◉ 1860 Peking Convention

◖ 1876 Chefoo Convention

▲ 1897 Sino-French
Trade Convention

○ additional ports
opened by 1911

● other towns and cities

y of Nerchinsk, 1689: Russia
gnizes Chinese border along
e Argun and Amur rivers

MANCHURIA

Amur

629–30
HORCHIN

Mukden
(capital, 1625–44)

KOREA
Manchu invasions,
1627, 1636–7
vassal status
1637

1645
SHANTUNG

Eight Trigrams
rising, 1813

1645
KIANGSU

1646
CHEKIANG

1646
FUKIEN

TAIWAN
Dutch, 1624–62; Ming
loyalists, 1662–83;
occupied by Ch'ing,
1683

rising of Heaven
and Earth
Society, 1787–8

etnamese
rate raids,
1800–9

in which foreigners enjoyed extra-territorial rights.
More seriously, it served to weaken imperial authority and encouraged the Taiping rebellion (1850–64),
the most serious of the many revolts that shook
Manchu power. The Taiping and Nien uprisings
alone left 25 million dead. These grave disorders also
convinced the Western powers that Ch'ing China
stood on the verge of collapse and encouraged them
to secure a share: Russia gained the Amur basin, the

Maritime Province (1858–60) and, temporarily, the Ili
valley in Turkestan (1871–81); France occupied Indo-
China (1884–5); Britain took Burma (1886); Japan
annexed Taiwan (1895) and Korea (1910) (map 2).
These losses convinced many Chinese that radical
changes were inevitable, and when in 1911 a small
mutiny broke out among the Manchu army, disaffection spread rapidly throughout the whole country
and the imperial government collapsed (page 130).

1707–1947

India

George V was crowned King Emperor of India at a durbar, or assembly of notables, in Delhi in 1911. In an effort to placate nationalist emotions, the annulment of the unpopular partition of Bengal was announced at the durbar .

2 India in 1857

- territory under British rule in 1805
- territory under British rule at close of Lord Dalhousies administration, 1856
- - - main area affected by Indian Mutiny, 1857
- • main centres of rebellion

PUNJAB
NW PROVINCES
BAHAWALPUR
Meerut
Delhi
Bulandshahr
Aligarh
Bareilly
Agra
Fatehgarh
RAJPUTANA
Mainpuri
OUDH
Lucknow
AJMER
Gwalior
Cawnpore
SIND
Jhansi
Kalpi
Allahabad
NEPAL
CHINA
ASSAM
BIHAR
BENGAL
BURMA
KUTCH
GUJERAT
CENTRAL INDIA
AGENCY
NAGPUR
KATHIAWAR
BERAR
Arabian Sea
BOMBAY
Bombay
HYDERABAD
Calcutta
ARAKAN
GOA Portuguese
MADRAS
MYSORE
COCHIN
TRAVANCORE
Ceylon

Shortly after Aurangzeb's death in 1707 (page 62), Mughal power declined. In the north, Oudh and Bengal became effectively independent, owing only nominal allegiance to Delhi; in the centre, the power of the Maratha confederacy increased; in the south the Muslim state of Mysore expanded rapidly. Meanwhile European influence in India continued to increase, with both the French and English East India Companies acquiring new territory in the southeast. Robert Clive's victory at Plassey in 1757 gave the English control over the lands and resources of Bengal, Orissa and Bihar, allowing the Company to maintain an army of over 100,000 men – most of them Indian soldiers (sepoys) trained to fight in European fashion – with which they not only destroyed France's Indian ambitions but also extended their control over the entire eastern coast of the subcontinent (map 1). Mysore went down to defeat in 1799, the Marathas in 1805, both delivering extensive new territories to British control, and most other major Indian rulers soon recognized British suzerainty.

Over the next half-century the conquest of Sind (1843) and the Punjab (1849), brought the dominions of the Company up to the country's natural frontier in the northwest, while a war with Nepal (1814-16) extended them to the Himalayas. To the east the

British clashed with the Burmese empire and in 1824-6 annexed Assam and Arakan (page 89). Within India, the 'Doctrine of Lapse' introduced by Governor-General Dalhousie (1847-56) resulted in the absorption of autonomous but dependent states, such as Oudh and several Maratha kingdoms, into the directly administered territories (map 2). Not surprisingly, this policy provoked disaffection which found violent outlet in 1857. Beginning as a mutiny of the Company's native soldiers, the revolt soon involved princes, landlords and peasants throughout northern India; but the loyalty of the Sikhs and the passivity of southern India enabled the British to restore control after 14 months of bitter fighting.

The mutiny proved a watershed in the history of British India. It thoroughly discredited the Company and in 1858 the London government assumed direct control. The subcontinent now acquired a pivotal position in Britain's Imperial system, leading to intervention in Afghanistan to block Russian expansion into central Asia (page 114), and in Burma to counter French influence in South-East Asia. From East Africa to China, the Indian army regularly acted to advance British interests. Within India, the autonomy of the princes was henceforth respected and active steps were taken to develop the economy: the construction of first-class roads and a major rail network, together with the opening of the Suez Canal in 1869, made possible the exploitation of raw materials and the introduction of export crops, such as tea. Between 1869 and 1929 India's foreign trade increased sevenfold. However, although some modern industries developed under Indian entrepreneurs, most of the trade involved importing British manufactures and exporting raw materials; and in most areas neither the character of the economy nor traditional agriculture experienced any basic change

3 British India, 1931

- territory under British rule
- territories permanently administered by Government of India (mostly tribal)
- states and territories administered by local Indian rulers
- Portuguese enclave
- French enclave
- Hindu majority provinces
- Muslim majority provinces
- area of Buddhist predominance
- area of large Sikh population

manufacturing products

- cotton textiles
- woollens
- tea
- chemicals
- metals
- machinery and transport material
- tobacco
- sugar
- rice mills
- iron and steel (large scale)
- shipping
- mills (various grains)

(map 3). The Gross National Product increased only slowly, while from 1921 (thanks to sustained population growth) per capita income declined.

The rise of a new middle class, partly through industry but more through the recruitment of educated Indians into the colonial administration, coupled with overt British racism, awakened a new political consciousness. The Indian National Congress (established with official blessing in 1885) at first accepted British rule, but soon developed an extremist wing which questioned the foreigners' right to rule India. The decision to partition the province of Bengal in 1905 provoked mass agitation and terrorist attacks; and from 1919, under the leadership of Mohendas K. Gandhi (1869-1948), Congress fought actively for home rule and, after 1929, for independence. Profiting from the unrest caused by unemployment and the world economic depression, Gandhi launched a civil disobedience campaign (1930-4) that galvanized the Indian masses, and forced Britain to pass the Government of India Act (1935) which provided a framework for participation in central and provincial government.

By 1937 Congress controlled 11 of the 14 provincial administrations, but failed to represent adequately the interests of the large Muslim minority whose leaders in 1940 passed a resolution calling for an autonomous Islamic state in the subcontinent: Pakistan. In 1942 Gandhi launched a 'Quit India' campaign and in 1946-7, faced by massive disaffection, a naval mutiny, and strong pressure from the United States, the British drew up hasty plans for partition along sectarian lines. India and Pakistan became independent in 1947, Burma and Ceylon in 1948 (page 162).

1 The growth of British power to 1805

- territory ceded to Britain by 1805 with dates
- British victories with dates

INTERNET LINKS

www.timelines.info/history/
ages_and_periods/the_age_
of_revolution/ —
A timeline of revolutions

The age of revolution

The later 18th century saw an unprecedented wave of uprisings throughout the western hemisphere (map 1). Many reflected a long-standing desire for independence, as in Corsica (1755, 1793), Haiti (1791), Sardinia (1793), Ireland (1798), Serbia (1804) and Spain (1808). Most, however, owed something to the Enlightenment, a European intellectual movement which emphasized certain fundamental rights of human beings and rejected traditional authority. Paradoxically, this could lead to rebellions by conservative elements against reforming rulers – such as the Austrian Netherlands (1787) and Hungary (1790) against the 'Enlightened' policies of Emperor Joseph II – or the resistance of colonial societies to the centralizing policies of the home government – as in North America after 1775 (page 104) and in South America after 1808 (page 112). More commonly opposition came from the middle classes: against a closed patriarchate in the Dutch Republic (1785-7); against the absolute monarchy and its aristocratic supporters in France.

In France, between 1789 and 1791 a representative assembly, summoned to solve a financial crisis, abolished feudalism, and created a constitutional monarchy and equality before the law. The king, however, refused to cooperate and was deposed in 1792, provoking Austrian, Prussian and (from 1793) British attempts to overthrow the Republic by force. They failed: instead, the revolutionary government in Paris purged its opponents at home and, by mobilizing unprecedented numbers of its citizens, conquered the Low Countries, Switzerland and Italy, imposing satellite republics.

In 1799 a successful general, Napoleon Bonaparte, took power as military dictator. He secured peace abroad (1802), and reorganized French local government, laws and education. But Britain declared war again in 1803 and, although her command of the seas (confirmed at Trafalgar, 1805) provided immunity from invasion, Napoleon defeated her continental allies – Austria, Prussia and Russia – in a brilliant series of battles (1805-7). Next, in order to create a continental blockade against British trade, Napoleon overran Spain (1808) and extended France's frontiers to Catalonia, the Baltic and Rome (1809-10). However Britain supported his opponents in the Iberian peninsula, expelling French forces by 1814. Meanwhile Russia's refusal to cooperate in the continental blockade led to a French invasion in 1812 which, although it reached Moscow, exhausted Napoleon's resources and led to his defeat and abdication in 1814 and again in 1815 (the 'Hundred Days').

Nevertheless, despite his failure, Napoleon's achievements inspired even his enemies: throughout the 19th century, Spanish, German and Italian reformers envisaged the state in essentially Napoleonic mode (page 116), while his administrative, legal and educational reforms in France survived the restoration of royal power.

1 Revolts and revolutions in Europe and America *(below and right)*

— borders, 1789

areas of nationalist revolt

areas of peasant revolt

areas of anti-colonial resistance

areas of revolt against royal authority

FINLAND

• Helsinki • St Petersburg

NORWAY (Danish)

SWEDEN

• Stockholm • Revel

Pskov •

R U S S I A N

• Gothenburg

• Aarhus

North Sea

Baltic Sea

Riga •

• Moscow (captured) 1812 ☒

• Dvinsk

Borodino 1812 ☒ • Maloyaroslavets 1812 ☒

DENMARK

• Copenhagen • Malmö

to Sweden

Königsberg

Nieman

Vitebsk • Smolensk (captured) 1812 ☒

E M P I R E

Tilsit

REPUBLIC OF DANZIG

☒ Friedland 1807

Eylau 1807

• Vilna

Berezina (crossed) 1812 ☒ Krasnoi 1812 ☒

• Lübeck

• Hamburg

PRUSSIA

GRAND DUCHY OF WARSAW

Berezina

• Minsk

• Kursk

• Hannover

• Berlin

• Poznań

• Brest-Litovsk

Rhine

Waterloo 1815 ☒

• Brussels

WESTPHALIA

Dresden 1813 ☒

Lützen 1813 ☒

• Warsaw

Laon 1814 ☒ Ligny 1815 ☒

Hanau 1813 ☒ Bautzen 1813 ☒

CONFEDERATION OF THE RHINE

Château Thierry 1814 ☒

Rheims 1814 ☒

Jena/ Auerstädt 1806 ☒

Leipzig (Battle of the Nations) 1813 ☒

• Cracow

Paris 1814 ☒

Champaubert 1814 ☒

Prague 1813

Austerlitz 1805 ☒

Montereau 1814 ☒

La Fère Champenoise 1814 ☒

Ratisbon 1809 ☒

Eckmühl/ Ebersberg 1809 ☒

Montmirail/ Vauchamps 1814 ☒

Ulm 1805 ☒

Wagram 1809 ☒

• Tours

NEUCHÂTEL

Hohenlinden 1800 ☒

Aspern/Essling 1809 ☒

F R E N C H

HELVETIC REPUBLIC

Zurich 1799 ☒

• Vienna

• Buda • Pest

• Geneva

Castiglione 1796 ☒

Lonato 1796 ☒

A U S T R I A N   E M P I R E

• Bordeaux

E M P I R E

• Lyons

Marengo 1800 ☒

Lodi 1796 ☒

Rivoli 1797 ☒

Bassano 1796 ☒

H U N G A R Y

Mondovi 1796 ☒

Dego 1796 ☒

Arcole 1796 ☒

• Zágráb

• Toulouse

Montenotte 1796 ☒

KINGDOM OF ITALY

Danube

• Ruschuk

Saragossa (captured) 1809 ☒

• Marseilles • Toulon

LUCCA

ILLYRIAN PROVINCES

SAN MARINO

• Zara

Danube

• Belgrade

• Nish

• Varna

CATALONIA

Barcelona 1808 ☒

PIOMBINO

• Florence

Spalato •

O T T O M A N   E M P I R E

• Corsica

Rome •

Ragusa •

• Sofia

ncia

• Ajaccio

KINGDOM OF ITALY

MONTENEGRO

Mediterranean

PONTECORVO

BENEVENTO

Naples • • Bari

KINGDOM OF SARDINIA

• Cagliari

KINGDOM OF NAPLES

• Taranto

Adriatic Sea

Corfu

A L G I E R S

Palermo • • Messina

KINGDOM OF SICILY

T U N I S

Malta (British)

Mediterranean Sea

2 Napoleon and the reshaping of Europe

French territories ruled from Paris, c. 1812

states ruled by members of Napoleon's family, c. 1812

other dependent states, c. 1812

☒ French victory

☒ French defeat

☒ battles of the Italian campaign

☒ battles of the War of the Second Coalition

☒ battles of the War of the Third Coalition

☒ battles in the Austrian War, 1809

☒ battles in the Peninsular War

☒ battles of the Russian campaign

☒ battles of the War of Liberation from French rule

☒ battles in the defence of France

☒ battles in the War of the 100 Days

On 14th July 1789 a crowd of Parisians stormed the Bastille fort to release a handful of political prisoners housed there *(below)*. The incident sparked off a more widespread revolt against the authority of Louis XVI, which led, four years later, to his imprisonment and execution. Bastille Day became the symbol for liberation struggles worldwide.

VICE-ROYALTY OF NEW SPAIN

THIRTEEN COLONIES

• Boston

• New York

War of Independence, 1775

Gabriel's slave revolt, 1800

Mississippi

• Mexico City

• Port-au-Prince

HAITI Toussaint l'Ouverture's revolt 1791

• Santo Domingo

• Panama

• Caracas

• Santa Fé de Bogotá

VICE-ROYALTY OF NEW GRANADA

• Quito

S O U T H   A M E R I C A

Pacific Ocean

• Lima

VICE-ROYALTY OF PERU

VICE-ROYALTY OF BRAZIL

• La Paz

• Bahia

VICE-ROYALTY OF RIO DE LA PLATA

• Santiago

• Buenos Aires

INTERNET LINKS

www.wsu.edu/~dee/
ENLIGHT/INDUSTRY.HTM
The industrial revolution

C. 1750–1914

The industrial revolution in Europe

1765 Watt develops improved steam engine

1781 Steam engine first used in Europe

1825 First steam railway opened in England

1828 First modern blast furnace (Silesia)

1849 Iron first produced from coke on the Ruhr

1855 Bessemer steel process developed by Krupp

1885 Benz develops first petrol-driven car

1890 First electric tram, Florence

1896 Marconi builds first radio transmitter

1 The pattern of industrial expansion, 1800
population per sq. mile in 1801

- under 50
- 50–100
- 100–150
- 150–200
- 200–260
- 260–390
- 390–800

▲ iron ore mining
☾ copper mining
▬ lead mining
◇ tin mining
⊟ salt mining
⟨ slate mining

— canal
■ expanding port
● expanding town
⠂ coalfields

James Watt's rotative steam engine. In 1765 Watt developed his first steam engine, used initially to drive pumps. In 1776 it was applied to the iron industry, but with the rotative steam engine in 1781 it was possible to power machinery, making possible the shift to large scale production.

explains its pre-eminence in the age of imperialism (page 118). Britain's precedence rested upon many factors. On the one hand, unlike much of the rest of Europe, it boasted abundant coal, iron and other basic materials, and it enjoyed an advantageous position in the Atlantic trade which generated much capital. On the other hand, it possessed several unique advantages. First, it escaped direct damage from the various wars that ravaged Europe between 1690 and 1815; second, unlike most continental states which bristled with customs barriers and internal frontiers, after the union of England and Scotland in 1707 Great Britain formed a single economic unit; third, again in contrast to continental Europe, the early disappearance of serfdom in England meant that the surplus labour released by rising agricultural productivity could move, without legal obstacles, to

The industrial revolution, which began in England in the later 18th century, became the catalyst of the modern world. Nevertheless the speed of change can be exaggerated. Even in continental Europe its impact remained limited before 1850 to a few enclaves; and not until the last quarter of the century did the great surge forward occur. Outside Europe, except for the United States, industrialization took place even later (page 120). In 1895, even in Germany, one-third of the population still worked on the land, and most of eastern and southern Europe remained virtually untouched by industry.

Until 1900, when its lead began to be challenged by Germany and the United States, Great Britain remained the workshop of the world and its industrial strength, which enabled it to dominate world markets, the growing industrial centres. Finally, England possessed a unique network of navigable rivers and canals (map 1), which proved of immense importance before the railway age for moving both raw materials and finished goods.

In its earliest phase, English manufacturers had also relied on water as a source of energy; but in the century to 1870 industrial power depended on steam, generated by the combustion of coal. At first, except in Britain and (from 1820) Belgium, steam power came only slowly, held back by political fragmentation, lack of capital and, above all, poor communications which severely limited markets. The steel firm of Krupp, founded in 1811 and later to be a giant of German industry, still employed only 7 men in 1826 and 122 in 1846. The pace of industrialization only accelerated with railway development. Between 1830 and 1870 the rail networks of Britain, Belgium and Germany became virtually complete, and construction began elsewhere. At much the same time, barriers to trade came down: France demolished her

internal tariffs in 1790, Prussia followed suit in 1818 and in 1834 joined the German Customs Union, which included 17 states and some 26 million people.

A new period, sometimes called the Second Industrial Revolution, opened in the 1870s (see map 2). The new German empire (page 116) led the way, increasing its coal output from 38 million tons in 1871 to 279 million tons in 1913, and its iron output from 1.5 million tons to 15 million tons. But it also led in new areas of industrial enterprise, especially chemicals, electricity and steel. By 1910, Krupp employed 70,000 men. At a time of growing international tension (page 124), such rapid economic growth was bound to produce a reaction among Germany's neighbours and Russia began a campaign of rapid industrialization in 1890 (page 114), France in 1895 and Italy in 1905. In all these states, much heavy industry was keyed to armaments. Although the bulk of the population of Europe remained largely untouched, industrialization had both changed the face of the continent and rendered its future uncertain.

2 The industrialization of Europe, 1870–1914

- areas of industrial concentration 1870–1914
- + centres of textile industry
- o coalfields
- ⊞ centres of engineering, armaments and metal industries
- △ iron ore fields
- ◔ lignite fields
- ◔ potash fields
- ╏ centres of petroleum industry
- —— railway network, 1870

INTERNET LINKS

www.spartacus.schoolnet.
co.uk/slavery.htm —
Online resources on the
slave trade, 1700–1930

1696 Britain begins official
balance-of-trade statistics

1763 Treaty of Paris
delivers most of Northwest
America to Britain

1750 Britain bans iron and
steel-making in American
colonies

1765 English East India
Company annexes Bengal

1783 French slave trade
act

1807 Britain and US
abolish slave trade

1830 Last Caribbean
pirate hanged

C. 1775
The emerging global economy

1 The Atlantic economy

→ exports of goods in £
(x 30 for approximate modern
equivalent)

→ movement of migrants and slaves

sugar New World export commodities

GUIANA areas linked economically with
Europe

In 1775, the areas of Spanish conquest and settlement in central and south America still ranked as the
most valuable European overseas possession, thanks
to the silver production of Mexico and Peru and the
gold exports of Brazil, most of which went to Europe
in return for manufactured goods. Along the Atlantic
coast from Brazil to the Chesapeake, but above all
in the Caribbean islands, plantation societies had
developed to meet the rising demand both in Europe
and in British North America (where over 2 million
whites now dwelt) for tropical agricultural produce:
cacao, tobacco, cotton and (especially) sugar. Since
most plantations depended on the labour of African
slaves, increased consumption in Europe meant
increased shipments of slaves from Africa.

A closely integrated Atlantic economy had thus
emerged. By 1775 the mainland colonies throughout
the Americas were generally self-sufficient in food

and some supported limited manufacturing. But their
white populations consumed prodigious quantities
of imported European manufactured goods, and
prosperity almost everywhere depended on the
ability to export to Europe. Transatlantic commerce,
in turn, contributed substantially to the economic
development of Spain, France and Britain (almost 40
per cent of whose total exports in 1775 went to
America).

In Asia, although the volume of European
trade also greatly increased in the 18th century, it
remained largely confined to ports or small coastal
enclaves to which Asian merchants delivered goods.
The Dutch and English East India Companies, founded
in 1600-2 (page 80), still dominated trade with
maritime Asia, but the shipment of spices to Europe
had by the 18th century been overtaken by a boom in
textiles (above all silks and cottons) and new drinks

(tea and coffee). Since, however, in contrast to the Americas, few European manufactures proved competitive in Asia (except in the Mediterranean ports of the Ottoman empire), increased imports of Asian goods generally depended on shipments of American silver, either re-exported from Europe or carried across the Pacific to the Philippines and thence to China.

European trade also stimulated the demand for export commodities from, and injected large quantities of silver into, India and China; but most of Asia's economic life remained relatively unaffected by contact with the West, and much of its long-distance trade continued to be conducted by Asian merchants using their own pack-animals or ships. However, conditions were changing rapidly in two areas of great economic importance: the British had gained control of Bengal, a major centre of textile

The loading plan of a slave ship *(below)* shows how many slaves could be crammed below decks. The crowding marked a callous compromise between the slavers' desire to ferry as many slaves as possible and the need to ensure as many as possible of those embarked survived the voyage. By the late 18th century most ships lost less then 10 per cent of their human cargo. In earlier times, however, losses had sometimes exceeded 30 per cent, leading the Portuguese to refer to their slave ships as *tumbeiros* – coffins.

manufacture, in the 1760s and now used its huge tax revenues to maintain a substantial army ready to annex other areas of the subcontinent; and the Dutch in Java could impose commercial controls and receive commodities (above all coffee) as tribute.

Only Africa remained almost totally resistant to European penetration. Although the slave trade reached its apogee in the 18th century, with some 2.3 million slaves shipped out between 1770 and 1800, the prices paid by the Europeans for each slave steadily rose – suggesting that the African rulers who dealt in slaves more than held their own, despite the disruption arising from wars and slave-raiding, and the sustained loss of population.

In short, Europe's rapid commercial expansion overseas (for better or worse) hastened the economic integration of the world. The Americas outside the plantations enjoyed a degree of self-sufficiency, but Europe still determined the economic development of much of the continent. Although, except in Bengal, Java and the Philippines, the West could not yet shape the economies of Asia and Africa, with Britain now poised to conquer India (page 96) and with the Industrial Revolution underway in Europe (page 100), the stage was set for the creation of an integrated global economy.

2 The trading worlds of Asia and Africa

— routes of European trade

routes of trade primarily of African and Asian merchants

coffee African and Asian export commodities

• centres of European trade in Africa and Asia

INTERNET LINKS

www.bbc.co.uk/history/
british/empire_seapower/
rebels_redcoats_01.shtml
The American War of
Independence

1775–1865

The United States

The disputes and difficulties leading to the American War of Independence and the foundation of the United States began almost immediately after the English victory over France in the Seven Years' War (page 86). Britain began to reorganize her vastly expanded North American possessions, establishing a huge Indian reserve west of the Alleghenies (1763) and extending the boundaries of Quebec (formerly French Canada) to the Mississippi and Ohio rivers (1774). The 'thirteen colonies' bitterly resented both this check to their westward expansion and the simultaneous insistence by Britain that its colonies should henceforth bear a greater share of the costs of their defence. Armed opposition began at Lexington and Concord in Massachusetts in 1775 (map 1). The colonies' representatives declared Independence in 1776, compelled the main British field army to surrender at Yorktown (1781), and fought on until the Treaty of Versailles (1783) recognized their sovereignty and extended the frontiers of the 'United States of America' to the Great Lakes and the Mississippi.

Expansion now proceeded rapidly. In 1783 the new republic comprised some 800,000 square miles (2,072,000 km^2) of territory, but the purchase of Louisiana from France (1803) more than doubled its size. West Florida was taken by force in 1812 and East Florida (60,000 square miles, 155,400 km^2) during the presidency of James Monroe. Thereafter extensive territories in the south and west were added, largely at the expense of Mexico (map 2), and in 1846 a compromise with Britain was reached over Oregon, increasing the number of states from 13 to 34. The population expanded from 3 million in 1783 to 31 million in 1860, fuelled by the arrival of a new wave of European immigrants, predominantly German and Irish.

These developments had important political consequences. The ruling elites of the southern states, with their plantation economy and large black slave population, felt increasingly threatened by the industrializing north and the growing Midwest. This, rather than the issue of slavery, underlay the American Civil War (1861-5); but the issues in fact proved inseparable because, with over 90 percent of

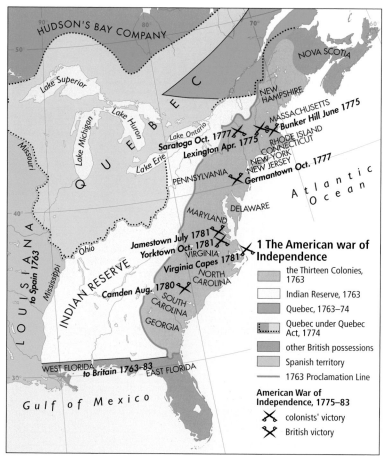

1 The American war of Independence

	the Thirteen Colonies, 1763
	Indian Reserve, 1763
	Quebec, 1763–74
	Quebec under Quebec Act, 1774
	other British possessions
	Spanish territory
—	1763 Proclamation Line

American War of Independence, 1775–83

⚔ colonists' victory

⚔ British victory

Dead soldiers at Gettysburg
(below). The small market town of Gettysburg, Pennsylvania, was the scene of the greatest battles of the war. Lee, advancing into the North to force Lincoln to negotiate peace on the basis of Southern independence, attacked General Meade's Union army, but in the course of a three-day battle was comprehensively beaten. The Union lost 23,000 men, the Confederacy 28,000.

the black population living in the South, the moral question was also a regional question. Abraham Lincoln, elected President in 1860 by the votes of the Northern states, was right to claim that the nation could not permanently remain 'half slave and half free'.

Soon after Lincoln's election, South Carolina seceded from the Union and was quickly joined by ten other states which came together as the Confederate States of America with their capital at Richmond, Virginia (map 4). For Lincoln the fundamental issue was whether a constitutional republic could preserve its territorial integrity; he recognized no constitutional right of secession. By 1863, however, pressure from radical Republicans added the aim of freeing the slaves in the rebel states to the commitment to restore the Union. Thanks to the superior military skill of their commanders, and to their shorter lines of communications, the confederacy fought on for four years (1861-5). The Northern strategy was to deny the South vital resources by a naval blockade, to gain control of key river routes and forts in the west and to capture Richmond. Eventually the superior demographic and economic resources of the North prevailed – albeit at the cost of 635,000 Union and 383,000 Confederate military casualties – and created the 'second American Revolution' which, by crippling the southern ruling class and liberating its labour force, determined that the thrusting, urban, industrialized North, with its creed of competitive capitalism, would stamp its pattern (for good or ill) on the entire United States.

4 Comparative resources: Union and Confederate states, 1861

Union States	Confederate States	
Total pop.: 2.5 to 1	Naval ship ton.: 25 to 1	Farm acreage: 3 to 1
Male adult pop.: 4.4 to 1	Factory prod.: 10 to 1	Draft animals: 1.8 to 1
Free men 18–60 yrs in military service: 1864 44% 90%	Textile prod.: 17 to 1	Livestock: 1.5 to 1
Wealth produced: 3 to 1	Iron production: 20 to 1	Wheat prod.: 4.2 to 1
Railroad mileage: 2.4 to 1	Coal production: 38 to 1	Corn production: 2 to 1
Merchant ship ton.: 9 to 1	Firearms prod.: 32 to 1	Cotton prod.: 1 to 24

2 Land cessions and density of settlement

expansion of white settlement by:

	1750		1850		largely unsettled by 1890
	1790		1890		

Oregon Country 1846
1818
Louisiana Purchase from France 1803
Mexican Cession 1848
Gadsden Purchase 1853
Texas annexed 1845
Mississippi
USA 1783
West Florida annexed 1812
East Florida annexed 1819

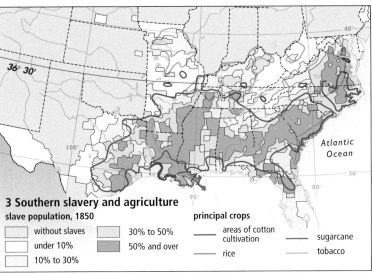

3 Southern slavery and agriculture

36° 30'

Atlantic Ocean

slave population, 1850

	without slaves		30% to 50%
	under 10%		50% and over
	10% to 30%		

principal crops

areas of cotton cultivation — sugarcane
— rice — tobacco

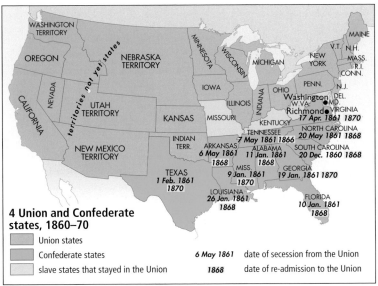

4 Union and Confederate states, 1860–70

WASHINGTON TERRITORY
OREGON
NEBRASKA TERRITORY
MINNESOTA
WISCONSIN
MICHIGAN
MAINE
V.T. N.H.
NEW YORK
MASS.
R.I. CONN.
NEVADA
CALIFORNIA
UTAH TERRITORY
IOWA
PENN.
N.J.
OHIO
DEL.
Washington MD.
W. VA.
Richmond
17 Apr. 1861 1870
VIRGINIA
KANSAS
MISSOURI
KENTUCKY
ILLINOIS
INDIANA
territories not yet states
NEW MEXICO TERRITORY
INDIAN TERR.
ARKANSAS 6 May 1861 1868
TENNESSEE 7 May 1861 1866
NORTH CAROLINA 20 May 1861 1868
ALABAMA 11 Jan. 1861 1868
SOUTH CAROLINA 20 Dec. 1860 1868
TEXAS 1 Feb. 1861 1870
MISS. 9 Jan. 1861 1870
GEORGIA 19 Jan. 1861 1870
LOUISIANA 26 Jan. 1861 1868
FLORIDA 10 Jan. 1861 1868

	Union states		6 May 1861	date of secession from the Union
	Confederate states		1868	date of re-admission to the Union
	slave states that stayed in the Union			

105

FROM 1788

Australia and New Zealand

1769–70 James Cook maps east coast of Australia

1788 Penal colony established at Sydney Cove, New South Wales

1840 Treaty of Waitangi; Wellington settled

1851 Gold Rush in Victoria and New South Wales

1860–5 Taranaki and Waikato land wars

1882 First frozen meat exports from New Zealand

1901 Commonwealth of Australia created

1975 Waitangi Tribunal established

1992 Mabo judgement on native title in Australia

1 The European settlement and development of Australia

- native land rights claims, Jan. 1997
- more than 2 persons per square mile 1961 (by statistical division)
- no significant use, c. 1960
- ■ penal settlements
- ● settlements

railways
- —— before 1881
- –·–·– 1881–1900
- - - - 1901–1920
- ·········· after 1920

minerals
gold	tin	zinc
copper	U uranium	oil
lead	blast furnace	N nickel
natural gas	iron ore	A alumina/bauxite
T tungsten	silver	M manganese

Although Australia and New Zealand were reconnoitred by the Dutch explorer Abel Tasman in 1642, colonization only began in 1770 when James Cook raised the British flag at Botany Bay. New South Wales served as a penal colony from 1788 to 1839, as did van Diemen's land (later Tasmania) from 1804 to 1853, but in 1829 the British government, in order to forestall the French, claimed the whole Australian continent. Fear of France also led to the annexation of New Zealand in 1840. However, the geographical obstacles, the lack of exportable goods (at first chiefly seal products and sandalwood), and (especially in the case of New Zealand) the opposition of the indigenous population complicated the colonization process in both territories. In 1850, the total white population of Australia still numbered only 350,000, and that of New Zealand was less than 100,000.

The discovery of gold in New South Wales and Victoria in 1851 initiated a new phase, and encouraged the growth of the inland population. Even more important was the rapid growth of sheep-farming: in 1850 Australia sent 17,000 tons of wool to Great Britain, but 134,000 tons in 1879. Nevertheless, as centralizing systems of communications and transportation developed, the dominance of the coastal cities – especially Sydney and Melbourne – increased. By the 1890s, two-thirds of Australia's population lived in urban areas along the coast (a pattern that steadily intensified throughout the 20th century.) In New Zealand, where wool remained largely a South Island product, exports rose in value from £67,000 in 1853 to £2.7 million twenty years later. The development of the North Island, which was held back by the bitter Maori Wars (1860–71), only came after the introduction of refrigeration, which made possible the export of frozen lamb, butter and cheese. Dairy farming developed rapidly, and the North Island now drew ahead of the South in population.

Political development kept pace with economic growth. In 1855 New South Wales, Victoria, South Australia and Tasmania became self-governing colonies, followed by Queensland in 1859; in 1901 they joined together to form the Commonwealth of Australia. New Zealand, which had been divided in 1852 into six provinces, each with an elected council, became a united Dominion (after measures had been taken to safeguard the rights of the Maori population) in 1876. Both countries achieved sovereign status under the Statute of Westminster in 1931. The economy of both dominions remained heavily dependent on primary exports – wool, meat, grain and dairy products – which enjoyed preferential treatment in the British market. Even the spectacular discoveries of minerals, coal, oil and gas in and about Australia after 1950 went largely into exports. However Britain's decision to join the European Economic Community and dismantle 'imperial preference' in 1973 (page 166), coupled with the conviction that the countries of the Pacific Rim would become the economic hub of the world in the 21st century, drove both Australia and New Zealand to develop new economic activities and to foster trade with countries outside the British Commonwealth.

This romanticized picture of an attack on a Maori *pa* (fort) during the first New Zealand War suggests the storming of a castle. In fact, recent research has revealed that the *pa* evolved rapidly into sophisticated trench and bunker systems which anticipated those of the Western Front by over 50 years. By the end of the conflict large tracts of Maori land had been confiscated by the colonial government.

2 The development of New Zealand to c. 1875

- ● pioneer sheep regions 1840s
- ● sheep
- ▲ timber
- ◪ gold rushes

1850 date of foundation of city

Marsden's first mission 1814

Russell *first capital 1840–1*

NORTH ISLAND

Auckland *second capital 1841–65*

Thames 1867–71

AUCKLAND

New Plymouth *1841*

TARANAKI (NEW PLYMOUTH)

Cook's landfall 1769

WELLINGTON

Napier *1855*

HAWKE'S BAY

Nelson *1841*

Blenheim *1855*

NELSON

MARLBOROUGH

Wellington *capital since 1865*

West Coast 1864–68

Hokitika

Tasman's landfall 1642

WESTLAND

Christchurch *1850*

Akaroa *French colony 1840*

CANTERBURY

OTAGO

SOUTH ISLAND

SOUTHLAND

Dunedin *1848 NZ's largest city 1861– c. 83*

Invercargill *1857*

Stewart Island

3 The development of New Zealand since 1875

- ◑ major sheep regions
- ○ coal c. 1880–1914
- 🐄 dairying (periods shown)
- ◪ gold-dredging 1880s–1960
- ▲ forest products since 1950
- ⚘ wine
- 🍎 horticulture
- ⊗ hydro-electricity since 1930
- ⊢——⊣ main trunk railways

Marsden Point *oil refinery 1965*

NORTH ISLAND *majority of population since 1901*

since 1920s

Polynesian migration since 1950s

Auckland *largest city since mid 1880s*

Glenbrook *steel mill 1969*

Hamilton

since 1920s

Arapuni *first major h.e. station 1929*

75% of Maoris north of line 1980s

New Plymouth

since 1880s

Wellington–New Plymouth railway 1886

North Island main trunk railway 1908

since 1900

Palmerston North

Napier

Wellington–Napier railway 1891

Westport Nelson Picton

Wellington urban area second largest since 1906

Greymouth

Christchurch–Picton railway 1945

Cook Strait

rail ferry 1962, h.e. cable 1965

Lake Coleridge *first government h.e. station 1914*

Cheviot

Christchurch *largest South Island city since 1895*

SOUTH ISLAND *majority of population 1861–1901*

Christchurch–Bluff railway 1879

Manapouri

N.Z.'s largest h.e. station 1971

Port Chalmers *first export of frozen meat 1882*

Dunedin

Edendale *first dairy export factory 1882*

Bluff *aluminium smelter 1971*

1798–1923

The decline of the Ottoman empire

The period between 1798 and 1923 saw the disintegration and final collapse of the Ottoman Empire, the major power in West Asia since the 16th century (see page 70). Plagued by foreign invasions, wars, and the revolts of subject peoples demanding national independence, the empire steadily lost territory.

In 1798 a French army led by Napoleon Bonaparte invaded Egypt and Syria, only to be defeated by the British. Peace was arranged in 1802 and three years later the sultan appointed Mohammed Ali governor of Egypt. Under his rule, however, the province

gained de facto independence and in 1841 Mohammed was recognized as hereditary viceroy. Meanwhile, between 1830 and 1847 the French conquered Algeria, and in 1881 they annexed Tunis; the following year the British occupied Egypt. There were also wars with Russia, rebellions in the Arab provinces and almost constant revolts in the Balkans – starting with the Greek War of Independence in 1821, which resulted (following the pressure of foreign powers) in the recognition of a sovereign Greek state in 1830. Foreign intervention also

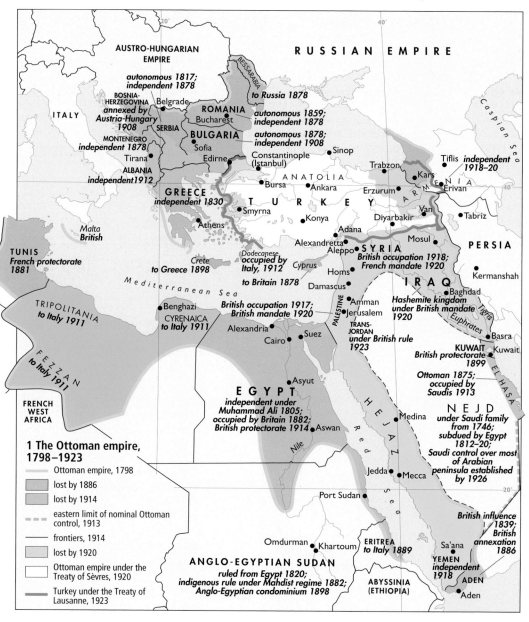

1 The Ottoman empire, 1798–1923

- Ottoman empire, 1798
- lost by 1886
- lost by 1914
- eastern limit of nominal Ottoman control, 1913
- frontiers, 1914
- lost by 1920
- Ottoman empire under the Treaty of Sèvres, 1920
- Turkey under the Treaty of Lausanne, 1923

precipitated the Crimean War (1853-6) and the Lebanese crisis of 1860-1, while Russian and Austrian demands helped secure the independence of Montenegro, Serbia and Romania by 1878. By 1882, the Ottomans had lost 40 per cent of their empire.

Their finances also deteriorated rapidly until in 1875 the state became virtually bankrupt and the Sultan suspended payment of the interest due on the Ottoman debt. In 1881, he agreed to supervision of his treasury by European bankers: the empire's survival became dependent on foreign governments which preferred the preservation of a weakened Ottoman state to the dangerous power vacuum that would follow Turkish collapse. Nevertheless, further territorial losses followed: Italy annexed Libya in 1911 and, at the end of the Balkan wars in 1913 (page 124), the Ottomans surrendered Crete, most of the Aegean islands, Thrace, Macedonia and Albania. In all, between 1908 and 1911, the Turks lost 30 per cent of their remaining possessions.

Throughout the 19th century the sultans made various attempts to modernize their empire, but not always successfully: Selim III, who aimed to create a modern army, was deposed in 1807 when his troops mutinied against the proposed reforms. The Janissaries rebelled in 1826 against reforms decreed by Mahmud II, but this provoked their abolition.

After a decade of agitation, in 1876 Sultan Abdul Hamid II introduced a constitution, and a Parliament met the following year; but it was dissolved almost immediately and only pressure by the Ottoman Society for Union and Progress (the 'Young Turks') forced its restoration in 1908. The following year Abdul Hamid abdicated, and the Young Turks came to dominate the administration. However, their nationalist policies and opposition to any further surrender of territory contributed substantially to the Arabs' willingness to seek accommodation with the Turks' enemies, once the Ottoman empire entered World War I on the side of Germany and Austro-Hungary (page 132).

Despite tenacious resistance, the Turks were eventually defeated and West Asia (despite earlier promises to the Arabs) came under the control of the victorious French and British governments. The Sultan collaborated with Great Britain after his defeat, and in 1920 agreed to the treaty of Sèvres which would dismember the empire. However, the arrival of Greek troops at Izmir provoked a nationalist uprising which crystallized around the Turks' only undefeated general, Mustafa Kemal. The sultanate was abolished and, after some reverses, Turkish forces drove back the Greeks and their allies and secured recognition of the sovereignty of the Turkish Republic at the treaty of Lausanne in 1923.

Mustafa Kemal, or Atatürk *(above),* – 'father of the Turks', as he styled himself – was an Ottoman commander in the First World War. His effective leadership of Turkish forces in 1922 led to his becoming president of the new Turkish republic that year. He was determined to turn Turkey into a modern, industrialized, Western-style secular state.

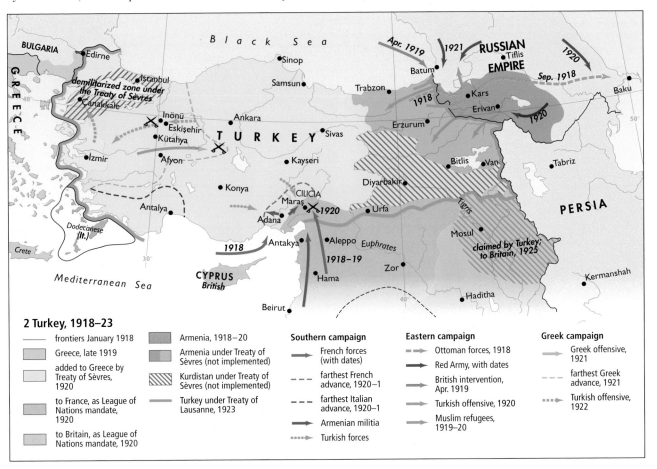

2 Turkey, 1918–23

——	frontiers January 1918	
▬	Greece, late 1919	
▬	added to Greece by Treaty of Sèvres, 1920	
▬	to France, as League of Nations mandate, 1920	
▬	to Britain, as League of Nations mandate, 1920	

▬	Armenia, 1918–20
▬	Armenia under Treaty of Sèvres (not implemented)
▨	Kurdistan under Treaty of Sèvres (not implemented)
▬	Turkey under Treaty of Lausanne, 1923

Southern campaign
- → French forces (with dates)
- - - - farthest French advance, 1920–1
- – – farthest Italian advance, 1920–1
- → Armenian militia
- ••••• Turkish forces

Eastern campaign
- - - → Ottoman forces, 1918
- → Red Army, with dates
- → British intervention, Apr. 1919
- → Turkish offensive, 1920
- → Muslim refugees, 1919–20

Greek campaign
- → Greek offensive, 1921
- - - - farthest Greek advance, 1921
- •••• Turkish offensive, 1922

INTERNET LINKS

www.bbc.co.uk/worldservice/
africa/features/storyofafrica
/index_section11.shtml
Africa and Europe,
1800–1914

Africa in the 19th century

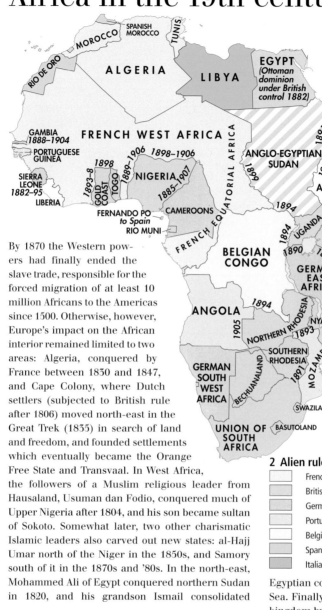

1804 Usuman dan Fodio establishes the Fulani empire

1806 Cape Colony captured by the British

1824 British agents establish post in Natal: first Anglo-Ashanti war

1830 French occupy Algiers

1852 South African Republic (Transvaal) established

1881 French establish protectorate over Tunisia

1882 Britain occupies Egypt

1883-6 Discovery of gold in the Transvaal

1884-5 Berlin Conference on West Africa

1896 British reconquest of Sudan: Italian invasion of Abyssinia defeated at Adowa

1898 Fashoda incident: France confronts Britain on the Nile

1899-1902 South African War between Britain and the Boer Republics

By 1870 the Western powers had finally ended the slave trade, responsible for the forced migration of at least 10 million Africans to the Americas since 1500. Otherwise, however, Europe's impact on the African interior remained limited to two areas: Algeria, conquered by France between 1830 and 1847, and Cape Colony, where Dutch settlers (subjected to British rule after 1806) moved north-east in the Great Trek (1835) in search of land and freedom, and founded settlements which eventually became the Orange Free State and Transvaal. In West Africa, the followers of a Muslim religious leader from Hausaland, Usuman dan Fodio, conquered much of Upper Nigeria after 1804, and his son became sultan of Sokoto. Somewhat later, two other charismatic Islamic leaders also carved out new states: al-Hajj Umar north of the Niger in the 1850s, and Samory south of it in the 1870s and '80s. In the north-east, Mohammed Ali of Egypt conquered northern Sudan in 1820, and his grandson Ismail consolidated

2 Alien rule in Africa, 1913

French		Anglo-Egyptian condominium
British		
German		independent
Portuguese	1882–95	date of determination of colonial boundary
Belgian		
Spanish	——	frontiers, 1914
Italian		

Egyptian control over much of the littoral of the Red Sea. Finally, in the south, the formation of the Zulu kingdom by Shaka in 1818 led to widespread disruption as neighbouring peoples moved away from the aggressive new state.

Meanwhile, the progress of industrialization in Europe (page 100) created a demand for new sources of raw materials and new markets, while the mass-production of quinine (which offered protection against the malaria endemic in Africa) and machine-guns gave the Europeans the ability to satisfy these demands by force. In the 1870s the French advanced inland from Senegal while the British began the conquest of Nigeria. In 1882 the British invaded and occupied Egypt, and the Belgians advanced up the Congo river. Next, Germany laid claim to Togoland, the Cameroons, Southwest Africa and

The Battle of Isandhlwana on 22 January 1879 was the first major engagement of the Zulu war *(right)*. A British force of 1700 white and African troops under Lord Chelmsford was routed by 20,000 Zulu, the consequence rather of British arrogance and carelessness than of overwhelming numbers. It demonstrated the continuing possibility that African tactics and weaponry could triumph over well-armed European forces.

1 The partition of Africa

colonies or settlements, 1880

French
British
Portuguese

★ anti-European resistance

African states or empires

colonial penetration

→ French
→ British
→ Portuguese
→ German
→ Italian
→ Spanish
→ Belgian

Tangier *international zone* **1923**
MOROCCO 1912 *French protectorate*
Algiers **French occupation 1830**
Tunis
ALGERIA 1870
TUNIS
Marrakesh
SPANISH HARA *12*
TRIPOLITANIA
Tripoli *1911*
Benghazi *1912*
CYRENAICA Alexandria
Ghadames
British invasion and occupation 1882
Cairo
In Salah **French 1901**
FEZZAN
EGYPT
Nile
Red Sea
S a h a r a
Taoudenni *occupation 1906*
Tamanrasset **French 1902**
Bilma
SUDAN
Anglo-Egyptian Condominium *established 1899*
Suakin
Massawa
CH SUDAN **1894** *e of Ahmadu Sefu f al-Hajj Umar)*
Timbuktu
Agadès
Omdurman
Khartoum
Adowa **1896** *Italian invasion defeated*
Aden (British)
Ségou
r's e
Gao
NIGER
Sokoto **British 1903**
Zinder **French 1899**
Kano **British 1902**
Fort Lamy
RABIH'S DOMAIN
Mahdist state in the Sudan 1881–98
Berbera
ABYSSINIA
1883
UPPER VOLTA
Say **French 1896**
SOKOTO CALIPHATE
Northern Nigeria claimed by Royal Niger Company (1886–1900)
SHOA
Djibouti
Addis Ababa
IVORY COAST *891*
Kumasi **1896**
Nikki **French 1894**
N I G E R I A
NUPE
ILORIN
failed attempt by Marchand to take Fashoda for France, 1898
Fashoda **British 1898**
Ethiopian expansion under Emperor Menelik
ITALIAN SOMALILAND 1889–92
GOLD COAST **1874**
Accra
TOGO
DAHOMEY
YORUBA
Lagos
IBO
Lokoja
CAMEROONS
Gondokoro
SIDAMA KINGDOMS
Mogadishu
Fernando Po **Spanish**
Principe **Portuguese**
Sao Tomé **Portuguese**
Douala
German occupation 1884
RIO MUNI
GABON
UGANDA **1893**
Kampala **British 1890**
BRITISH EAST AFRICA (KENYA)
Nairobi
Imperial British East Africa Company 1888–93

East Africa, each move provoking parallel actions by other powers. Portugal revived her effort to colonize the interior of Angola and Mozambique, while Britain claimed parts of East Africa (later Kenya and Uganda) and, on the initiative of the Cape politician and industrialist Cecil Rhodes, central Africa (later Zimbabwe, Zambia and Malawi).

Even larger gains accrued to the French, who swept into sub-Saharan Africa from three directions and gained control over almost one-third of the continent (map 1). With the conquest of Libya and Cyrenaica by Italy in 1911 and the partition of Morocco between France and Spain in 1912, of the 40 political units into which Africa had been arbitrarily divided, only two could claim any real independence: Ethiopia, which had defeated an Italian attempt at annexation in 1896, and Liberia, which enjoyed financial support from the United States. In little more than a generation, the Europeans had gained control over an additional 12 million square miles (31 million km²) of territory.

FRENCH CONGO
Congo
CONGO FREE STATE *penetration by King Leopold's agents (became Belgian Congo in 1908)*
TIPPU TIB'S DOMAIN
Cabinda
GERMAN EAST AFRICA (TANGANYIKA)
Mombasa
Lake Victoria
Lake Tanganyika
Zanzibar **British 1890**
Dar es Salaam **German occupation 1888**
Luanda
Indian Ocean
KATANGA
ANGOLA
Benguela
Moçâmedes
NORTHERN RHODESIA
British Central Africa (Nyasaland) Protectorate 1891
Lake Nyasa
Ruvuma
Zomba
Mozambique
Zambezi
Salisbury
Quelimane
MOZAMBIQUE
Tamatave
Tananarive
MADAGASCAR
MERINA KINGDOM
SOUTHERN RHODESIA
Beira
Swakopmund
GERMAN SOUTH WEST AFRICA
Walvis Bay **British 1878**
Rhodes' British South Africa Company 'Pioneer Column' 1890
Pretoria
TRANSVAAL
Johannesburg
Delagoa Bay
Vaal
Lüderitz **German 1884**
Orange
BRITISH BECHUANALAND
ORANGE FREE STATE
NATAL
Durban
Kimberley
CAPE COLONY
East London
Cape Town
Port Elizabeth

111

INTERNET LINKS

www.tamu.edu/ccbn/dewitt/
mexicanrev.htm
The struggle for Mexican
independence

1808–1929

Latin America

Napoleon's invasion of Spain and Portugal in 1808 (page 98) enabled these countries' American colonies to gain independence. The revolt began in Argentina in 1810 and in Venezuela in 1811, helped by the decision of Great Britain and the United States to oppose intervention by the Iberian powers. The fall of Lima (1821) and Simón Bolívar's victory at Ayacucho (1824), deprived Spain of control over South America. In the North, early rebellions in Mexico were suppressed, but in 1823 a republic was proclaimed, and a last Spanish attempt at reconquest in 1829 met with defeat. Only Brazil made the transition to independence peacefully, as Portugal agreed to provide a constitution and in 1822 the Portuguese king's eldest son became Emperor Pedro I of Brazil. Only in 1889 when, following the abolition of slavery (1888), disgruntled plantation owners rose in revolt, did a federal republic replace the empire.

Independence remained in essence a political movement confined to the colonial aristocracy, who desired a transfer of authority without social change. The next half-century was dominated by military dictators who ruled in the interests of the privileged classes and squandered their assets on repeated territorial disputes. Mexico lost most, forfeiting vast territories to the United States (see page 104); but it was also the first state to introduce limited social reforms after the election of the Indian Benito Juarez as President in 1861.

A subsistence economy still prevailed in most areas. Although Brazil with its slave-operated coffee plantations offered an exception, elsewhere the great rural estates showed little interest in producing for the market. After 1880, overseas investment increased rapidly, but selectively, concentrated mainly in Argentina, Brazil, Mexico and Chile. Moreover, even there, the foreign stimulus shifted those economies sharply towards the export of primary products: grain and meat from Argentina, nitrate from Chile, coffee and rubber from Brazil, oil from Mexico, and fruit from the so-called 'Banana Republics' of the central isthmus.

Most of these countries modernized and commercialized their production, and built docks and railways to expedite the export of food and raw materials. This attracted a new wave of immigrants and created a new urban and industrial proletariat as well as a middle class prospering from the export trade; but it left the majority of the rural population in abject poverty. Mexico under the repressive regime of Porfirio Díaz (1876-1911) exemplified these trends until in 1910 the country erupted in revolution: eventually, in 1917, a constitution incorporating major social and political reforms was adopted. Elsewhere, as long as prosperity continued – that is, until the Great Crash of 1929 (see page 138) – political and social pressures remained under control (albeit sometimes only thanks to armed intervention by the United States); but rapid and unbalanced economic expansion steadily undermined the regimes that promoted it.

abbreviations to map below

A	AGUASCALIENTES	N	NUEVO LEÓN
C	CAMPECHE	P	PUEBLA
G	GUANAJUATO	Q	QUERÉTARO
H	HIDALGO	S	SAN LUIS POTOSÍ
ME	MÉXICO	T	TLAXCALA
M	MORELOS	V	VERACRUZ

CALIFORNIA

UTAH

ceded to USA by Mexico 1848

sold by Texas to USA 1850

UNITED STATES

NEW MEXICO
San Diego
sold to
USA 1853

TEXAS
independent
republic 1836–45
to USA 1845

Texas 1850

Rio Grande

LOWER CALIFORNIA

SONORA

CHIHUAHUA

COAHUILA

Carranza 1913

BAHAMA IS.
(British 1629)

PUERTO RICO (Spanish) to USA 1898

Pancho Villa
1914

M E X I C O
1821

SINALOA
DURANGO
ZACATECAS
N
TAMAULIPAS

Ten Years' War
1868–78

CUBA
1898
US protectorate
1898–1903

ANTIGUA
(British)

Santa Anna
1834–55

TEPIC
JALISCO
A
S
G Q H

liberal reform 1855–7
War of Reform 1857–60
Benito Juárez 1861–72

YUCATAN

Caste war
of Yucatán
1848

REPUBLIC OF
HAITI
1804

DOMINICAN
REPUBLIC
1844
to Spain 1808–1822
to Haiti 1822–1844

VIRGIN IS.
(British)

GUADELOU
(French)
MARIE GAL
(French)

COLIMA
MICHOACAN
ME
M
T
V
P

TABASCO

JAMAICA
1656
(British)

SABA (Dutch)
ST EUSTATIUS (Dutch)
ST CHRISTOPHER (British)
NEVIS (British)
ST VINCENT (British)
BONAIRE (Dutch)
CURAÇAO (Dutch)

DOMINICA
(British)
MARTINIQU
(French)

Madero
1911

GUERRERO

OAXACA

CHIAPAS

C

BRITISH
HONDURAS

ARUBA (Dutch)

ST LUCIA (Bri
BARBADO
(British)

Zapata
1910

GUATEMALA
1838

HONDURAS
1838

MOSQUITO
COAST
to Nicaragua
1860

GRENADA (Br
TRINIDAD
(British)

EL SALVADOR
1838

NICARAGUA
1838

Morelos
1811–15

(see map right)

(see map left)

COSTA
RICA
1838

PANAMA
1903

Cartagena · Maracaibo · Caracas

Panama

Mompos · Orinoco · Angostura

Antioquia

VENEZUELA *1830*

Georgetown

▽ **Páez 1830–48**

▽ **Guzmán Blanco 1870–88**

◇ *violent constitutionalism*

Bogotá

COLOMBIA
1830

to Britain 1904 · BRITISH · DUTCH · FRENCH

1873 · GUIANA · Cayenne

1900

☐ **Cabanagem 1835–40**

☐ **Balaiada 1839**

☐ **Confederation of Equator 1824**

▽ **García Moreno 1860–75**

Quito

ECUADOR
1830
ORIENTE

Guayaquil

1907

to Ecuador 1880

Manaus

Amazon

RIO GRANDE DO NORTE

PARÁ

MARANHÃO

CEARA

Iquitos · Tabatinga

to Ecuador 1880

RIO NEGRO
(later Amazonas)

B · R · A · Z · I · L

PARAIBA

PERNAMBUCO

ALAGOAS

SERGIPE

ACRE
1899–1903

to Bolivia
1867

1822
(empire 1822, republic 1889)

PIAUI

☐ Sabinada
1837

▽ **Castilla 1845–62**

to Perú
1909
to Peru
1902

Lima · *1824*

Callao · Cuzco

P · E · R · U

BAHIA

GOIAS

☐ Praieira
1848–9

Santa Cruz

La Paz

MATO GROSSO

☐ *Liberal revolution 1842*

MINAS GERAIS · Minas Novas

Diamantina

ESPIRITO SANTO

Tacna
to Peru 1929 · Arica

BOLIVIA
1825

Potosí

Corumbá

RIO DE JANEIRO

Rio de Janeiro

Chilean gains 1883

1870 · *1870*

GRAN
CHACO

Concepción

SÃO PAULO

São Paulo

▽ **Melgarejo 1864–71**

Jujuy

PARAGUAY
1811

1874 · Asunción

Ciudad Real

☐ **Farroupilha revolution 1835–45**

○ **Batlle 1903–15**

1874 · *1927*

SANTA
CATARINA

Simón Bolívar (1783–1830)
(below) became known as 'The Liberator' for his role in the emancipation of South America from Spanish rule. After participating in several unsuccessful revolts, he and his army defeated the Spanish at Boyacá in 1819 and organized the republic of Gran Colombia. In 1821, he defeated the Spanish near Carabobo, ensuring Venezuelan independence. Between 1822 and 1824 he also helped free Ecuador and Peru. Southern Peru became a new republic, named Bolivia in his honour.

1818

RIO GRANDE
DO SUL

Córdoba

URUGUAY *1828*
part of Brazil
1816–28

1 Latin America: political development from 1824 *(above and left)*

Valparaíso · Mendoza

Santiago · San Luis

Constitución

Rosario

C · H · I · L · E

◇ *aristocratic presidentialism*

A · R · G · E · N · T · I · N · A

Buenos Aires

Montevideo

Río de la Plata

1816

	boundary of Mexico, 1824
▪	Mexico 1867
1821	date of independent statehood
	Republic of Gran Colombia, 1821–30
	United Provinces of Central America, 1823–38
	later Brazilian acquisitions
	areas affected by Mexican revolution from 1910
	disputed between Ecuador and Peru
	disputed between Bolivia and Paraguay
▽	*caudillismo*
○	revolutionary movements
◇	constitutionalism
☐	radical reformism
	French territory
	British territory
	Dutch territory
	Spanish territory

Valdivia

War of the Desert 1880–81

▽ **Rosas 1829–52**

◇ *conservative republic 1826–1910*

United Provinces of Rio Plata 1819–25
Argentine confederation 1825–53
Argentine republic from 1853

P · A · T · A · G · O · N · I · A

settled by Argentina by late 19th C

settled by Chile through 19th C

FALKLAND IS.
(Islas Malvinas)

colonized by Britain 1765–74; claimed by Spain to 1811, subsequently claimed by Argentina; British from 1833

113

The expansion of the Russian empire

INTERNET LINKS

www.yale.edu/lawweb/
avalon/econ/koval6.htm
Origins, growth and
abolition of Russian serfdom

1825 Nicholas I becomes
tsar: 'Decembrist' uprising
suppressed

1853-5 Defeat in Crimean
War against France and
Britain

1861 Emancipation of the
serfs

1881 Alexander II,
the 'reforming tsar'
assassinated

1904-5 Russia defeated in
war with Japan

1905 Revolt forces
constitutional reform

1914 Russia enters First
World War

Feb. 1917 Tsar Nicholas
II overthrown by popular
revolution

For 40 years after the Congress of Vienna (1815) Russia remained the strongest military power in Europe, focusing her interests on the Balkans and on the straits leading from the Black Sea. Since most Balkan subjects of the Ottoman empire were Orthodox Slavs, Russia considered herself their natural protector; and because Turkey lay in the way of Russia's access to the Mediterranean, it desired Constantinople to remain amenable to Russian influence alone. However, France and Austria also had imperial ambitions in these areas, while Britain opposed any further Russian expansion. In 1854, therefore, following Russia's invasion of Turkey's Danubian provinces and destruction of the Ottoman fleet, France and Britain (supported by Austria) declared war and invaded the Crimea, eventually forcing Russia to evacuate the Balkans and to dismantle its Black Sea fleet. A further Russian attempt to liberate the Balkan Slavs from Turkish rule in 1877-8 also failed (page 108).

Russia proved far more successful in Asia (map 1). Her forces subdued the Kazakhs (1816-54), completed Russian control of the Caucasus (1857-64) and annexed the khanates of central Asia (1865-76). The imperial frontier now reached – and sometimes penetrated – the great mountain chains that separated it from Persia, Afghanistan, India and China. The colonization of North America also continued into the early 19th century, and forts were built as far

south as California; but most were soon abandoned and Alaska was sold to the United States in 1867. On the other hand, China ceded to the Tsar the Amur basin and parts of the Pacific coast (where Vladivostok was founded in 1860), and leased Port Arthur (1898). This warm-water harbour, unimpeded by winter ice, was soon linked to the main Trans-Siberian railway (completed in 1903). But Russian expansion conflicted with Japanese designs. The two powers had already clashed over their interests in Korea and south Manchuria, following Japan's victory over China in 1894-5 (page 130), and in 1904-5 Japan attacked Russia, forcing her to abandon most of her gains in the Far East and to cede south Sakhalin.

This humiliating defeat fanned the flames of domestic unrest. Shaken by the backwardness exposed in the Crimean War, Tsar Alexander II (1855-81) had initiated a number of reforms in the 1860s: new local government organizations; educational improvements; and radical changes to the legal system. The emancipation of the serfs in 1861 was the cornerstone of the reforms (map 2). However, still confined to their villages, many peasants felt aggrieved that they often had to acquire by purchase less land than they had previously worked. From 1890 the government embarked on an industrialization programme with railways at its centre. Many of the lines aimed to facilitate the movement of troops to frontier areas in case of war, but they allowed not

1 Russia in Asia, 1815–1900

- the Russian empire, 1815
- acquisitions 1816–56
- acquisitions 1856–76
- acquisitions 1877–1900
- vassal khanates
- railway

Map 3 - Russian Empire (revolution of 1905)

Vyatka · Motovilikhinskiy
Vyborg · Votkinskiy
Åbo · Sveaborg · St Petersburg · Izhevskiy
Kronstadt · Kostroma · Kazan
Revel · Narva · Ivanovo-Voznesensk · Yaroslavl · Surmovo
Riga · Vladimir · Nizhniy Novgorod
Dvinsk · Moscow · Orekhovo-Zuyevo · Samara
Kaluga · Kolomna
Smolensk · Tula · Ryazan · Penza
Grodno · **R U S S I A N   E M P I R E** · Ural
Bobruysk · Kursk · Voronezh · Saratov
Baranovichi · Lugansk
omzha · Belostok · Tsaritsyn
Warsaw · Kiev · Kharkov
odz · Rovno · Berdichev · Poltava · Kadiyevka
Ostrog · Kremenchug · Yenakiyevo
Dnieper · Yekaterinoslav · Rostov-on-Don
Dniester · Yuzovka · Mariupol · Taganrog
Aleksandrovsk
Odessa · Nikolayev · Yekaterinodar
AUSTRIAN EMPIRE · Feodosiya · Novorossiysk · Stravropol
Sevastopol · Sochi
Kutaisi · Vladikavkaz
B l a c k   S e a · Batum · Baku
Tiflis
OTTOMAN EMPIRE · Kars

Caspian Sea

3 The revolution of 1905

→ voyage of the battleship *Potemkin*

▨ peasant unrest and land seizures

▲ workers' soviets

■ army mutinies

⊡ naval mutinies

★ major strikes and armed workers' uprisings

Map 2 - Serfdom in Russia, 1860

ARCHANGEL
FINLAND · OLONETS · VOLOGDA
ST PETERSBURG · PERM
ESTONIA · NOVGOROD · VYATKA
LIVONIA · YAROSLAVL
COURLAND · PSKOV · TVER · KOSTROMA · KAZAN · UFA
KOVNO · VITEBSK · MOSCOW · VLADIMIR · NIZHNIY NOV-GOROD
VILNA · SMOLENSK · KALUGA · RYAZAN · SIMBIRSK · ORENBURG
GRODNO · MOGILEV · TULA · PENZA · SAMARA
MINSK · OREL · TAMBOV · SARATOV
VOLHYNIA · CHERNIGOV · KURSK · VORONEZH
PODOLIA · KIEV · POLTAVA · KHARKOV · DON
BESSARABIA · KHERSON · YEKATERINOSLAV · ASTRAKHAN
TAURIDA · KUBAN · STAVROPOL
Black Sea · TEREK · *Caspian Sea*
TRANS-CAUCASIAN PROVINCES

2 Serfdom in Russia, 1860

serfs as a percentage of the population

▨ over 50   ▨ 10–30

▨ 30–50   ☐ under 10

—— boundary of Russia, 1871

serfs' obligations

◆ *obrok*: dues in kind or cash

◇ *barshchina*: labour service to landlord

⬖ both *obrok* and *barshchina* dues

only migration from overcrowded central Russia to western Siberia, but also the movement of peasants to urban areas to man a growing number of factories. Between 1863 and 1914 Russia's urban population increased from 6 to 18.6 million.

In 1905, in the wake of Japan's victory, revolutionary parties proved quick to exploit the low incomes and general hardships created by these rapid changes, while the new professional classes pressed for political reform (map 3). Unrest in the towns spread to the countryside, to the army and even to the Black Sea fleet, led by the battleship Potemkin, forcing Tsar Nicholas II (1894-1917) to grant a constitution, including a duma, or parliament; but by 1907 the government had regained full control. Nevertheless the 1905 revolution irreparably weakened the old order, and after 1912 another wave of social unrest swept the empire. Internally, Russia was in no position to meet the challenge of the First World War in 1914.

Although mobilization took place with a rapidity that took the Germans by surprise (page 132), the tsar's government proved incapable of supplying its millions of troops with equipment, munitions or (eventually) with food.

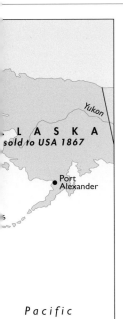

Map - Alaska

Yukon
A L A S K A
sold to USA 1867
Port Alexander
Pacific Ocean

'It is better to abolish serfdom from above than wait for it to abolish itself from below,' declared Alexander II *(left)* in 1857. Four years later Alexander did indeed free the serfs. He soon found that it was one thing to emancipate them, another to feed, clothe and educate them. Radical though they were in Russian terms, Alexander's reforms failed to address the core problems facing his country.

Nationalism in Europe

www.fordham.edu/halsall/
mod/modsbook3.html#
Nationalism

INTERNET LINKS

Online resources on
nationalism

Nationalism flourished in Europe in the wake of the French Revolution (page 98), but it remained confined largely to the middle classes and proved relatively short-lived. The Great Powers at the Congress of Vienna in 1815 aimed to restore Europe (as far as possible) to its pre-war condition by combating both liberalism and nationalism and by creating a barrier around France. To that end Holland received the Austrian Netherlands (later Belgium); Prussia took over Westphalia and much of the Rhineland; Sardinia-Piedmont annexed Genoa; Russia retained Finland and most of Poland; and Austria gained Venetia and Lombardy.

By 1830, however, when a new wave of liberal and national agitation arose, the Great Powers no longer worked in unison, enabling Greece (page 108) and Belgium to obtain independence. In 1848-9, when an outburst of nationalism erupted into full-scale revolution, the solidarity of the conservative powers – coupled with divisions among the nationalists themselves – still sufficed to maintain the status quo. Shortly afterwards, a new generation of statesmen began to use nationalism for their own ends. Cavour

Known as the 'Iron Chancellor', Otto von Bismarck *(above)* became minister-president of Prussia in 1862. After wars against Denmark (1864) and Austria (1866), he formed the North German confederation (1867) and after the Franco-Prussian war (1870-1) inaugurated the German empire. As German chancellor (1871-90) he played a leading role in the European alliance systems of the 1870s and 1880s.

2 The unification of Germany, 1815–71

Prussia in 1815	● free city
acquired by Prussia, 1815–66	━━ German Empire, 1871
━ German Confederation, 1815	⬅ Austro-Prussian forces attack on Denmark, 1864
--- North German Confederation, 1867	⬅ Prussian armies in the war with Austria, 1866
Imperial territory of Alsace-Lorraine, 1871	⬅ German armies in the Franco-Prussian war, 1870–71

1 The unification of Italy, 1859–70

- French from 1768, formerly Genoese
- Kingdom of Sardinia in 1815
- territory annexed 1859
- territory annexed March 1860
- territory annexed November 1860
- territory lost to France 1860
- territory annexed 1866
- territory annexed 1870
- Austrian empire, 1815
- Italian border, 1914

SWITZERLAND

AUSTRO-HUNGARIAN EMPIRE

TYROL

Trent (Trento)

Udine

Görz (Gorizia)

Trieste

VENETIA

Bergamo

Como

Monza

Brescia

Verona

✕ Custoza 1848, 1866

Fiume

SAVOY

Aosta

PIEDMONT

LOMBARDY

Magenta 1859 ✕ Milan

Novara 1849 ✕

Solferino 1859 ✕

Mantua

Padua

Venice

Pola

Susa

Turin

Alessandria

PARMA

Parma

Guastalla

Ferrara

ROMAGNA

Modena

Bologna

MODENA

KINGDOM OF SARDINIA

Genoa

LIGURIA

Pontremoli

La Spezia

Rimini

SAN MARINO

Pesaro

Zara

NICE

Monaco

Nice

Pisa

Lucca

Arno

Florence

Arezzo

Livorno (Leghorn)

Siena

Elba

TUSCANY

Urbino

Ancona

Castelfidardo

MARCHES

UMBRIA

Spoleto

STATES

Lissa 1866 ✕

F R A N C E

CORSICA

Civitavecchia

Mentana

Rome

PAPAL

Tiber

Rieti

Dalmatia

OTTOMAN EMPIRE

Adriatic Sea

Tyrrhenian Sea

Pontecorvo

Terracina

Gaeta

Volturno 1860 ✕

Benevento

Bari

KINGDOM

Naples

Castellammare

Salerno

Potenza

NAPLES

Taranto

OF

THE

Mediterranean Sea

Sassari

KINGDOM OF SARDINIA

Cagliari

Cosenza

TWO

Lipari Is.

Aspromonte 1862 ✕

Messina

Reggio

Palermo

SICILIES

Marsala

Catania

Syracuse

sought a unification of Italy along conservative lines, in the interests of Piedmont-Sardinia, and was hostile to the more revolutionary nationalism of Garibaldi and Mazzini. Bismarck in Prussia wanted unification to achieve his aim of a conservative, Prussian-dominated German state. Both used diplomacy and war to achieve their objectives: Cavour allied with France before attacking Austria in 1859, securing the unification of Italy (except for Venetia and the Papal States) by 1861 (see map 1). Bismarck allied with Austria in order to defeat Denmark (1864), then in concert with Italy attacked Austria (1866), and finally defeated France (1870-1), achieving in the process the unification of Germany (map 2).

Liberal nationalists later endorsed both achievements, but neither satisfied the nationalism they had aroused. Italy still laid claim to the Alto Adige and Istria; Bismarck's 'Small German' solution, which excluded Austria, disappointed those who hankered after a Greater Germany. Nevertheless, the four short wars fought between 1859 and 1871 solved the Italian and German questions, and re-drew the map of Central Europe. Moreover, the Great Powers now remained at peace for over four decades and although nationalist grievances continued to fester, territorial disputes within Europe ceased to divide most governments.

INTERNET LINKS

www.fordham.edu/halsall/
mod/modsbook34.html
Online resources on
imperialism

1830–1914
Imperialism

Until 1830, the search for oriental luxuries remained the driving force behind European imperialism, and (with the important exception of India: page 96) the European stake in Asia and Africa remained confined to trading stations and the strategic outposts necessary to protect trade. Thereafter two new factors transformed the situation. First came the enforced 'opening' of key markets – Turkey and Egypt (1838), Persia (1841), China (1842), Japan (1858) – to European, particularly British, commerce. Then, from the 1870s, a new phase of the Industrial Revolution (page 100) provoked a search for raw materials to feed the new industries. In the scramble for these resources between 1880 and 1914, Europe added almost 9 million square miles (23.4 million km^2) – one-fifth of the land area of the globe – to its overseas colonial possessions.

France and Britain took the lead. The former conquered Algeria after 1830, annexed Tahiti and the Marquesas in the 1840s, expanded its colony in Senegal in the 1850s and began the conquest of Indo-China in 1859. Britain, both to forestall the French and to safeguard its position in India, claimed sovereignty over Australia and New Zealand (page 106), and acquired Singapore (1819), Malacca (1824), Hong Kong (1842), Burma (1852), and Lagos (1861) (map 1).

1 Colonial penetration, 1815–79
see key right

2 The closing of the world system

major powers

British	Ottoman	Belgian
French	Dutch	Russian
German	Italian	USA
Portuguese	Spanish	Danish
		Japanese

1893 date of European control

[1902] date of independence

princely states of India

○ treaty ports

------ sphere of effective

▓▓▓▓ proposed spheres of influence

⚑ major investments of European colonial powers outside Europe

── major sea routes

major raw materials exported to Europe

⬰ grain		▬ jute
◑ meat		◀ silk
T tea		○ rubber
▥ cane sugar		◔ veg oil
🐄 dairy produce		◐ copra
▶ cotton		◠ wool

The same imperatives underlay British expansion after 1880, except that the number of competitors to forestall increased. Thus the French empire grew between 1871 and 1914 by nearly 4 million square miles (10.4 million km²) and 47 million people (mainly in north and west Africa and Indo-China, where Laos and Tongking were added to Cambodia and Cochin-China, but it also secured Madagascar and some Pacific islands); Germany also acquired an empire of 1 million square miles (2.6 million km²) and 14 million colonial subjects (in South-West Africa, Togoland, the Cameroons, Tanganyika and the Pacific islands); Italy obtained several outposts in Africa; the United States annexed the Philippines, Guam, Hawaii and some Caribbean islands; and Russia began to expand in central Asia. Britain too managed to acquire extensive new territories in Africa which almost linked Cape Town with Cairo, more Pacific islands (including Fiji), and parts of the Indonesian archipelago (map 2). It added 88 million subjects to her empire and, by 1914, exercized authority over a fifth of the world's landmass and a quarter of its peoples.

In retrospect, the fragility of these European empires, so hastily assembled, is obvious. None of the imperial powers possessed the resources to govern them effectively and European imperialism proved more ephemeral than anyone at the time imagined; yet it left an indelible mark on the peoples of Africa and Asia, propelling them willingly or unwillingly into the 20th century.

Advertisements often unconsciously reflect the assumptions on which societies operate. The Victorian tobacco advert *(left)* shows the wealthy European manufacturers receiving the raw material from crudely parodied native growers, to whom the finished product will eventually be resold.

INTERNET LINKS

www.wyomingtalesandtrails.
com/sherman2.html —
The building of the
Pacific railroads

1865–1929
North America

26 Apr. 1865 The South
surrenders; end of Civil War;
Reconstruction begins

1867 Canadian Federation
formed; USA purchases
Alaska from Russia

1869 First trans-
continental railroad in
USA completed

1870-1 Manitoba and
British Columbia join
Canadian Federation

1877 Reconstruction
formally comes to an end

1885 Canadian-Pacific
railroad completed

1898 USA annexes
Hawaii: Cuba and the
Philippines seized from
Spain

1914 Canada and (1917)
USA join World War I

Although the United States made a remarkably rapid recovery after the Civil War (page 104), development remained very uneven. In the defeated South, the period of Reconstruction (1865–77) proved a bitter experience. South Carolina, which in 1860 had ranked third in the nation in per capita wealth, ranked 40th ten years later; and other once-prosperous states did scarcely better. The 4 million liberated black slaves fared worst, being left (as Frederick Douglass wrote) without money, property or friends. Although the population of the Union surged from 31 million in 1861 to 92 million in 1910, most of the increase by-passed the South and concentrated wealth and power in the north-east and the upper Mid-West. Only around 1920 did cheap labour attract textile industry to the South (map 1).

The settlement of the Great Plains, made possible by the railway boom after 1870, constituted perhaps the most striking achievement of the post-war period. The track in operation increased from 30,000 miles (48,000 km) in 1860 to 163,000 (262,000 km) in 1890 (at which point it exceeded the size of the entire European rail system); the number of farms rose from 2 million in 1860 to 6 million in 1910; and the population living west of the Mississippi grew from 6 million to 26 million. Yet the bulk of the population remained concentrated in the north-east (map 3), and most of the 25 million immigrants arriving between 1870 and 1914 stayed there, providing cheap labour for American industry.

Railways played an even more prominent role in the development of Canada. The United States made no secret of its hope to absorb the provinces and thus create a continent-wide empire. After the acquisition

Pittsburgh, Pennsylvania, surrounded by huge coal-fields and beds of iron and at the confluence of two important rivers, became the leading centre of iron and steel production in the United States. So vast and dramatic was the sight of its blast furnaces and coke ovens at work that early 20th-century artists and commentators began to refer to it as 'Hell with the lid off.'

2 Canada, 1867–1929

land occupied;
- prior to 1851
- 1851–1871
- 1871–1901
- 1901–1921

population of towns, 1871;
- 25,000-100,000 people
- over 100,000 people

population of towns, 1911;
- 25,000-100,000 people
- over 100,000 people

railways 1916:
- Canadian Pacific Railway
- Canadian Northern (Main Line)
- National Trans-continental Railway
- main industrial regions

ALBERTA 1905 date of accession to Dominion of Canada

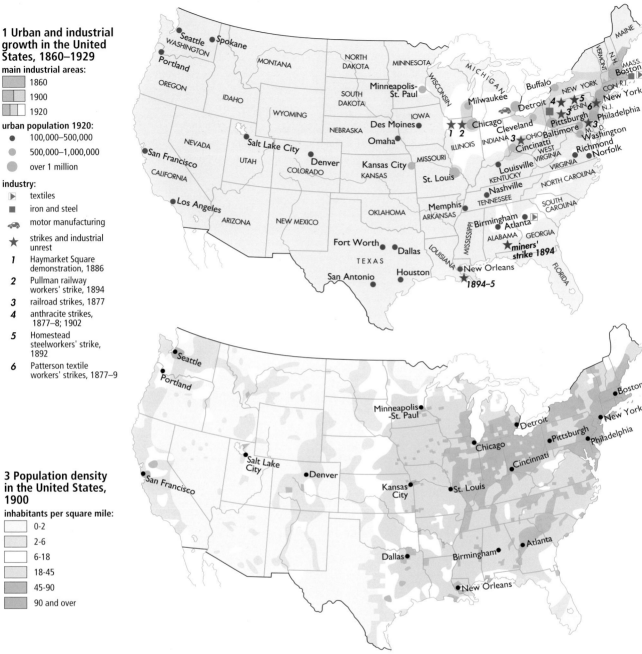

1 Urban and industrial growth in the United States, 1860–1929

main industrial areas:
- 1860
- 1900
- 1920

urban population 1920:
- 100,000–500,000
- 500,000–1,000,000
- over 1 million

industry:
- ▷ textiles
- ■ iron and steel
- 🚗 motor manufacturing
- ★ strikes and industrial unrest

1 Haymarket Square demonstration, 1886
2 Pullman railway workers' strike, 1894
3 railroad strikes, 1877
4 anthracite strikes, 1877–8; 1902
5 Homestead steelworkers' strike, 1892
6 Patterson textile workers' strikes, 1877–9

3 Population density in the United States, 1900

inhabitants per square mile:
- 0-2
- 2-6
- 6-18
- 18-45
- 45-90
- 90 and over

of Alaska by the United States (1867), this pressure grew, but the Canadians frustrated their neighbours' intentions by forming the Canadian Federation in 1867, completed by the purchase of Rupert's Land from the Hudson's Bay Company (1869) and the adhesion of Manitoba (1870) and British Columbia (1871). The great transcontinental railways – the Canadian Pacific (completed 1885) followed by the Canadian Northern and the National Trans-continental – became the lifeblood of the new Dominion, opening Manitoba and Saskatchewan, and turning Canada into one of the world's leading wheat producers. It also facilitated the exploitation of rich mineral deposits, particularly copper and nickel (map 2). Overall, Canada's industrial output increased from $190 million in 1890 to over $500 million in 1914.

This achievement was dwarfed, however, by the economic and territorial growth of the United States. Output of iron and steel increased 20-fold between 1870 and 1913, by which time steel production exceeded that of Britain and Germany combined, and the United States remained the world's leading agricultural producer. Meanwhile, in 1898 (following a successful war with Spain), the Philippines, Guam, Puerto Rico and Hawaii were annexed, the latter after many years of American encroachment in the islands' affairs; and in 1903 Cuba and the Panama Canal Zone became protectorates. The United States now possessed the political and economic might to intervene almost anywhere on the world stage: in Mexico in 1914 and again in 1916, and – on a far greater scale – in Europe in 1917-18 (page 132).

(INTERNET LINKS)

http://afe.easia.columbia.edu
/japan/japanworkbook/
modernhist/meiji.html —
The Meiji restoration and
modernization

1868–1941
Japan

1868 Tokugawa shogu-
nate ends and the Meiji
emperor assumes power

1894–5 Sino–Japanese
War; Japan occupies
Formosa

1904–5 Russo–Japanese
War; Japanese success
stimulates Asian nationalism

1910 Japan annexes Korea

1914 Japan takes over
German concessions in
China

1920 Japan given permanent seat on the League of
Nations

1931 Japan occupies
Manchuria

1937 Sino–Japanese War

1940-1 Japan occupies
French Indo-China

7/8 Dec. 1941 Japanese
air forces attack Pearl
Harbor & Philippines

The Tokugawa shoguns (page 88) gave Japan over
two centuries of peace and prosperity. In 1868,
however, internal tensions, combined with the
pressure of Western powers to open Japan to foreign
trade, resulted in a revolution (known as the Meiji
Restoration) which replaced the shogun and the feudal
structure with a modern system of government. The
new Japanese leaders implemented widespread
reforms in the belief that a modern economy and
military would ensure Japan's international independence and equality. They instituted a national
education system (which by 1900 provided teaching
for 90 per cent of children), a conscript army, and a
navy with modern ships. Legal codes, largely based
on French and German models, were introduced
from 1882. The economic reforms were wide-reach-
ing; the first railway opened in 1872 and by 1906 the
system linked most parts of the country; up to one-
third of state expenditure went on developing
commerce and industry (map 1); and a land tax
reform in 1873 provided a secure source of revenue
for the government. The shifting structure of
Japanese foreign trade (see table 3) illustrates
the dramatic impact of these changes.
Whereas by 1878-82, manufactured
goods represented half of all imports
but only 7 per cent of exports, in
1918-22 the ratio had reversed:

1 Industrial Japan
town population, 1918
- ● less than 50,000
- ● 50,000–100,000
- ● 100,000,–500,000
- ■ 500,000–1 million
- ■ over 1 million

railways in 1906

additions to railways
1906–1918

main manufacturing
areas

KYOTO   prefecture

industries:
- ■ metal
- ⚓ shipbuilding
- ✛ textiles
- ⬧ wood
- ◀ silk
- ⬧ ceramics
- ■ chemicals
- ⬧ food
- ⊞ machinery
- ■ manufac-
turing
industry

minerals:
- ● coal
- C copper
- ▲ iron
- ⬧ oil

**The battle of Tsushima
Strait,** in May 1905, was one of
the most complete naval
victories in history *(right)*. The
Russian fleet, in dire need of
mechanical overhaul, was
outmanœuvred by the Japanese
Togo, and forced to surrender after
the sinking of six of its battleships. The war was over – the
first time that an emerging Asian
power had defeated a Western
one; the news resounded
throughout the colonial world.

finished manufactures now accounted for over 40 per cent of sales and only 15 per cent of purchases. Moreover the total value of Japan's exports rose in this period from 30 million to 1.8 billion yen.

International recognition of Japan's new status was nevertheless slow in coming: consular jurisdiction survived until 1894, and the unequal treaties negotiated in the 1850s with the Western powers remained in force until 1911. As Japan's strength and confidence grew, however, so did nationalist and imperialist ambitions. In 1894-5 a victorious war against China, arising from disputes in Korea, ended in a treaty granting Taiwan to Japan. Russo-Japanese rivalry over Manchuria culminated in Japanese victory in the war of 1904-5. The Treaty of Portsmouth (1905) gave Japan a lease of territory in China and extensive rights in South Manchuria. In 1910 she acquired Korea. Japanese support for the victorious Western powers in World War I brought few further rewards, however, and the country's military leaders became frustrated. After 1931, under the impact of the Great Depression (page 138), Japan overran first Manchuria and then – despite strong opposition from the United States – northern China in an attempt to achieve economic self-sufficiency (map 2). Germany's victory over France and the Netherlands in 1940 offered an opportunity to expand southwards – thereby gaining control over valuable oil fields in Borneo and Burma – precipitating full-scale war with the Western powers (page 142). Paradoxically, Japan's total defeat and the ensuing American occupation propelled her even more decisively into the modern world than the Meiji restoration had done.

2 Japanese expansion from 1914

- Japanese territory by 1914, with dates of acquisition
- spheres of Japanese influence, 1918
- expansion to 1933
- expansion to Nov. 1941
- ✳ Japanese conflict with USSR
- → Japanese attacks
- ■ Chinese capitals
- ▪ Allied bases
- — railways

3 Structure of Japanese trade

food, drink | raw materials | semi-manufactured goods | finished goods | other

1878-82
export
import

1918-22
export
import

0%   25%   50%   75%   100%

### Map labels

U S S R
KARAFUTO 1905
Amur
MANCHURIA
Manchukuo (Japanese protectorate proclaimed 1932)
Nomonhan 1939
Japanese forces defeated by Red Army under Zhukov
Vladivostok
Changkufeng 1938
Sea of Japan (East Sea)
Tokyo
Changchun
1933
SOUTH MANCHURIA
Mukden
KOREA (CHOSEN) 1910
Pusan
J A P A N
Russian support for China, 1935
Peking
Tientsin
Kwantung leased territory 1905
SHANTUNG
Tsingtao
Yellow R.
Yellow Sea
Ryukyu (Loochoo) Is.
1932
1937
Shanghai 1937
Nanking
C H I N A
1941
Nanchang
Chungking
FUKIEN
Amoy
TAIWAN (Formosa) 1895
Pacific Ocean
Yangtze
Burma Road
Swatow
1941
8 Dec. 1941
Nanning
Canton
Kunming
Hong Kong
1941
PHILIPPINE IS. (USA)
Japanese support for independence movements
Hanoi
Hainan
South China Sea
Manila
occupied by Japan, 1940
F R E N C H   I N D O - C H I N A
Franco-Japanese agreement permitting occupation, 1941
S I A M
under Japanese influence, 1941
Bangkok
Saigon

INTERNET LINKS

www.worldwar1.com/
tlindex.htm
Information on the lead-up
to the First World War

1878–1914
European rivalries and alliances

The unification of Germany and Italy (page 116) seemed for a time to have resolved the major questions which had disturbed the peace of Europe since 1848. Bismarck, the architect of German unification, concentrated after 1871 on building a system of alliances that would ensure the future of the new empire, mainly by isolating France, which proved unable to reconcile itself to the rise of the new German empire, and for almost 20 years he succeeded in convincing the rest of Europe of Germany's conservative and pacific intentions. In time, however, the alliances that had seemed defensive became aggressive and destabilizing.

Meanwhile, although the achievements of Bismarck and Cavour reduced nationalist fervour in central Europe, they stirred up a hornet's nest in the Balkans, where the struggles of various national groups for independence from the Turks inevitably involved the neighbouring powers, Russia and Austria (which, after its exclusion from Germany in 1866 became far more interested in the Balkans).

Revolts in the Balkans between 1875 and 1878, culminating in Russian intervention and war with the Turks, resulted in the treaty of Berlin (brokered by Bismarck) which either confirmed or established the independence of Serbia, Montenegro, Romania and Bulgaria and granted Austria a mandate to govern Bosnia and Herzegovina. In 1879 Germany and Austria signed a defensive alliance, expanded to include Italy in 1882 (map 1). Russia, satisfied that Slav interest had been met in the Balkans, turned increasingly to Central Asia and the Far East. The main European rivalries were now between Britain and Russia in Asia, and Britain and France in Africa. Britain remained isolated in Europe, while France and Russia signed an alliance in 1894 as a counterweight to the strength of the alliance bloc based around Germany.

The situation changed after 1897, however, when Germany began to seek a 'place in the sun'. This was not unreasonable; but by then most places in the sun had been occupied by others, and German policy – which involved building a High Seas Fleet to rival that of Britain – therefore seemed to constitute a threat to the established imperial powers. As a result, Britain resolved its differences with France in 1904,

1 European alliance systems, 1882–1914

— frontiers, 1912

The Triple Alliance, 1882

The Triple Entente, 1912

The Balkan League, 1912

AUSTRO-HUNGARIAN EMPIRE

Budapest

Lake
Balaton

Sava

Banja Luka

BOSNIA-
HERZEGOVINA
administered by Austria-
Hungary 1878; annexed 1908

Sarajevo

Belgrade

principality 1817;
independent 1878

S E R B I A

Nish

MONTENEGRO

Kotor
(Cattaro)

Cetinje

Scutari

Tirana

to Serbia
1913

Uskub
(Skoplje)

Monastir

Adriatic
Sea

ALBANIA
principality
1913

Koritsa

to Bulgaria 1913

Macedonia

Carpathian Mts

Jassy

MOLDAVIA
semi-independent
1829

Galatz

R O M A N I A
united 1859; independent 1878;
kingdom 1881

WALLACHIA
semi-independent
1829

Bucharest

Vidin

Danube

Sofia

B U L G A R I A
principality 1878
independent 1908

EASTERN
RUMELIA
to Bulgaria 1885

Maritsa

Balchik

Varna

Burgas

Black
Sea

Kavalla

to Bulgaria 1913

Adrianople

T h r a c e

Constantinople

to Greece 1913

EPIRUS

Corfu

Yannina

Preveza

to Greece 1864

Arta

THESSALY
to Greece 1881

Larissa

Salonica

Thasos

Lemnos

to Greece 1913

Mytilene

O T T O M A N

E M P I R E

to Greece
1864

K I N G D O M   O F   G R E E C E

independent 1830

Patras

Athens

Piraeus

Tripolis

Aegean
Sea

Chios

Smyrna

Ionian
Sea

Ionian
Islands

Nikaria

to Greece 1913

to Greece 1864

CRETE
independent 1898
to Greece 1913

Candia

Dodecanese

Rhodes
occupied by Italy
1912

and with Russia in 1907, and France settled its long-standing dispute with Italy in 1902. Thereafter, the Triple Entente with France and Russia became the lynch-pin of British foreign policy, the only firm assurance against the German 'threat'. Germany, on the other became concerned with the danger of 'encirclement' by a hostile ring constructed by Great Britain (map 1).

As a result, a dangerous simplification of alignments occurred into a bi-polar system: the Triple Alliance and the Triple Entente drew tighter, and Germany in particular grew closer to its only dependable ally, Austria. When Austria annexed Bosnia and Herzegovina in 1908, Germany gave her qualified support, though it rekindled Austro-Russian antagonism in the Balkans. During the Balkan wars (1912-13), in which a Russian-sponsored Balkan League consisting of Serbia, Greece and Bulgaria attempted to drive the Turks out of Europe, the two diplomatic systems still cooperated; but Austria stood aghast at the consequent enlargement of Serbia – which almost doubled its size – and feared Serb agitation for an independent south Slav state (map 2).

The assassination of the heir to the Austrian throne in Sarajevo (Bosnia) in June 1914 provided what seemed to the Austrian government like its last chance to deal with Serbia before it grew too powerful, and Germany threw its entire weight behind its ally. Russia, however, could not afford to leave Serbia in the lurch and began to mobilize against Austria. Germany regarded this as a direct threat, and also began to mobilize. However, to forestall an attack from Russia's allies in the West, German Grand Strategy called for an immediate attack on France – in the hope that it could be knocked out of the war before Russia advanced in force. On 28 July, Austria declared war on Serbia; on 1 August 1914 Germany declared war on Russia, and two days later on France. The diplomatic system created by Bismarck, coupled with the volatile situation in the Balkans, had produced a world war (page 132).

---

2 The Balkans, 1878–1913

- – – frontier of Ottoman empire, 1800
- —— frontier of Ottoman empire, 1885
- —— national frontiers after the Balkan wars 1912–13

HMS Temeraire, depicted on a pre-war postcard. Britain responded to Germany's increased warship building after 1900 with a rival programme based on the most modern Dreadnought battleships. The Royal Navy was fully mobilized for exercises at the outbreak of war.

INTERNET LINKS

www.ucs.mun.ca/~jcraig/
marconi.html
The first wireless
communication

1870–1914

The formation of a world economy

The integration of the global economy into a single interdependent whole formed one of the principal developments of the period 1870-1914. Europe (and to a lesser extent the United States) stood at the heart of this process, emitting the impulses that opened up the remaining areas of the globe to Western exploration and exploitation.

Three interrelated aspects deserve special attention. First came the development of better means of communication. In 1870, railways remained largely confined to Europe (60,400 miles, 97,250 km of track) and North America (56,300 miles, 90,600 km): the rest of the world could boast only 9100 miles (14,650 km). By 1911, however, the total network of tracks had increased to 657,000 miles (1.06 million km) – 175,000 miles (280,000 km) of them outside Europe and North America – and included some spectacular transcontinental links: across the United States (four between 1869 and 1893), Canada (1885), Russia (1904) and the Andes (1910). The expansion of world shipping was equally striking, with not only a spectacular rise in the total tonnage, but a shift from sail to steam which increased the speed and regularity of shipments. However, the main shipping traffic, both passenger and freight, took place among the advanced countries and the white dominions, or between them and the producers of the raw materials they required. Canal construction also continued apace – above all the Suez Canal, completed in 1869, which carried 437,000 tons in 1870 and over 20 million in 1913; and the Panama Canal, completed in 1914, which carried 5 million tons of cargo in its first year. These spectacular totals reflected the enormous savings in distance – 41 per cent for vessels sailing from Liverpool to Bombay, 60 per cent for vessels sailing from New York to San Francisco.

Finally, messages travelled around the world with increasing speed. Cables laid beneath the oceans linked the continents – between Britain and North America (1866); from Vancouver to Brisbane (1902) – followed by telephones (with international lines from 1887) and wireless stations (from 1897).

These developments paralleled a boom in commerce. Foreign trade tripled in volume between 1870 and 1914, although (again) most of the activity occurred among the industrialized countries, or between them and their suppliers of primary goods or their new markets. In 1913, only 11 per cent of the

1 The development of the world economy

foreign investment, 1914
(in $ million)

535	United Kingdom	420	United States
3180	France	1050	Germany

—— busiest shipping routes
—— other major shipping routes, c. 1900
—— international telegragh cables

Colonial empires in 1900

Belgian	Japanese
British	Ottoman
Danish	Portuguese
Dutch	Russian
French	Spanish
German	USA
Italian	other countries

Panama canal, 1914

3 The share of world trade

1860
total
$8 billion

Others, United Kingdom, USA, France, Russia, Spain, Austria-Hungary, Italy, Scandinavia, Germany, Holland and Belgium, Switzerland world's trade took place between the primary producers themselves. Britain ranked as the world's largest trading nation in 1860, but by 1913 it had lost ground to both the United States and Germany: British and German exports in that year each totalled $2.3 billion, and those of the United States exceeded $2.4 billion.

Britain remained the world's financial capital, however, as well as its largest lender, with almost $20 billion in foreign investments by 1914 – slightly more than those of France, Germany, Holland and Belgium combined. The United States and Russia were in fact net borrowers of foreign capital. Investments within Europe and North America on the whole assisted and accelerated economic advancement, helping to create the costly infrastructure (such as railways and other public works) for developing nations that would in time repay these debts. By contrast, investments in non-industrial regions (such as the Russian and Ottoman empires) and overseas territories that lacked both the knowledge and the power to direct the capital flow, served to colonize rather than develop them, destroying native industries and creating dangerous political and economic pressures which would, in time, produce conflict between rich nations and poor nations and demands for a new economic order (page 174).

2 Foreign Investment in 1914 (in $ million)

Russia	500
Belgium	900
USA	3,510
Holland	4,100
Germany	5,650
France	9,280
United Kingdom	19,935

300 NEW ZEALAND

COMMONWEALTH OF AUSTRALIA 1700

GERMAN NEW GUINEA

DUTCH NEW GUINEA

JAPAN 500

DUTCH BORNEO
SARAWAK

200
200
600 INDO-CHINA
SIAM
BURMA

MONGOLIA

CHINA

550
400
2400

RUSSIAN EMPIRE

INDIA 1850

Indian Ocean

investment in the rest of Europe

NORWAY 535
SWEDEN 1050

UK
GERMANY 750
FRANCE
AUST.-HUNGARY 450
650 OTTOMAN EMPIRE
ITALY
SPAIN ARABIA

PERSIA

Suez canal, 1869
Mediterranean Sea

200
200 EGYPT 500

ALGERIA LIBYA

100
FRENCH WEST AFRICA

ANGLO EGYPTIAN SUDAN

ABYSSINIA

600 BRITISH EAST AFRICA

MADAGASCAR

NIGERIA

all of Africa

CONGO FREE STATE
500 GERMAN E. AFRICA

ANGOLA RHODESIA

GERMAN SOUTH WEST AFRICA
1550 UNION OF SOUTH AFRICA from 1910

Miners at the Republic Gold Mining Company in the Transvaal, South Africa, fuelled the economic engine that drove the Gold Standard. This originated in Britain in 1821, but until Germany joined the system in 1871, most other countries remained on a bi-metallic standard, gold and silver.

FOUR
The Modern World

By making the world one, the European powers stirred up forces that eventually caused their own eclipse. The world wars between 1914 and 1945 whittled away their resources and Europe's exhaustion benefited the Soviet Union and the United States, the two superpowers on the eastern and western flanks, whose rivalry produced an age of bipolarity. But bipolarity, too, proved to be temporary. The recovery of Europe, the emancipation of Asia and Africa, the rise of Japan and finally the collapse of the Soviet empire brought a new constellation into being, and with it the threat of confrontation between rich and poor nations and of the exhaustion of global resources through overpopulation. No one can foretell the shape of things to come. All this section can do is show, in historical perspective, how the world of the 20th century changed and chart the emergence of significant new factors in the 21st century.

Devastation inflicted by the first atomic bomb
Hiroshima, 1945

INTERNET LINKS

www.spartacus.schoolnet.
co.uk/CHINAkuomintang.htm
The Kuomintang

1911–1949

The Chinese Republic

1915 Japan issues its 'Twenty-One Demands'; Japanese dominance in Shantung, Manchuria and Inner Mongolia

1919 'May 4th' nationalist movement founded

1921 Chinese Communist party founded

1926 Chiang Kai-shek begins reunification of China

1927 Nationalist purge their Communist supporters

1934 'Long March' of China's communists begins

1937 Start of Sino-Japanese war

1945 Defeat of Japan

1946 Civil war in China begins

1949 Communist victory in China

1 The Nationalist (Kuomintang) regime, 1928–37

occupied by Japan by 1933

area in which Japan attempted to establish a puppet North China state, 1935

areas of effective control of Nationalist government

from 1928

added 1929–34

added 1935–7

brought under Nanking influence, 1935–7

By 1911 the imperial government of China was thoroughly discredited (page 94) and an army mutiny led to the emperor's abdication. But the Republic proclaimed in 1912, with Sun Yat-sen as its first president, was overwhelmed by its inherited problems, and Sun was soon deposed by Yuan Shih-k'ai, the most powerful general of the old regime. After Yuan's death in 1916 power passed to provincial warlords, whose armies caused untold damage and millions of casualties. Compounding this misery were the expansionist policies of Japan and the foreign powers, based in the Treaty Ports (page 88), which interfered in the Chinese economy and in Chinese politics.

In 1919, the refusal of the Paris Peace Conference to abrogate foreign privileges provoked spontaneous urban uprisings (the 'May 4th' movement). These provided a new opportunity for Sun Yat-sen, who in 1923 reorganized his Nationalist (Kuomintang; KMT) Party, allied with the Chinese Communist Party (founded 1921), and prepared to reunite the country. But Sun died in 1925 and it was Chiang Kai-shek, the Moscow-trained general of the KMT army, who in 1926 marched northwards to eliminate the warlords. Helped by peasant and workers' uprisings along his route, Chiang proved remarkably successful, but in 1927 he turned on his allies, massacring the Communists in

Shanghai. However KMT direct rule remained limited to the lower Yangtze (map 1). Nevertheless, the Japanese, fearing the potential challenge from a reunited China, decided to reinforce their hold in the north and overran Manchuria (1931) and Jehol (1933).

Although KMT purges had virtually eliminated Communism from the cities, peasant disaffection – arising from the absence of land reform – offered an alternative constituency. From his base at Chingkang Shan, Mao Tse-Tung and others created a new centre of revitalized communism, developing a peasant-based party rather than an urban, proletarian party on the Russian model. In 1929 KMT pressure

2 The Chinese Communist movement to 1945

- abortive urban insurrections after the break with Kuomintang 1927
- position of early Communist army groups
- early Soviets (self-governing Communist areas) 1927–35
- route of the 'Long March', Oct. 1934–Oct. 1935, of Chinese Communists after Kuomintang assaults on Kiangsi Soviet area
- main Communist base area, governed from Yenan 1935–45
- area occupied by Japan end 1941
- area occupied by Japan during 1944 offensives
- 'liberated areas' dominated by local Communist groups by 1945
- railways in 1937
- main industrial areas 1937
- main industrial centres 1937
- other industrial centres 1937

U S S R

MANCHURIA

Manchouli   Hailar

Tsitsihar   Kiamusze

OUTER MONGOLIA
(independent 1921)   Harbin

Kirin

Changchun

Mukden   Fushun
Chinchow Penki
          Anshan
       Yingkow Antung

KOREA
Japanese
1910–45

Kalgan

Peking
Tatung   Tangshan   Dairen
Paotow   Tientsin   Port Arthur
                        (Lüshun)

SHEN-KAN-NING
Taiyuan
Yenan   Pao-an: Soviet
         1930–5   Tsinan
                  Tsingtao
Lanchow   Yellow River
            (Hwang Ho)
         Kaifeng   Lienyünkang
Sian   Loyang Chengchow
                Hsü-chou
                (Suchow)
4th army group,
Chang Kuo-tao
Hsü Hsiang-ch'ien   Nanking Soochow
                              Shanghai
         Wuhan   Hangchow
C H I N A   Ningpo
Chengtu
                Kiukiang   East China
Chungking   Nanchang   10th army group,   Sea
            Aug. 1927   Fang Chih-min
Tsunyi   W. Hunan
Jan. 1935 Changsha Chingkang Shan,
         Hengyang   Mao Zedong and
                    Chu Teh, 1927–9
Kweiyang   Jui-chin Foochow
                  (Juikin) Kiangsi Soviet under
                            Mao Zedong and Chu Teh,
Kunming   1929–34
                    Amoy   TAIWAN
                            Japanese
                            1895–1945
         Canton
         Dec. 1927   Swatow
                  Hailufeng Soviet under
Hong Kong   P'eng P'ai, 1927–8
BURMA   British

FRENCH
INDO-CHINA

THAILAND   Hainan   South China Sea

Yellow Sea

compelled Mao and his followers to move first to Kiangsi, and then in 1934 to the north-west (the 'Long March': map 2).

In 1937 Japanese forces invaded northern and central China and the KMT retreated to the interior, where they remained until the Japanese surrender in 1945. A race to occupy the liberated areas now ensued, with the Communists gaining much of the north and most of Manchuria, and the KMT re-occupying the south. In 1946 hostilities between the two sides erupted into a civil war from which the Communists emerged victorious. The People's Republic of China was proclaimed in October 1949, and soon afterwards the KMT fled to Taiwan. For the first time in a century, a strong regime controlled all of mainland China – albeit most of the country had been devastated by the warlords, the Japanese occupation and the civil war.

A poster from c.1927 showing Sun Yat-sen (top centre) and Chiang Kai-shek (on horse) about to set out with Kuomintang forces on the 'Northern Expedition' of 1926–8.

INTERNET LINKS

www.bbc.co.uk/history/
worldwars/wwone
In-depth coverage of the
First World War

1914–1918

The First World War

All the war-plans of the Great Powers in 1914 envisaged a short war. The German Schlieffen Plan called for an attack on northern France through Belgium, leading to the rapid collapse of the French government before Russia had time to mobilize (page 125). It almost succeeded: the Germans came within 40 miles of Paris, but not before Russian armies had invaded East Prussia. Although their advance was halted at Tannenberg (August), important German reserves were diverted from the Western front just as a spirited counter-attack by French and British troops began at the Marne (September). The two sides now spread their forces out and dug in, until their trenches stretched from the Channel coast to Switzerland.

The war in the west (map 2) turned into a war of attrition. Each side launched repeated offensives, with appalling casualties but little gain, for railways were able to bring up reinforcements before the slow-moving front-line troops could make good any advantage. In 1916 the British, under Sir Douglas Haig, made a major frontal assault on German lines at the river Somme. On the first day of the battle 60,000 British casualties were mowed down as they advanced through the barbed wire. Haig threw his forces into an unwinnable conflict for another four months. Both sides experienced terrible losses and achieved little. Neither side could break the trench

stalemate by pursuing alternative strategies. The British and French attempted a series of attacks from the rear: in the Dardanelles and Mesopotamia against the Ottoman empire, which entered the war in November 1914 on the side of the Central Powers (Germany and Austria); on Austria's southern frontier after Italy declared war in May 1915; at Salonika in Greece in support of Serbia. All failed. The Germans countered by building a fleet of submarines with the express intention of bringing Britain to its knees by attacking vulnerable food imports on which Britain relied. In 1917 unrestricted submarine warfare failed to halt Britain's food supply, but provoked the United States into war with Germany.

On the eastern front, which stretched for twice the distance of that in the west, warfare remained more mobile and both Germany and Austria scored major successes. In 1915 the former overran a huge area of Poland, whose resources it ruthlessly exploited, while the latter occupied most of Serbia. In 1917 the combination of huge losses and economic chaos broke the fighting spirit of the Russian forces and provoked revolution and military collapse (page 134). At the peace of Brest-Litovsk in March 1918 Germany gained the Ukraine, Poland, Finland and the Baltic provinces.

NORWAY
Bergen
Kristiania

FINLAND
Helsingfors
St Petersburg (Petrograd)
Revel

SCOTLAND
Scapa Flow
Glasgow
Edinburgh

naval blockade of Germany effective end 1916
1916: Battle of Jutland

SWEDEN
Gothenburg
Stockholm

1918

R U S S I A N

1914: Russian offensive in East Prussia
Pskov
Dvinsk
Moscow
Smolensk
Tula

UNITED KINGDOM
Newcastle

IRELAND
Belfast
Dublin
Liverpool
Manchester

WALES
ENGLAND
Birmingham
Bristol
London

NORTH SEA

DENMARK
Aarhus
Copenhagen
Malmö
Kiel

1917: Riga offensive

Baltic Sea
Memel
Riga
Gumbinnen
Vilna
Königsberg

Minsk

E M P I R E
Volga

1914: Tannenberg counter-offensive
Hamburg
Bremen
Danzig
Masurian Lakes
Tannenberg

Stettin
Berlin
Hanover
Posen
Warsaw
Brest-Litovsk

Kursk

Amsterdam
NETHERLANDS
Rhine
Cologne
Dresden
Elbe

POLAND
Lodz
1914
Kiev 1918
Kharkov

BELGIUM
Brussels
LUXEM-BOURG
Metz
Strassburg

Prague
Cracow
Tarnow
Lemberg
Gorlice
1917

1916: Brusilov offensive
UKRAINE
Dnieper

Rouen
Seine
Paris
see inset below left

1915: Gorlice campaign
Vienna
Munich
Danube

AUSTRO-HUNGARIA
1917
Budapest

1918: Central Powers advance through Ukraine
Kishinev
Dniester

Nantes
Orléans
Loire

SWITZERLAND
LIECHTENSTEIN
Innsbruck
Berne
Caporetto
1915 Isonzo

EMPIRE
Kolozsvár
Odessa

F R A N C E
Bordeaux

1916: Asiago offensive
Venice
Trieste
1918
Zagreb

1915: conquest of Serbia
Belgrade
ROMANIA
Sebastopol

Geneva
Bologna

Kolubara
1914
Sarajevo
BOSNIA-HERZEGOVINA
MONTE-NEGRO

Bucharest
BLACK SEA

1916: Central Powers conquest of Romania

Bilbao
Toulouse
Marseilles
Nice
MONACO
ANDORRA

I T A L Y
Rome
San Marino
Corsica

SERBIA
Danube
BULGARIA
Sofia
Burgas

Madrid
Valencia
Barcelona
SPAIN

1916
Tirana
Skopje
1918: Allied advance into Serbia
Constantinople

Balearic Is.

Sardinia
Cagliari

Naples
Bari
Brindisi
ALBANIA
Monastir
Salonica
Gallipoli
OTTOMAN
Angora

M E D I T E R R A N E A N

1915: British land at Salonica to support Serbia
1915: Gallipoli offensive
Smyrna
EMPIRE

Palermo
Sicily
Messina
SEA

GREECE
Athens

Crete
Dodecanese (It.)
Cyprus (Br.)

Instead of moving its forces across to the West, however, Germany sent its troops to occupy these new territories – even Finland – and at the same time launched a final, all-out offensive in the West, in an attempt to break the deadlock. Once again it came close to success but the Allied line held and in July, aided by tanks and reinforced by American forces and money, a counter-attack began that pushed the German army back towards the German frontier. Morale collapsed: by October 1918, with Austria close to disintegration and with Germany facing a grave political crisis at home, the Berlin government sued for an unconditional armistice, granted on 11 November 1918.

At the peace conferences held in and around Paris in 1919, the victors imposed upon Germany, Austria, Hungary, and Bulgaria notable losses of territory, huge reparations and stringent reductions in their armed forces. The draconian nature of the settlement made it inevitable that, although over 9 million men had perished in the fighting, and the financial cost of the war totalled over $186 billion worldwide, it would not be (as so many had hoped) 'the war to end all wars'.

1 The Great War in Europe, 1914–18

Entente Powers

Central Powers

major Entente Power offensives

major Central Power offensives

farthest advance by Entente Powers: (east 1914, west 1918)

farthest advance by Central Powers: (west 1914, east 1918)

★ battle

✦ battle costing over 250,000 lives

⚓ naval base

The Menin Road *(left),* vividly recalled by the British painter Paul Nash, saw some of the Western Front's worst fighting. In the second half of 1917, a British campaign to re-capture seven miles of Flanders towards Menin and Passchendaele flounderd in heavy rain and mud. The British lost 265,000 men and Menin remained in German hands

The USSR from Lenin to Stalin

INTERNET LINKS

www.spartacus.schoolnet.
co.uk/RUScivilwar.htm
Comprehensive account of
the Russian civil war

Feb. 1917 Tsar Nicholas II abdicates

Oct. 1917 Lenin and the Bolsheviks seize power

1918 Treaty of Brest-Litovsk: Russia withdraws from the First World War

1918-20 Russian civil war

1921 Lenin introduces New Economic Policy

1922 Stalin appointed Secretary General

1924 Death of Lenin

1928 Start of first Five Year Plan

1929-33 Soviet agriculture collectivized

1941 German invasion of the Soviet Union

1945 Russian troops occupy Berlin; German unconditional surrender

2 Collectivization, 1923–39

- ▬ 2-10% of all farms collectivized by 1928
- 25-50% of all farms collectivized by 1933
- 50-70% of all farms collectivized by 1933
- 70-85% of all farms collectivized by 1933
- famine areas, 1932
- *Kraslag* labour camp admin. zone
- ☠ corrective labour camps, 1932

By 1917 the strain of war had fatally weakened the Tsarist government: liberals, businessmen, generals and aristocrats all plotted its overthrow. In the end sheer hunger turned a general strike and bread queues into a revolutionary movement which in February forced the Tsar to abdicate, and power passed to a provisional government of prominent *duma* (parliament) politicians. The revolutionary committees (soviets) did not disband, however, and gradually the 'peace, bread and land' programme of the Bolshevik group, led by V. I. Lenin, gained support. In October, the Bolsheviks seized control of strategic points in Petrograd (formerly St Petersburg), arrested the Provisional Government, and assumed power in the name of the soviets. The same soon happened in other cities (map 1).

No one thought they would retain power for long. The overriding need was for peace, and Lenin accepted the onerous terms imposed by Germany in the treaty of Brest-Litovsk (March 1918: page 133); but almost immediately the Bolsheviks (who now took the name 'Communists') faced massive invasions by forces loyal to the Tsar and assisted by troops from

Britain, France, Czechoslovakia, Poland and other anti-Bolshevik powers. Nevertheless, by 1920 the civil war had been won, albeit at the cost of 13 million lives and immense damage to property. Lenin now introduced his 'New Economic Policy', which by 1925 allowed the Russian economy to regain its pre-war industrial level. In 1928 Lenin's successor, Joseph Stalin, introduced a Five Year Plan of industrialization, and the following year embarked on the forced collectivization of agriculture, which transformed small, individual peasant holdings into huge state collective farms. The results of the policy proved disastrous, however. It was implemented without adequate machinery, and poorly organized. Crop yields fell, and a great famine in 1932-3 claimed millions of victims. This rural catastrophe caused some 40 million people to move into the cities, where their fresh labour was used mainly for construction, making the industrial growth rates of the Soviet economy under the first and second Five Year Plans (1928-37) look both startling and unique amid the Great Depression that prevailed elsewhere.

This industrialization took place against a background of state-directed terror as Stalin consolidated the Communist dictatorship. The security forces (the NKVD) executed perhaps 12 million people, while a further 10 million suffered imprisonment in forced labour camps (see map 2). Russia survived the German invasion in 1941 (page 140), partly because over 1500 factories were moved to safety further east, but the setback remained undeniable. A further 20 million Soviet citizens died in the conflict and, although the USSR mobilized more fully than any other state in World War II, its industrial output in 1946 stood at only 70 per cent of the 1940 level.

A poster of Stakhanov, a model mine-worker who exceeded his norm through exceptional efforts. He became a hero of the Soviet State and a propaganda tool in Communist efforts to increase worker participation.

1919–1939
European political problems

The collapse of the Central Powers in the autumn of 1918, and the subsequent peace treaties (page 133), brought about major frontier changes, the emergence of several new states, and the enlargement of others on the winning side (see map 1). The dismemberment of the Austro-Hungarian empire, the disarmament and the imposition of reparation payments on Germany and her allies, and the effects of the Russian Revolution and civil war (page 134) completely altered the balance of political power in Europe. In terms of population and industrial strength, however, Germany, although weakened, still had no rival in central Europe. The only hope of those who stood behind the peace treaties was the maintenance of overwhelming collective military strength against any revival of German strength. France tried to restrain Germany by signing alliances with the new states of Poland and Czechoslovakia, but Britain proved reluctant to enter into new continental commitments, and the United States withdrew into isolationism. However, Germany's formal recognition of the post-war frontier settlements with France and Belgium by the Locarno treaties (1925) inaugurated a new spirit of cooperation and it was welcomed back into the community of nations. After 1928 many nations signed the 'Kellogg-Briand Pact', which outlawed aggressive war.

But indications of stability proved illusory. Many

PLEBISCITES AND TERRITORIAL DISPUTES

1 plebiscite Feb. 1920: divided between Denmark and Germany
2 occupied by France 1923–5
3 to Belgium 1919
4 to Belgium 1919
5 evacuated 1930, remilitarized, 1936

6 League of Nations Mandate by plebiscite to Germany 1935
7 to France 1919
8 divided between Germany and Poland by plebiscite Mar. 1921
9 Allied occupation 1920–3, annexed by Lithuania 1923, autonomous 1924,

to Germany 1939
10 to Germany July 1920
11 to Poland Dec. 1918
12 partitioned between Czech-oslovakia and Poland 1920
13 to Hungary 1921
14 to Austria 1920
15 occupied by Poland 1920,

annexed by Poland following elections 1922
16 to Greece from Bulgaria 1919
17 demilitarized 1924, remilitarized 1936
18 Greek-Bulgarian conflict, 1925

states, especially in eastern Europe, displayed alarming political instability; and all European participants emerged economically weakened from the World War. Italy – which had run up huge debts and lost 600,000 men in the war, but gained only 9000 square miles (14,400 km²) of new territory at the peace – soon became ungovernable, with civil war between left- and right-wing extremists prevailing in many cities until in 1922 the Fascist party, led by Benito Mussolini, took power. In other parts of Europe, the cost of the war and the defects of the peace settlements, coupled with the strains of economic readjustment and disastrous inflation, strengthened anti-parliamentary and revolutionary movements of both left and right. And with the onset of the Great Depression in 1929 (page 138), financial and economic chaos returned to the entire continent. Unemployment rose drastically, especially in Germany where after 1930 the anti-parliamentary movements of both right and left, the Nazis (National Socialists)

Adolf Hitler (1889-1945) is greeted by a crowd in the Sudetenland, shortly after its occupation by Germany in 1938. Born in a small Austrian town, Hitler fought in the German army in the First World War. In 1919 he joined a small radical nationalist party in Munich. During a two-year jail sentence for his part in an unsuccessful coup in Munich in 1923, he wrote his major work *Mein Kampf*. In it he called for revenge for Germany's defeat in 1918 by building a racially strong Germany and overturning the Versailles settlement. His message proved attractive to the conservative masses in the Depression after 1929 an in January 1933 he assumed the chancellorship.

and the Communists, increased their strength enormously until in 1933 the Nazi leader, Adolf Hitler, became Chancellor and proceeded to absorb or abolish all the other parties.

Hitler's victory, combined with the economic weakness of Britain and the political instability of France, irretrievably damaged the precarious balance of peace in Europe. The League of Nations, created in 1920 to regulate international disputes and protect member states from aggression, remained only as strong as its members. Its failure to prevent Italy's annexation of Ethiopia in 1935-6, and Germany's remilitarization of the Rhineland in 1936 encouraged further aggression (map 2 and inset). Hitler, who rapidly increased and modernized Germany's armed forces, annexed Austria and parts of Czechoslovakia in 1938, then Bohemia and Memel in spring 1939, while Italy invaded and occupied Albania (1939). Whether an early alliance between the western democracies and the Soviet Union would have halted the aggressors is a matter of dispute. However, fearing that he might be next in line, and already engaged in hostilities with Hitler's ally, Japan, in August 1939 Stalin signed a non-aggression pact with Germany. The collapse of the unstable system created after World War I was now unavoidable.

1 National conflicts and frontier disputes, 1919–36

- —— German empire, 1914
- —— Austro-Hungarian empire, 1914
- —— Russian empire, 1914
- —— post-settlement frontiers
- ▲ plebiscites held

- new states
- areas of dispute
- areas temporarily autonomous or independent
- areas under armed occupation
- areas under League of Nations High Commissioners

2 Axis expansion, 1935–9

- Germany, 1935
- —— frontiers, 1937

German annexations:
- Mar. 1938
- Oct. 1938
- Mar. 1939
- → Italian campaigns 1935–6

INTERNET LINKS

www.english.uiuc.edu/maps/
depression/overview.htm
The Depression and its
effects in the US

1929–1939
The Great Depression

The New York Stock Market crash in October 1929 reflected deep weaknesses in the world economy. Commodity prices world-wide had been falling since 1926, reducing the capacity of exporters such as Australia and Latin America to buy products from Europe and the United States. Within the latter, wages lagged behind profits, impairing the development of domestic markets and limiting the potential of new industries, such as automobiles, to replace old ones, such as textiles. International finance never recovered from the strains of World War I, which caused a dramatic increase in productive capacity, particularly outside Europe, without a corresponding increase in sustained demand. Fixed exchange rates and free convertibility gave way to a compromise – the Gold Exchange Standard – that lacked the stability necessary to rebuild world trade.

In the scramble for liquidity that followed the Great Crash, funds flowed back from Europe to America and Europe's fragile prosperity crumbled. In many industrial countries one-quarter of the labour force was thrown out of work. Prices and wages plummeted, industrial production fell to 53 per cent of its 1929 level in Germany and world trade sank to 35 per cent of its 1929 value (see map 1). Early attempts to solve the problem did more harm than good. In 1930 the United States imposed the highest tariff in its history; in 1932 Britain responded with the Ottawa agreements, a series of preferential tariffs for the Commonwealth. Britain also left the

Gold Standard in 1931, followed by other countries, dividing virtually the entire world into closed currency blocs which inhibited trade still further. Only Soviet Russia, largely isolated from the world economy, continued to increase its industrial production (page 134).

Economic nationalism fostered political nationalism, just as mass unemployment and the erosion of middle-class living standards fostered political extremism. In Japan, the fall of the Hamaguchi government in 1931 marked the end of constitutional democracy and the beginning of aggression in

1 The world economy, 1929–39

major currency blocs:
- gold bloc
- yen bloc
- dollar area
- sterling area
- areas of shifting allegiance due to German-American rivalry
- areas of loose currency bloc allegiance

production indices:
- 1929=100
- 1930
- 1932
- 1934
- 1936
- 1938

CANADA
NETHERLANDS
UK
SWEDEN
USSR
GERMANY
USA
BELGIUM
JAPAN
FRANCE
ITALY
BRAZIL
SOUTH AFRICA
AUSTRALIA
NEW ZEALAND

farm workers begin organizing, 1933
San Francisco general strike, May–July 1934

WASHINGTON
Seattle
Columbia
OREGON
IDAHO
NEVADA
CALIFORNIA
Los Angeles
ARIZONA
Phoenix
Salt

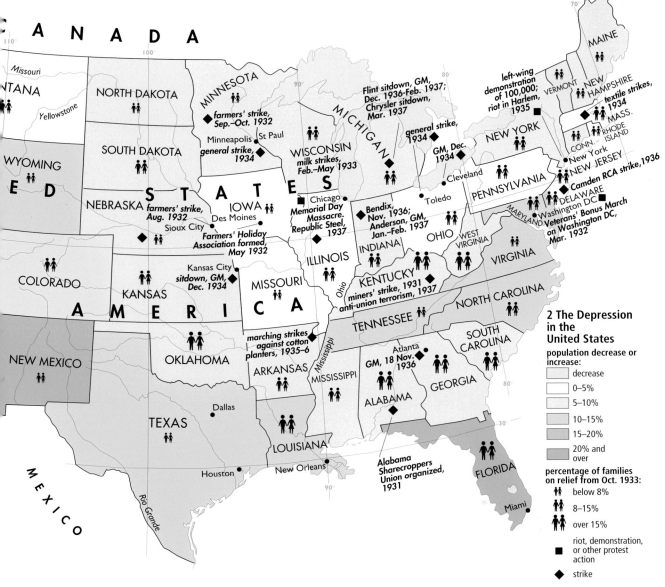

CANADA

MINNESOTA

NORTH DAKOTA

farmers' strike,
Sep.–Oct. 1932

Minneapolis ■ St Paul

SOUTH DAKOTA

Minneapolis
general strike,
1934

WISCONSIN
milk strikes,
Feb.–May 1933

MICHIGAN

Flint sitdown, GM,
Dec. 1936-Feb. 1937;
Chrysler sitdown,
Mar. 1937

left-wing
demonstration
of 100,000;
riot in Harlem,
1935

VERMONT

MAINE

NEW
HAMPSHIRE

textile strikes,
1934

MASS.

general strike,
1934

GM, Dec.
1934

NEW YORK

CONN.

RHODE
ISLAND

New York

NEW JERSEY

Camden RCA strike,1936

DELAWARE

Washington DC

Veterans' Bonus March
on Washington DC,
Mar. 1932

Missouri

NTANA

Yellowstone

WYOMING

E D

NEBRASKA   farmers' strike,
Aug. 1932

Des Moines

Sioux City

IOWA

Farmers' Holiday
Association formed,
May 1932

Chicago
Memorial Day
Massacre,
Republic Steel,
1937

Cleveland

Toledo

PENNSYLVANIA

MARYLAND

Bendix,
Nov. 1936;
Anderson, GM,
Jan.–Feb. 1937

OHIO

WEST
VIRGINIA

COLORADO

KANSAS

Kansas City
sitdown, GM,
Dec. 1934

MISSOURI

S T A T E S

ILLINOIS

INDIANA

Ohio

KENTUCKY

miners' strike, 1931
anti-union terrorism, 1937

VIRGINIA

A M E R I C A

TENNESSEE

NORTH CAROLINA

NEW MEXICO

OKLAHOMA

marching strikes
against cotton
planters, 1935–6

ARKANSAS

Mississippi

MISSISSIPPI

Atlanta

GM, 18 Nov.
1936

SOUTH
CAROLINA

GEORGIA

Dallas

TEXAS

LOUISIANA

ALABAMA

Houston

New Orleans

Alabama
Sharecroppers
Union organized,
1931

FLORIDA

Miami

Rio Grande

M E X I C O

2 The Depression in the United States

population decrease or increase:

- decrease
- 0–5%
- 5–10%
- 10–15%
- 15–20%
- 20% and over

percentage of families on relief from Oct. 1933:

- below 8%
- 8–15%
- over 15%

■ riot, demonstration, or other protest action

◆ strike

Manchuria (page 123). In Europe, Hitler rose to power in 1933 partly in response to the deflationary policies of his predecessors that raised unemployment from 3 million in 1930 to 6 million in 1932 (page 137). Even in Britain and the United States, fascist movements exercised considerable pressure. In the former, a right-wing National Government, formed in 1931, preserved democratic rule; in the latter, President Franklin Roosevelt, elected in 1932, implemented a 'New Deal' that laid the foundations for recovery. Nevertheless in 1934 some 20 billion days were lost in the US through industrial action and in 1938 over 10 million Americans remained out of work (map 2). Only World War II, and the boost it gave to production, pulled the United States out of the Depression.

By 1932 two out of every five Germans were out of work, and many of the rest were on short time. Here (*right*) the unemployed queue for newspapers carrying lists of jobs. Official efforts were made to limit the employment of women and to give preference to unemployed men.

3 World commodity production, 1926–38

stocks
production
prices

1926 28 30 32 34 36 38

*base inex 1929 = 100

4 World unemployment in the 1930s

%

1930 32 34 36 38

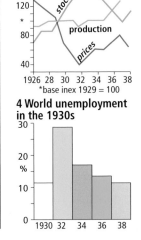

INTERNET LINKS

www.bbc.co.uk/history/
worldwars/wwtwo—
In-depth coverage of the
Second World War

1939-45

The Second World War: the West

Hitler's accession to power in 1933 added a new dimension to international politics. At first his expansionist designs had to await economic recovery, but his virtually unopposed annexation of Austria and Czechoslovakia (1938-9) and the Nazi-Soviet Pact of August 1939 (page 137) led him to expect similar acquiescence when, the following month, he invaded Poland. This time he miscalculated: the western democracies declared war (though this did nothing to aid the Poles).

Over the next two years, Germany rapidly secured first Denmark and Norway, then France and the Low Countries, and finally Yugoslavia and Greece, while Italy annexed Albania and invaded Egypt (map 1). Despite the Nazi-Soviet pact, however, Hitler's ultimate goal was the conquest of Russia: his operations in the West, like the Schlieffen Plan in 1914 (page 132),

merely aimed to eliminate Germany's western enemies before the main struggle began in the east. In this Hitler failed because Britain – though defeated on the continent and subjected to sustained aerial bombing – refused to concede defeat. Nevertheless, in June 1941 Hitler launched his forces on Russia and, thanks to the

Timeline

Sep. 1939 Germany invades Poland; Britain and France declare war

May 1940 Fall of France

Jun. 1941 Germany invades USSR

Sep. 1942–Feb. 1943 Battle of Stalingrad

Nov. 1942 Anglo-American landings in North Africa

Jun. 1943 Combined Allied Bomber Offensive launched

Jul. 1943 Battle of Kursk: USSR defeats Germany

Sep. 1943 Italy surrenders to Allies; occupied by Germans

6 Jun. 1944 D-Day: Allied invasion of France

2 May 1945 Fall of Berlin

8 May 1945 German surrender

1 The Axis advance, 1939–41

- Axis territory, 1 Sep. 1939
- Axis co-belligerents
- occupied by Axis after Sep. 1939
- Vichy France and territories
- Soviet annexed territory, 1939–41
- neutral powers
- frontiers, 1 Sep. 1939
- Axis advances, 1939
- Axis advances, 1940
- Axis advances, 1941
- Axis airborne landings
- Allied forces
- Soviet advances, 1939–40
- Allied retreat and withdrawal
- major cities severely damaged by bombing

combination of strategic surprise and tactical superiority, made rapid progress, taking over 3 million Russian prisoners-of-war. But the winter killed many Germans, who had far outrun their logistical support and lay stranded outside Moscow, Leningrad and Rostov. At precisely this point, on 7 December 1941, Japan attacked the United States (page 142), and Hitler – in an act of egregious folly – also declared war.

Although Germany launched another major thrust in Russia in 1942, reaching the Volga at Stalingrad, that too failed, with the loss of a major army, and its troops fell back in the face of superior Soviet forces, supplied both by the industrial complex built up beyond the Urals (page 134) and by the United States. Meanwhile, Anglo-American troops cleared Axis forces first from Africa and then from Sicily in 1942-3, leading Italy to make peace (though German forces there fought on); partisans gradually took over Yugoslavia; and from June 1944 allied armies liberated France and Belgium before moving into Germany. They met the Soviets on the Elbe in May 1945.

The costs of the war were appalling: 15 million military personnel and 35 million civilians perished, 20 million of them Soviet citizens. The Germans murdered prisoners of war

(Canadians, Americans and Britons in the West as well as Russians in the east); they murdered all captured partisans and members of the communist party; and they murdered all Jews they could find, many in mass shootings and at least 6 million in special extermination camps. However, they also lost heavily: the Anglo-American strategic bombing offensive reduced most of their major cities to rubble, and the Soviet troops carried out a systematic campaign of destruction as they advanced in 1944-5. By war's end, almost all Europe lay in ruins, yet already the differences between the victors had appeared which would darken the post-war years (page 164).

German troops fighting on the Eastern Front in June 1943. From early in 1943 the Soviet army experienced an almost uninterrupted run of successes against the Germans. In 1944 the Red Army pushed as far west as Warsaw, and in 1945 into Germany itself. Nearly 3 million German soldiers died during the war.

2 The defeat of Germany, 1942–5

- ☐ Grossdeutsches Reich, 1942
- ← Axis attacks
- ⇠ Axis withdrawals
- ← Allied attacks
- ⚑ major cities under heavy air attack
- ✳ major battle with date
- ✊ partisan/resistance movements
- ● commando raids
- V1 launching sites
- V2 launching sites
- — frontiers 1942

INTERNET LINKS

http://plasma.nationalgeo-
graphic.com/pearlharbor –
Footage, photos and
accounts from the attack on
Pearl Harbour

The Second World War: Asia and the Pacific

Japanese expansion in Asia after 1931 (page 123) stemmed from a desire for economic self-sufficiency, military security and a self-imposed leadership of East Asia. By 1940, however, with no end in sight to the Chinese war, Japan widened its ambitions to include the empires of the colonial powers – those of France and the Netherlands, recently defeated by her ally Germany, and those of Britain, at war with Germany (page 140) – as an alternative source of raw materials and markets that would free Japan from economic dependence on an increasingly unfriendly United States.

In September 1940 Japan occupied French Indo-China and the United States promptly placed an embargo on sending all iron and steel scrap to Japan. Next, following a sharp defeat in summer 1939 at Nomonhan (Kalkhin Gol), Japan concluded

a neutrality pact with Russia – which had been seen as the empire's principal potential enemy since the Russo-Japanese war (page 122) – and prepared to occupy the rest of the European colonies in South-East Asia. But first she felt it necessary to forestall a counterstrike by the United States: at dawn on 7 December 1941 her aircraft attacked and partially destroyed the US Pacific fleet at Pearl Harbor, Hawaii.

Japan hoped to fight the world's greatest industrialised power to a stalemate that would result in a negotiated peace recognizing Japanese hegemony in East Asia. Within six months, her forces had conquered the American outposts of Guam and the Philippines, and occupied the British and Dutch colonies throughout South-East Asia. Their forces also overran the Bismarck archipelago and much of New Guinea, and captured most of the island redoubts necessary to create a defensive perimeter in the mid-Pacific (map 1). In June 1942, however, at

On 2 September 1945
Japanese representatives finally
signed the act of surrender
(below) on board the battleship
USS Missouri in Tokyo Bay.

1 The Japanese advance, 1941–2

- - - Japanese empire, 1941
→ Japanese advance or strike
● Japanese base
■ Allied base
✕ battle

Midway Island, aggressive tactics shaped by superb intelligence allowed the aircraft carriers of the US Pacific fleet (which had not been in Pearl the previous December) to destroy a major Japanese carrier force. The United States, although following a 'Europe first' policy in the world war, still possessed abundant resources to advance on two distinct axes against Japan: in the south Pacific, an island-hopping strategy (by-passing the major centres of Japanese resistance and executed by amphibious forces) aimed for the Philippines; in the central Pacific, carrier-borne forces advanced towards the Marianas, from whose airbases bombing raids could be launched on Japan itself. At the same time, Allied forces moved from India into Burma; and in August 1945 Russia finally broke her neutrality pact and invaded Manchuria (map 2).

But Japan, though utterly exhausted, succumbed to none of these conventional threats: rather two atomic bombs, dropped on Hiroshima and Nagasaki in August 1945, precipitated the unconditional surrender of the millions of her troops still in arms.

The brief Japanese colonial adventure had caused almost as much destruction as Hitler's war in Europe; but it also unleashed forces of revolutionary nationalism that would shape events throughout Asia over the next five decades (page 162).

2 The Allied counter-offensive

- → Allied advance
- ┼ Allied air attack
- ■ Allied base
- ✶ atomic bomb target
- ● Japanese base
- ▣ Japanese base bypassed or neutralized
- ✕ battle

Japanese perimeters
- ⋯⋯ March 1944
- ⋅−⋅− October 1944
- −−− August 1945

143

INTERNET LINKS

http://nobelprize.org/nobel_
prizes/peace/laureates/1964/
king-bio.html
Biography of Martin
Luther King

1952 Eisenhower elected
president

1956 Federal Highways
Act

1960 Kennedy elected
president

1963 President Kennedy
assassinated; US build-up in
Vietnam begins

1968 Martin Luther King
assassinated

1973 US withdrawal from
Vietnam

1974 President Nixon
resigns after Watergate
scandal

1987 Stock Market crash

1994 NAFTA established

2001 Terrorist attack on
World Trade Centre

The United States since 1945

The requirements of wartime production solved the unemployment problem (page 138) of the United States at last, and the gigantic output achieved and allies demonstrated the economic potential which, when realized, would create an era of unprecedented prosperity for the United States. Gross National Product almost trebled in real terms between 1950 and 1990, while real income per head nearly doubled.

A number of factors brought about the economic surge: rapid population increase (from 132 million in 1940 to 281 million in 2000); technological advances coupled with the emergence of new consumer goods; the sudden spending of wartime savings; and the rearmament programmes connected with the Cold War and the Korean War (page 164 and 154). Affluence came to seem entirely normal and business confidence was seldom less than buoyant: on this basis of wealth and hope most American people began to transform their entire way of life. The expansion of the suburbs constituted perhaps the most obvious change. Easy credit, cheap fuel (both for homes and cars), mass production of housing and automobiles, and giant road-building programmes (40,000 miles of interstate highways by 1980), all helped encourage Americans in their millions to move off the farms and out of the cities into endless miles of suburbs. So although the population of the central cities grew from 48 million to 79 million between 1950 and 1990, that of their urban fringes also rose from 21 million also to 79 million (map 1).

By 1990, less than one-third of the US population lived in non-metropolitan areas, but the flight from the farms did not reduce productivity: on the contrary, the number of people fed by one farm worker doubled from 15 in 1950 to 30 in 1970. Thanks to mechanization,

improved seeds and fertilisers and government subsidies, the United States provided a significant proportion of the world's staple foods, such as wheat, maize and soya beans. The economy at large grew steadily, with the service sector (as in western Europe: page 166) expanding far more rapidly than manufacturing.

But beneath the prosperity lurked tensions. American capitalists tended to spend their profits rather than re-invest them, and industrial workers claimed higher wages and easier conditions of work without regard to the effect such claims (if successful) might have on prices and on the inter- national competitiveness of American industry. The Vietnam War (1965-73: page 162) created high inflation and bitter internal divisions. Explicit discrimination against Blacks and Asians exploded in urban riots during the 1960s and gave rise to a widespread movement for civil rights led by Dr Martin Luther King (map 2). Then came the policies of Presidents Ronald Reagan (1981-9) and George Bush (1989-93), who cut taxes by a third (releasing a flood of spending power on the markets), slashed welfare programmes (turning the inner cities into ghettoes), increased expenditure on armaments (so creating the biggest deficit in history), and failed to remedy the structural defects of American industry (so that the new purchasing power went overwhelmingly into imports, creating an equally unprecedented trade deficit).

Under the presidency of Bill Clinton (1993-2001), Americans rediscovered their national self-confidence. The United States played a decisive role in the conflicts in the Middle East and the Balkans and its economy boomed. Much of this prosperity depended on sales of computers and satellite communications, however, and when demand for these slackened in 2000, recession threatened. The terrorist attacks of September 2001, by shaking public confidence and precipitating a decline in consumer spending, turned the threat into reality.

On 11 September 2001, two planes hijacked by Islamic extremists were deliberately crashed into the World Trade Centre in New York, killing thousands of people. A third plane crashed into the Pentagon in Washington. The shock to a nation which had never suffered a peace-time atrocity on this scale was profound. Defence and the need to secure the nation against similar attacks immediately rose to the top of the political agenda. The blame for the assault was squarely laid on the Islamic al-Qaeda network led by Osama bin Laden and based in Taleban-ruled Afghanistan. An American-led bombing campaign which began in October led, by December, to the collapse of the Taleban regime and the destruction of much of al-Qaeda's infrastructure in Afghanistan.

144

3 Growth of consumer durables, 1950–2000

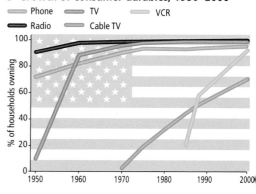

— Phone   — TV   — VCR
— Radio   — Cable TV

% of households owning

1950   1960   1970   1980   1990   2000

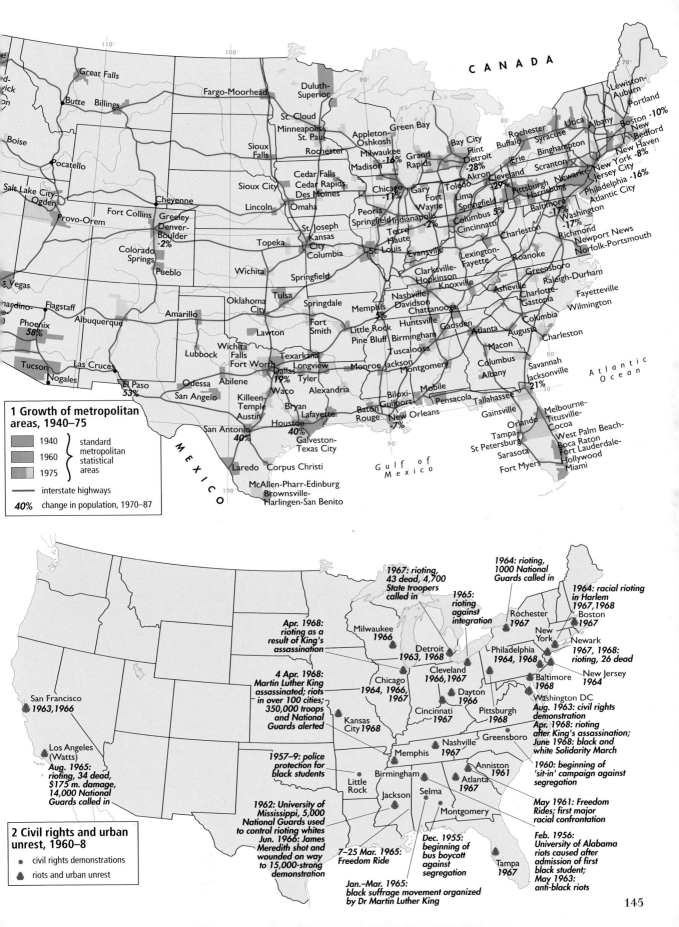

1 Growth of metropolitan areas, 1940–75

▨ 1940	standard metropolitan statistical areas
▨ 1960	
▨ 1975	

— interstate highways

40% change in population, 1970–87

Map labels (Map 1):

Great Falls, Butte, Billings, Boise, Pocatello, Salt Lake City–Ogden, Provo-Orem, Fort Collins, Cheyenne, Greeley, Denver-Boulder **-2%**, Colorado Springs, Pueblo, Las Vegas, Flagstaff, Albuquerque, Phoenix **58%**, Tucson, Nogales, Las Cruces, El Paso **53%**, San Antonio **40%**, Laredo, Corpus Christi, McAllen-Pharr-Edinburg, Brownsville–Harlingen–San Benito, Odessa, San Angelo, Abilene, Killeen-Temple, Austin, Bryan, Waco, Houston **40%**, Galveston–Texas City, Lafayette, Baton Rouge, New Orleans **7%**, Dallas **19%**, Fort Worth, Tyler, Longview, Texarkana, Monroe, Jackson, Alexandria, Lawton, Fort Smith, Oklahoma City, Tulsa, Springdale, Wichita, Springfield, Topeka, Kansas City, Columbia, St Joseph, Lincoln, Omaha, Sioux City, Sioux Falls, Fargo-Moorhead, Duluth-Superior, St. Cloud, Minneapolis–St. Paul, Rochester, Madison, Milwaukee **-16%**, Appleton-Oshkosh, Green Bay, Cedar Falls, Cedar Rapids, Des Moines, Chicago **-11%**, Gary, Peoria, Springfield, Indianapolis **-2%**, Terre Haute, St. Louis, Evansville, Clarksville-Hopkinson, Nashville-Davidson **5%**, Memphis **5%**, Chattanooga, Huntsville, Birmingham, Tuscaloosa, Montgomery, Mobile, Pensacola, Biloxi-Gulfport, Tallahassee, Gainsville, Pine Bluff, Little Rock, Fort Wayne, Detroit **-28%**, Bay City, Flint, Grand Rapids, Lima, Toledo, Akron, Cleveland **-29%**, Columbus **5%**, Cincinnati, Lexington-Fayette, Knoxville, Asheville, Charlotte-Gastonia, Columbia, Charleston, Augusta, Macon, Columbus, Albany, Savannah, Jacksonville **21%**, Orlando, Tampa, St Petersburg, Sarasota, Fort Myers, West Palm Beach–Boca Raton, Fort Lauderdale–Hollywood, Melbourne-Titusville-Cocoa, Miami, Erie, Scranton, Pittsburgh **-17%**, Harrisburg, Baltimore **-17%**, Washington **-17%**, Richmond, Newport News, Norfolk-Portsmouth, Roanoke, Greensboro, Raleigh-Durham, Fayetteville, Wilmington, Charleston, Buffalo, Rochester, Syracuse, Binghampton, Utica, Albany, Lewiston-Auburn, Portland, Boston **-10%**, New Bedford, New Haven **-8%**, New York **-8%**, Jersey City, Newark, Philadelphia **-16%**, Atlantic City

CANADA · MEXICO · Atlantic Ocean · Gulf of Mexico

2 Civil rights and urban unrest, 1960–8

● civil rights demonstrations

♣ riots and urban unrest

Map labels (Map 2):

San Francisco *1963, 1966*

Los Angeles (Watts) **Aug. 1965:** *rioting, 34 dead, $175 m. damage, 14,000 National Guards called in*

Apr. 1968: *rioting as a result of King's assassination* — Milwaukee *1966*

4 Apr. 1968: *Martin Luther King assassinated; riots in over 100 cities; 350,000 troops and National Guards alerted*

1967: *rioting, 43 dead, 4,700 State troopers called in* — Detroit *1963, 1968*

1965: *rioting against integration*

1964: *rioting, 1000 National Guards called in* — Rochester *1967*

1964: *racial rioting in Harlem 1967, 1968* — Boston *1967*

New York

Newark **1967, 1968:** *rioting, 26 dead*

New Jersey *1964*

Cleveland *1966, 1967*

Philadelphia *1964, 1968*

Baltimore *1968*

Chicago *1964, 1966, 1967*

Dayton *1966*

Cincinnati *1967*

Pittsburgh *1968*

Washington DC **Aug. 1963:** *civil rights demonstration* **Apr. 1968:** *rioting after King's assassination;* **June 1968:** *black and white Solidarity March*

Kansas City *1968*

1957–9: *police protection for black students*

Nashville *1967*

Memphis

Greensboro **1960:** *beginning of 'sit-in' campaign against segregation*

May 1961: *Freedom Rides; first major racial confrontation*

Anniston *1961*

Atlanta *1967*

Birmingham

Little Rock

1962: *University of Mississippi, 5,000 National Guards used to control rioting whites* **Jun. 1966:** *James Meredith shot and wounded on way to 15,000-strong demonstration*

Jackson

Selma

Montgomery

7–25 Mar. 1965: *Freedom Ride*

Dec. 1955: *beginning of bus boycott against segregation*

Jan.–Mar. 1965: *black suffrage movement organized by Dr Martin Luther King*

Feb. 1956: *University of Alabama riots caused after admission of first black student;* **May 1963:** *anti-black riots*

Tampa *1967*

INTERNET LINKS

www.fordham.edu/halsall/
mod/1945YALTA.html —
The conditions of the
Yalta conference

1945–1973
Europe

World War II left Europe politically disorganized and economically prostrate, a situation greatly exacerbated by large-scale population movements. The German collapse released millions of incarcerated prisoners-of-war and slave-workers, and a further 5 million Russian prisoners, refugees and servicemen were repatriated. Two more lasting shifts of population also occurred: some 12 million Germans abandoned (voluntarily or forcibly) their pre-war homes in the east, especially in lands annexed by the Nazis after 1938; and over 2 million Russians moved into the territories annexed by the Soviet Union during its westward advance (map 1).

The political frontiers of the new Europe were established at conferences between the victors (USA, USSR, Britain and France) held at Yalta and Potsdam in February and July 1945: the union of Germany and Austria decreed by Hitler in 1938 was dissolved and Germany lost territory to Poland and the Soviet Union; both countries were divided into occupation zones under four power control. In Austria the system worked relatively smoothly, and in 1955 the country achieved independence, albeit as a permanently neutralized state; but co-operation between the USSR and her allies in Germany broke down in 1948. Britain and the United States had already amalgamated their

1 Post-war population movements and territorial change

Territorial change, 1945–9

- cities divided into four occupation zones
- frontiers, 1949
- Germany, 1937
- Allied control zones of Germany and Austria
- annexed by Soviet Union 1940–5
- states which became Communist, 1945–8
- Yugoslav gains from Italy, 1945
- Federal Republic of Germany from 1949
- German Democratic Republic from 1949

Population movements: peoples resettled, evacuated or expelled (with numbers):

- Germans
- Finns driven from area bordering Russia
- Baltic peoples
- Russians
- Russians forcibly repatriated
- Poles
- Czechs
- peoples settled by International Refugee Organisation

zones in 1947 and, in conjunction with France, they now prepared for the formation of a West German government (the Federal Republic: BRD). After an attempt to prevent this by means of a blockade on Berlin, the Soviets prepared their zone for quasi-independence as the German Democratic Republic (DDR): the two states came into existence in 1949 (map 1).

They immediately took their place in the two political blocs into which Europe had become divided. The eastern republics had all come under communist rule by 1948 and economic growth, though continuous, remained slow thanks to Stalinist methods of production. In the western democracies, thanks largely to lavish American aid (the Marshall Plan from 1947; map 3), an economic miracle took place, with smooth and rapid growth year after year. The two blocs had their own military groups – NATO in the west (1949) and the Warsaw Pact in the east (1955) – and their own economic organizations – in the east Comecon (1949) and in the west the European Community (six members 1957; 9 by 1973) and the less successful European Free Trade Association (map 4). However the growth surge suffered a serious check in 1973 when the Arab-led Organization of Petroleum Exporting Countries (OPEC) increased the price of oil by 250 per cent.

On 23 June 1948, the Soviet Union set up a blockade of the Western sectors of Berlin. The Western states mounted an airlift *(left)* until May 1949, which brought in 2.3 million tons of supplies.

2 Berlin, 1945–90

- American sector
- British sector
- French sector
- Soviet sector
- city borders
- the Berlin Wall, 1961–89
- Autobahn
- international railway
- ⊕ airport
- ■ headquarters
- ▫ allied HQ
- → air corridor

4 European military and economic trading blocs, 1947–73

military partitions

- Nato 1949– (including United States and Canada)
- ★ Warsaw Pact 1948–91

economic blocs

- Benelux customs union, 1947
- joined EEC, 1973
- founder members of European Free Trade Association (EFTA), 1960
- ▲ subsequent EFTA members
- Council for Mutual Economic Assistance (COMECON) members, 1949
- subsequent COMECON members
- original European Economic Community (EEC) members, 1957

3 The Marshall Plan

- applied for and received Marshall aid, with amounts (in US$)
- applied for Marshall aid but withdrew application
- did not apply
- 14.0% Net Marshall aid as percentage of national income 1948–9

ICELAND $24 m 5%

NORWAY $236 m 5.8%

SWEDEN $118 m 0.3%

DENMARK $257 m 3.3%

IRELAND $116 m 7.8%

UNITED KINGDOM $2,825 m 2.4%

NETH. $979 m 10.8%

BELGIUM $546 m 0.6%

WEST GERMANY $1,297 m 2.9%

FRANCE $2,445 m 6.5%

AUSTRIA $560 m 14.0%

POLAND applied for Marshall aid but received nothing

PORTUGAL $50 m

SPAIN denied Marshall aid because of Franco's pro-Axis sympathies

ITALY $1,314 m 5.3%

GREECE $515 m

TURKEY $152 m

INTERNET LINKS

www.bbc.co.uk/history/
historic_figures/stalin_
joseph.shtml —
Joseph Stalin and the
Soviet Union

1945–91
The Soviet Union ALASKA

1945-7 Soviet control established in eastern Europe

1953 Death of Stalin

1956 Khruschev launches 'de-Stalinization' campaign

1964 Brezhnev succeeds Khruschev as Soviet leader

1985 Gorbachev begins programme of reforms

1989 Soviet influence in eastern Europe ended

1991 Soviet Union dissolved

Despite the extensive loss of life and property inflicted on Russia during World War II (page 141 above), remarkable economic recovery began after 1945. The output of heavy industry rose steadily and light industry, neglected under Stalin (who died in 1953), also progressed under his successors. The agricultural problems created by collectivization (page 134) remained – grain production only increased in the late 1950s, and even then the USSR continued to depend on imports – but vast reserves of oil, gas and mineral ores were discovered and exploited in Siberia. Russia's east European satellites were obliged to supply high-quality engineering products and expert personnel (as well as more basic items), which immensely assisted the USSR's economic progress. The development of the atom bomb (1949), of the first satellite (the sputnik: 1957), and of the first manned space flight (1961) all indicated the ability of Russian science to innovate.

After 1945 the Soviet military became a central feature of the state. One-fifth of the budget was devoted to military spending while between 1952 and 1976 101 military leaders became full members of the Central Committee of the Communist Party. The Soviet Union, along with the United States, had become a 'superpower', with a comparable degree of military strength. Although its gross national product fell well short of its rival's, the USSR overtook the USA in the production of iron ore, cement, steel and oil. Nevertheless the Soviet economy entered a period of crisis in the 1970s. Increasingly, the USSR found the arms-race more costly than did the USA (not least because the latter enjoyed far better credit and so could finance much of its expenditure

1 The USSR and the world, 1945–85

- USSR and client states, 1938
- annexed 1944–5
- territorial ambitions thwarted, 1945–6
- unsuccessful attempt to gain or maintain control by 1949
- control or influence secured by 1954
- Warsaw pact, 1955
- turned antagonistic to USSR from the early 1960s
- acknowledgement demanded from China that 19th-century Russian annexations were by unequal treaties
- ties from USSR loosened from mid 1960s
- brought into or kept in Soviet sphere in 1970s by military intervention
- other allies in 1985
- **c,v** pro-Soviet regime maintained or installed by Cuban or Vietnamese forces, with date
- Soviet influence aborted or sought unsuccessfully, 1960–85
- Soviet forces in action or deployed in confrontation, with date
- ⊕ foreign aircraft downed, with detail
- frontiers, 1985

through loans: page 144), and the position became critical when the USA threatened to extend its defence system into outer space (the 'Strategic Defense Initiative'). In 1985 a new Soviet leader, Mikhail Gorbachev, came to power with a programme of reform designed to achieve a 'revolution within the revolution'.

From 1985 to 1990 Gorbachev successfully improved relations with both China and the west in order to provide peaceful external conditions for reconstruction. He introduced *glasnost* (openness) in the media to encourage criticism of deficiencies in the economy and society; but he could not assure an

A May Day parade in Moscow, 1983 *(left)*. After the war the Communist Party became the dominant presence in Soviet society. Under Stalin, large numbers of workers and peasants entered the party. But by the 1980s it perpetuated an elite and gave few opportunities for social mobility

2 State tyranny under Stalin

Deportations

- deported minorities (with numbers and dates of deportation)
- direction of deportation

The Gulag

- prison camp
- prison zone
- maximum German advance, 1942
- Soviet Union, 1945

3 The Soviet economy, 1950–85					
YEAR	steel (million tons)	coal (million tons)	exports (million roubles)	cars (thousands)	televisions (thousands)
1950	27.3	261	1.6	65	12
1960	65.3	509	5.0	139	1726
1970	116.0	624	11.5	344	6682
1980	148.0	716	49.6	1327	7528
1985	155.0	726	72.7	1332	9371

adequate supply of food, and unrest in the cities grew. In desperation, in 1989 he withdrew Soviet forces from eastern Europe, hoping to reduce costs and thus improve the situation at home; but the resurgence of nationalism in many constituent republics began to threaten the entire union. The Soviet Union comprised many different ethnic, religious, linguistic and cultural groups (map 1). The majority of the population claimed Slavic origin, including the Russians (53 per cent) and Ukrainians (16 per cent) – by far the largest groups. But the minorities, especially those incorporated by force during the 19th century (page 114) and the Baltic states, violently annexed in 1945, eagerly anticipated the chance to assert their independence (page 168).

INTERNET LINKS

http://www-chaos.umd.
edu/history/prc3.html
The Chinese Cultural
Revolution

China since 1949

The establishment of the People's Republic of China in 1949 (page 130) marked a fundamental turning point in the modern history of China. After a century of severe internal conflict, usually provoked or exacerbated by external aggressors, China was now reunified and governed by leaders who possessed a decisive vision of the society they wished to create. Whatever the excesses and failures since 1949, not least the systematic repression of much of the population, that remains a fundamental achievement.

For a time, China closely followed the Soviet model of directed economic planning and achieved modest progress in developing heavy industries and raising agricultural production. In 1958, however, the communist leader Mao Zedong became impatient and sought to mobilize the revolutionary energies of China's vast population, launching the 'Great Leap Forward'. Rural China was divided into 26,000 communes, each required to abolish private property and meet huge targets in agricultural and industrial production. Some 600,000 backyard furnaces sprang up across the countryside. The experiment proved an unmitigated disaster: production declined sharply, 20-30 million people died from starvation or malnutrition, and the project was abandoned in 1961.

This failure strengthened the hands of moderate communists who preferred a more centrally-planned, Soviet-style development. Mao responded by forming an alliance with the People's Liberation Army (PLA) and with Chinese youth who, as 'Red Guards', faithfully supported his policies. In 1966 Mao launched the Great Proletarian Cultural Revolution. Red Guards were set loose to prevent the development of 'vested interests' and careerism in party and state by establishing permanent revolution. The guards killed thousands and forcibly resettled millions. Chaos followed throughout China, forcing Mao to call on the PLA to restore order (map 1).

Mao died in 1976 and his widow Jiang Qing with three allies (later denounced as the 'Gang of Four') tried to seize power; but by this time the PLA and the elite had had enough of revolution. The 'Gang of Four' were arrested, tried and expelled from the Communist Party.

In the late 1970s Deng Xiaoping became the dominant figure in China's politics. Following the visit of United States President Nixon in 1972, which began the process of re-opening China to the capitalist West, Deng launched a policy of economic liberalization. He created special economic zones in areas bordering the foreign colonies of Hong Kong and Macao and Taiwan, and in Shanghai, with inducements to encourage foreign investment. By 1992, $36 billion had been invested. Other reforms followed: peasants were permitted to own land and, by 1984, 98 per cent did so. The communes vanished and agricultural output increased by 49 per cent in five years. Private businesses, also now permitted, grew in number from 100,000 in 1978 to 17 million in 1985 (map 2).

Economic reforms led to demands for political liberalization. In December 1986, students demonstrated for democracy in 15 cities. Deng responded

Student demonstrators in
Beijing in 1989 *(left)*. Thousands
of students occupied Tiananmen
square for six weeks in May and
June to demonstrate for greater
democracy. On 3-4 June the
army violently ejected the
students. The death toll was later
estimated at 400-800.

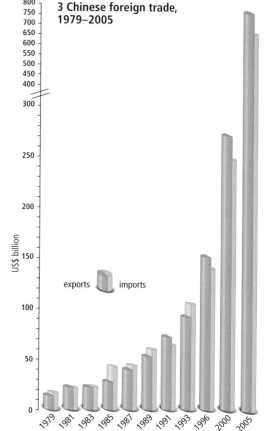

**3 Chinese foreign trade,
1979–2005**

US$ billion

exports   imports

1 The Cultural Revolution in China, 1966–76

★ fighting involving Red Guards and Army or workers, 1966–9

main areas of activity of Red Guards

movement of urban intellectuals to rural areas

with repression: he arrested 'troublemakers' and sacked Hu Yaobang, the liberal secretary-general of the Chinese Communist Party. When Hu died in April 1989, students used the occasion to demand democracy, gathering in Beijing's Tiananmen Square, at times numbering over a million, until in June Deng sent in the PLA and the movement was ruthlessly crushed.

After the Tiananmen massacre China swiftly reassured the world that it was a stable economic partner, and most of the world obligingly ignored human rights concerns in return for a share of China's economic boom. Foreign investment soared, and so did China's foreign trade (table 3). Further economic liberalization now took place as most of China operated a 'socialist market economy'. Growth rates, which averaged 10 per cent or more for the 1980s and 1990s, were only slightly affected by the economic turmoil which hit most of the rest of east Asia in 1997–8. In 1997, Britain returned its colony of Hong Kong, which retained a degree of self-government, and two years later Portugal surrendered Macao. With growing freedom in many areas of life, the issue of democracy remained the unfinished business of China's 20th-century achievement.

2 The Chinese economy, 1983–97

💰672 foreign investment, 1983-97, by province, in million US$

▢ Special Economic Zone (SEZ), 1984

GDP per capita <80% of national average, 1997

GDP per capita 80-120% of national average, 1997

GDP per capita >120% of national average, 1997

● open coastal city

● inland city with expanded authority

━ "golden triangle" development areas

▲ major oilfields

■ major coalfields

── frontiers, 1992

SINCE 1945
Japan and Korea

In the wake of the Second World War, United States support for Japan, South Korea and Taiwan, perceived after 1948 as its first line of defence in east Asia, transformed their economies.

Japan, like Germany (page 146), ended the war with its economy in ruins: most towns and industrial plants destroyed; nearly all foreign assets lost; domestic capital run down. Moreover, the victors demanded reparations and occupied the country following its surrender. The Far East Commission, which contained representatives of all the countries that had fought Japan but remained an American enterprise, sought to demilitarize Japan and create a peaceful, democratic state. It reformed the education system (removing from the syllabus all material that

had encouraged military and authoritarian values); abolished the divinity of the emperor and made the Diet (parliament) the highest political authority; established an independent judiciary and free labour unions; introduced a programme of land reform; and sought (with little success) to break up the great concentrations of corporate power. With the advance of the Chinese communists after 1948, however, the United States increasingly came to see Japan not only as the key bulwark of Western power in east Asia but also as one whose effectiveness depended on the reconstruction of its economic power. The occupation formally ended in 1951.

Japan's defeat also ended its harsh colonial rule of Korea (since 1910) and led to the peninsula's occu-

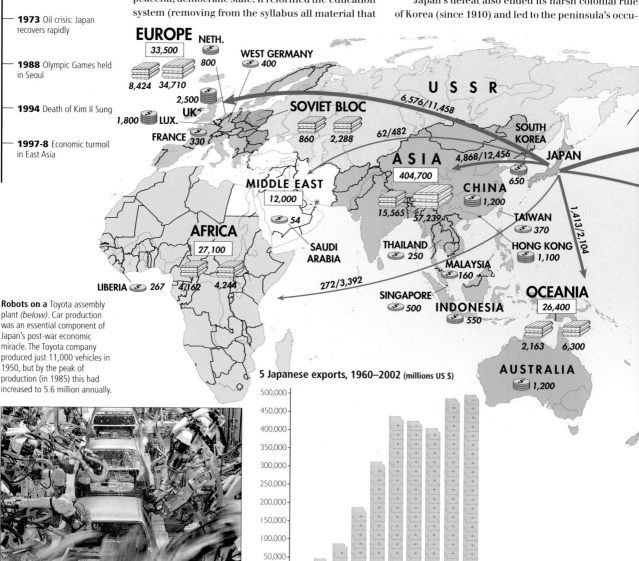

Robots on a Toyota assembly plant (below). Car production was an essential component of Japan's post-war economic miracle. The Toyota company produced just 11,000 vehicles in 1950, but by the peak of production (in 1985) this had increased to 5.6 million annually.

5 Japanese exports, 1960–2002 (millions US $)

pation by the victors: Japanese forces north of the 38th parallel surrendered to Soviet Russia, those in the south to the United States. The Soviets supported the establishment of a communist state in the north under Kim Il-Sung, a guerrilla leader who had spent considerable time in the Soviet Union; and the Americans retaliated by sponsoring a representative regime under Syngman Rhee, a strong anti-communist. Both new governments entertained strong ambitions to unite the country under their own rule, and in June 1950 the North attacked, pushing the South Korean and remaining United States troops back toward Pusan (map 1). The US forces counterattacked in September with a daring amphibious landing at Inchon, leading to a further offensive that promised to unify Korea. In November, however, the Chinese committed substantial forces and regained most of the north. A stalemate ensued until an armistice was signed in 1953.

The Korean War boosted the Japanese economy and initiated a period of exceptionally high economic growth – well over 10 per cent a year throughout the 1960s, and over 4 per cent annually between 1974 and 1985, faster than that of any other OECD country. A key feature of Japan's growth was its flexibility in pursuing economic objectives: in the 1950s it emphasized heavy industry, ship-building and iron and steel; in the 1960s it moved into high-technology consumer manufactures largely for export; from the 1970s it concentrated on technological innovation and higher value-added products while transferring the production of lower value-added goods overseas. Industrial production and exports soared (tables 3 and 5) and massive Japanese investment took place in Asia, Europe and North America. Yet by 2002, Japan, for so long boasting the world's strongest economy and the largest per capita GNP, had endured a decade of slow growth or recession, rising unemployment and deflation.

Korea epitomized the relative success of the communist and capitalist projects. Until 1970 North Korea had the higher GNP per capita, but by the 1990s GNP was declining at 5 per cent and the state, still communist, came close to economic and humanitarian disaster. From the mid-1960s South Korea embarked on rapid industrialization and by the 1990s boasted the world's 13th largest economy with great strengths in car manufacture, shipbuilding and semi-conductors (table 4). Its regime showed little tolerance of political dissent, however, and crushed open protest.

Although the economic turmoil that hit the east Asian economies in 1997 exposed serious structural weaknesses, particularly in the inefficient and debt-laden finance and banking sectors, the vast underlying strength of the region suggests that the Pacific Rim will remain a lynchpin of the global economic system.

3 Japanese industrial production

index of industrial production (1945=100)

2684.1 — 1980
1736.4 — 1970
487.8 — 1960
112.2 — 1950

2 Japanese investment overseas, 1970–98

15,565 57,239 — trade with region, 1970–4 and 1985–9 (billion Yen)

6,576/3,392 — value of Japanese direct foreign investment in region, 1987/1999 (US$ million)

1,200 — value of Japanese direct foreign investment in country, 1987 (US$ million)

404,700 — workers in Japanese-affiliated companies, 1980

CANADA 650

NORTH AMERICA 83,900

USA 14,700

17,170 75,190

15,357/21,873

4,814/6,479

BAHAMAS 730

CAYMAN ISLANDS 1,200

PANAMA 2,300

LATIN AMERICA 128,100

BRAZIL 230

2,024 2,372

4 The two Koreas; per capita GNP growth, 1945–99

thousand US$

$13,300 (1999)

South Korea
North Korea

1945 1950 1960 1970 1980 1990 1999

1 The Korean War

CHINA

UN maximum advance 2 Nov. 1950 before start of Chinese counter-attack

Chosan

Antung

Chinese intervention Oct. 1950

Iwon

Unsan

Hungnam

US airborne landings 20 Oct. 1950

landing of US 7 Division, 26 Oct. 1950

NORTH KOREA

Wonsan

Pyongyang

armistice line 27 July 1953

38th Parallel

Panmunjom

Seoul

Inchon

Chinese and North Korean maximum advance 25 Jan. 1951

Wonju

landing of US X Corps 15 Sep. 1950

Taejon

SOUTH KOREA

Pohang

North Korean maximum advance 15 Sep. 1950

Taegu

Pusan

Mokpo

INTERNET LINKS

www.bbc.co.uk/history/
historic_figures/gandhi_
mohandas.shtml
Biography of
Mohandas Gandhi

AFTER 1947
Retreat from empire

The Western empires created in the 19th century (page 118) remained intact in 1939, though most German and Ottoman possessions had passed to Britain, France and Japan as League of Nations mandates. The United States planned to grant independence to the Philippines, acquired in 1898, and did so immediately after World War II; but none of the seven remaining European colonial powers – Britain, France, Spain, Portugal, Belgium, Italy and the Netherlands – surrendered their empires voluntarily. Only Britain even conceived of independence as the ultimate goal, albeit with continued membership of the Commonwealth, a goal already attained in 1939 by Canada, South Africa, Australia and New Zealand. The continental colonial powers thought more in terms of evolution towards a common citizenship, with their colonies as overseas parts of the metropolitan territory. Such plans were complicated, however, by the resistance of European settlers, with consequent inter-racial tensions, and by clashes between the European ideal of evolution along Western lines (in education and economic development) and the powerful Hindu, Muslim, Buddhist and Confucian cultures of the 'subject peoples'.

1942 Japan overruns Europe's Far Eastern colonies

1947 India partitioned: India and Pakistan independent

1954 Communist Vietnamese defeat French at Dien Bien Phu: start of Algerian War

1957 Suez crisis; abortive French and English invasion of Egypt

1957-68 Independence for British African colonies

1960 Independence for all French sub-Saharan colonies and Belgian Congo

1962 France withdraws from Algeria

1965 Rhodesian white settlers make Unilateral Declaration of Independence resulting in guerrilla war

1975 Portuguese rule in Africa ends

1990 Namibia gains independence from South Africa

1997 Hong Kong returned to China

1999 Macao returned to China

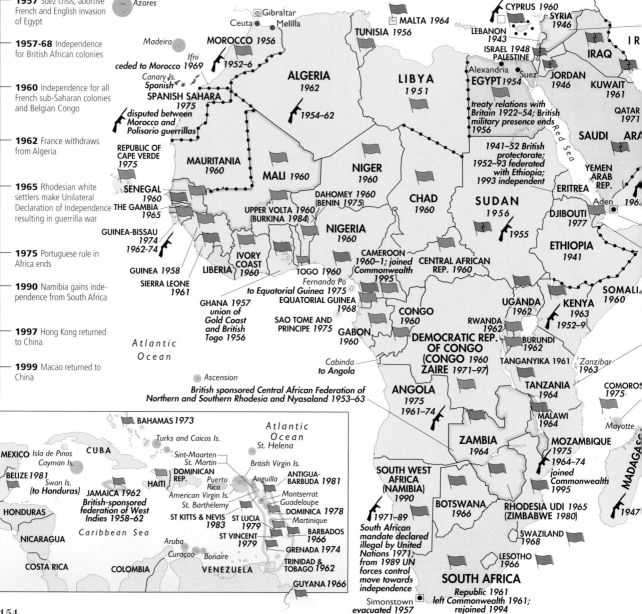

France fought stubbornly to maintain its control of Indochina (page 162), and the Netherlands struggled to contain the nationalists of Java, who had proclaimed the Indonesian Republic in 1945. Neither succeeded. Continual unrest forced Britain to grant independence to India and Pakistan (1947), followed in 1948 by Burma and Ceylon (page 162). Nevertheless Britain fought (and won) a long war against communist insurgents in Malaya, and resisted Indonesian attempts to annex Sarawak and Brunei. Only after the evacuation of Aden in 1967 did Britain abandon its presence east of Suez – save only for Hong Kong, retained until 1997, its economic success being of some benefit to Communist China.

In Africa resistance to independence was strongest in colonies with substantial white settler populations. In Algeria, with 1 million whites, a savage war of liberation occurred between 1954 and 1962; but conflict proved bitter, too, in Kenya and Rhodesia. However by 1974 all had achieved independence (page 160). By then, although Britain showed in the Falklands War (1982) its determination to fight on behalf of the few outposts still directly ruled from London, the formal structures of European imperialism had been dismantled and largely replaced by different forms of association such as the British Commonwealth or the French Community.

Mohandas Gandhi *(right)* became leader of the Indian nationalist movement in 1918, preaching non-violence *(satyragha)*. In 1922 he was imprisoned by the British authorities, but was released in 1924 on becoming president of the Indian National congress. He led a campaign to boycott British cotton imports, and in 1930 encouraged resistance to a proposed salt tax. Although he withdrew from formal politics in 1933 he remained the guiding influence of the nationalist movement, and was a key figure in the eventual negotiations for Indian independence and partition in 1946-8.

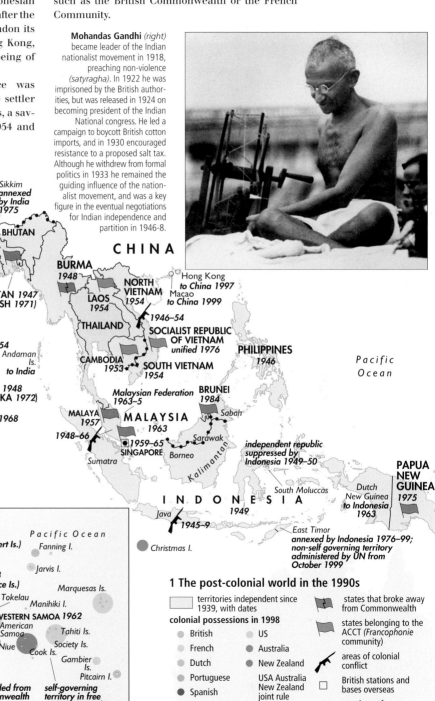

1 The post-colonial world in the 1990s

- territories independent since 1939, with dates

colonial possessions in 1998

- British
- French
- Dutch
- Portuguese
- Spanish
- US
- Australia
- New Zealand
- USA Australia New Zealand joint rule

- states within British Commonwealth
- states that broke away from Commonwealth
- states belonging to the ACCT (*Francophonie* community)
- areas of colonial conflict
- British stations and bases overseas
- members of abortive federations
- border conflict

www.ghazi.de/history.html
INTERNET LINKS

www.ghazi.de/history.html —
The Lebanese civil war

SINCE 1945
The Middle East

- **1948** Establishment of State of Israel: first Arab-Israeli war

- **1956** Suez crisis; second Arab-Israeli war

- **1967** Third Arab-Israeli war (the Six-Day War)

- **1973** Fourth Arab-Israeli war (Yom Kippur War)

- **1975-92** Lebanese civil war

- **1978** Egyptian-Israeli peace talks (Camp David)

- **1980-88** Iran-Iraq War

- **1982** Israel invades Lebanon: withdraws from Sinai

- **1988** PLO recognises State of Israel

- **1990-1** Iraq invades Kuwait: defeated by UN coalition

- **1993** Oslo Accords between PLO and Israel

- **1994/5** Limited Palestinian autonomy in Gaza strip and West Bank

- **1997** Khatami becomes Iranian president

- **2000** Israel withdraws from southern Lebanon

- **2003** US-led forces invade Iraq; Saddam Hussein captured

- **2004** Death of Yasser Arafat

- **2005** Elections in Iraq; civil war persists

- **2006** Second Israel-Lebanon war; Palestinians elect Hamas government

The Middle East has occupied world attention more consistently than any other region since 1945: Israel and its neighbours have fought four full-scale wars; Israel has invaded Lebanon twice; three Gulf wars have taken place; military coups have reinforced internal repression; refugees have fled; Western troops have intervened repeatedly.

American support for the state of Israel (founded in 1948), sponsorship of the Baghdad Pact (1955), and intervention in Lebanon (1958) alarmed the USSR and so it offered assistance to Syria, Egypt and (after 1958) Iraq. The Soviets also championed the Arab states during the Arab-Israeli war of 1967 but Israel still took and held the West Bank of the Jordan, Sinai and the Golan Heights (map 1). In 1973 an Egyptian and Syrian attack on Israel met with limited military success and opened the

1 Israel and Palestine, 1948–94

- Israel after Arab invasion and War of Independence, 1948
- Israeli conquests, 1967
- Land that would be annexed
- Egyptian re-conquests, and Israeli conquests, 1973

population movements:
- Jewish immigration, 1948–64
- Arab refugees, 1948 (total 750,000)
- Arab refugees, 1967 (total 250,000)

Sinai, the Israeli withdrawal:
- Egyptian frontline under second Sinai agreement, 1 Sept 1975
- Israeli settlements given up in 1982
- Israeli military and civil airports given up in 1982
- Israeli oil wells given up in 1982

way for negotiations. Egypt and Israel concluded the Camp David Accords (1978) which resulted in the return of Sinai in 1982; but the Israelis refused to return the other 'occupied territories' and instead installed many Jewish settlements. Moreover in 1982, to counter Palestinian guerrilla activity, they invaded and held south Lebanon until 2000. Meanwhile, in the wake of prolonged resistance to Israeli rule in the West Bank and Gaza, which excited much outside sympathy, after extended peace talks brokered by US (the 'Oslo accords') Israel allowed limited Palestinian self-rule from 1994-5. Although by 2002 relations with the Palestinian leadership under Yasser Arafat had collapsed completely, the death of Arafat in 2004 offered a chance to renew negotiations between Israel and the Palestinian Authority (map 1).

As open conflict between Israel and her neighbours abated, it began around the Persian Gulf. The replacement of the Shah of Iran by Ayatollah Khomeini in 1979 seemed to President Saddam Hussein of Iraq to offer the chance of territorial gain. He attacked in 1980. However, eight years of war achieved little and in 1990, in an attempt to gain resources to liquidate his war debts, Saddam invaded and annexed another neighbour, Kuwait. The United Nations, led by the US, pressured Saddam to withdraw and, when he refused, in 1991 used armed force to expel him. The invasion stopped at the Iraqi frontier and Saddam survived in power until 2003, although the victors' economic sanctions, military 'no-fly zones' and

'weapons inspectors' prevented him from rearming. Nevertheless, in 2003 the US alleged that Iraq possessed 'weapons of mass destruction' and constituted an immediate threat to world peace: it launched a second invasion that travelled straight to Baghdad (map 2). Inadequate planning for exploiting victory led to chaos that allowed Saddam's supporters (mostly from the Sunni minority) and Muslim opponents of the West from around the world to organize resistance to the US-led occupation. Although democratic elections took place in 2004, they produced no clear winner and religious divisions among Iraq's Muslims continued to threaten the country's stability.

Islamic fundamentalism destabilized many other parts of the Muslim world (map 3). After 1979 it became a badge of hostility towards the West in Iran and towards Russia in Afghanistan, and elsewhere toward the regime in power – unless, as in Iran, that regime was an Islamic theocracy. In the 1990s Islamic fundamentalism stimulated terrorist violence from Algeria to Indonesia. Although the collapse of the Soviet Union (page 168) ended superpower rivalry in the area, the Western powers remained engaged in order to safeguard the unequalled oil supplies of the area on which their economies depended. Oil and the enormous concentrations of conventional weapons – together with attempts to develop chemical, biological and nuclear weapons – in so many antagonistic states continued to keep the Middle East at the centre of world attention.

3 Islamic fundamentalism in the Middle East, since 1979

- countries with radical Islamic governments
- Islamic parties represented in parliament
- ✳ civil war
- 🖐 violent anti-government Islamic campaigns
- ▲ countries with significant Shia populations
- ✴ Islamic terrorist attacks

TURKEY

2002: Justice and Development (Islamist party) wins absolute majority in general election

SYRIA
Hama
Beirut
LEBANON ▲
Damascus
ISRAEL
Amman
Jerusalem 🖐
JORDAN

Feb. 1982: rioting by Islamic militants in Hama brutally supressed

1983: foundation of Hezbollah, radical Islamic movement; becomes principal proxy for Iranian-inspired terrorism in Lebanon

continuing anti-Israeli campaign of suicide bombings

Teheran ● ▲
I R A N

1979: following overthrow of shah, hardline Islamic fundamentalist government, headed by Ayatollah Khomeini, established
late 1980s: Iranian backing for the formation of HAMAS and Islamic Jihad, militant Palestinian Islamic groupings

AFGHAN. ▲

IRAQ
Baghdad ●
● An Najaf

Tripoli

LIBYA

'3: Qadhafi publishes Third Universal ...eory, declaring Islam the true path 1977 Libyan "cultural revolution" introduces Islamic socialism

Cairo ●

EGYPT

✴🖐 *original home of Muslim Brotherhood (founded 1920s), the region's most significant and widespread Islamic organization*
2000: members of Muslim Brotherhood elected to parliament standing as independents

Medina ●

BAHRAIN

autumn 1994: civil disturbances among Shia majority, Iranian instigation alleged

▲ **KUWAIT**

2001: radical Islamic Taliban regime overthrown following US-led campaign

PAK.

Persian Gulf

🖐 **QATAR**
Doha ●
Abu Dhabi ●
▲ **UAE**
Muscat ●

Riyadh ●

SAUDI ARABIA

1992: emergence of incipient Islamic political opposition
1996: Hizballah attack on US military complex at Khobar Towers

Mecca ●

Red Sea

▲

OMAN

SUDAN

✴ *June 1989: military coup brings National Islamic Front (NIF) to power, launches violent attempt to Islamicize rebel south Sudan*

Khartoum ●

ERITREA

San'a ●

YEMEN ✴ ▲

Arabian Sea

ETHIOPIA

Aden ●

1998: Islamic army of Aden kidnaps foreign tourists
2000: Islamist attack on USS Cole

Popular protest played a key role in the fall of the shah of Iran in 1979 and the rise to power of Ayatollah Khomeini. The picture was taken in 1987 on the eighth anniversary of the revolution. According to Khomeini, ultimate governmental authority should be vested in a supreme Islamic jurist. A rightly guided Iran should spread the message of true Islam to the rest of the Islamic world. But true Islam had first to be consolidated within Iran: an estimated 10,000 people had been executed by 1985 and 40,000 imprisoned.

T U R K E Y

secured, 11 Apr.
Mosul ☠
● Arbil

26 Mar. US 173rd Airborne Brigade

secured, 9 Apr.

36° N
(Northern no-fly zone, pre-war)

Kirkuk ●
☠ Sulaymaniyah
● Halabja

31 Mar: destroyed by US and Kurdish forces

Coalition special forces active before 19 Mar. and throughout conflict

Turkey blocks entry of US ground forces, Feb. 2003

S Y R I A

Tikrit ●
Samarra ●

I R A N

secured, 16 Apr.

Beirut ●

LEBANON

Damascus ●

Euphrates

2002–3: Increased US diplomatic pressure; agrees to close terrorist organization offices, 2003

Ar Ramadi ●

Karbala bypassed, 1 Apr.

Baghdad ●

19 Mar: 1st air attack
3 Apr: city reached by ground forces
9 Apr: city falls

ISRAEL

B-52 bombers from UK

Jerusalem ●
Amman ●

Karbala ●
Najaf ✳

33° N
(Southern no-fly zone)

Kut ●

B-52, B-1, B-2 bombers from Diego Garcia, Indian Ocean

J O R D A N

Special forces seize airfield; used by Coalition 26 Mar.

Coalition special forces active before 19 Mar. and throughout conflict

I R A Q

Samawah ●

Nasiriyah ●

secured, 7 Apr.

Basra ●

slowed by sandstorm (25–27 Mar.)

Umm Qasr ●

Coalition amphibious landings

Kuwait ●

KUWAIT

S A U D I A R A B I A

US 3rd Infantry Div. spearhead bypasses cities; 101st Air Assault later enters

US and UK combat aircraft from Kuwait and UAE

US Patriot anti-missile defences

---

2 The Invasion of Iraq, 2003

advances

- → US ground force
- → UK ground force
- → Kurdish and Coalition special forces
- ⚓ US Navy carriers, Tomahawk-launching ships and submarines, based in the Mediterranean, Gulf, and Red Sea
- ✳ Coalition airstrikes
- ☠ Ansar-al-Islam and terrorist camps

157

INTERNET LINKS

www.hartford-hwp.com/
archives/43b/index-ab.html
Various online resources on
the Cuban revolution

1950-4 Attempted
reforms in Guatemala

1955 Overthrow of Perón
regime in Argentina

1959 Cuban revolution

1973 Overthrow of
Allende regime in Chile

1982 The Falklands War

1982-9 Return to civilian
rule in Bolivia (1982),
Argentina (1983), Uruguay
(1985), Chile (1989)

Latin America since 1930

The Great Depression (page 138) struck Latin America a shattering blow, cutting off supplies of foreign capital and lowering the price of its primary products in the world markets. Chile's exports fell by over 80 per cent between 1929 and 1933; those of Bolivia and Peru by 75 per cent. Only oil-exporting Venezuela more or less weathered the storm. The economic collapse led to widespread disillusion with middle-class liberal or radical parties: in 1930 and 1931, 11 of the 20 republics south of the Rio Grande experienced revolutionary changes in government. Mexico, where Lázaro Cárdenas (1934-40) revived the land distribution policies of 1911 (page 112), experienced a shift to the left; but elsewhere the swing was mainly to the right. The new dictators tended to be populists, appealing directly to the masses and cooperating with organised labour. They also introduced programmes of industrialization – following Soviet or, more often, Fascist models – to reduce dependence on overseas markets and hasten economic development.

Manufacturing industry received a further boost during World War II, which cut off imported consumer goods and stimulated the industrial sector. But industrialization made Latin America dependent upon imported capital goods, raw materials, technology and finance – especially from the United States – creating enormous foreign debts (map 2). Multinational corporations exploited the cheap labour of Latin America without stimulating economic development. Social tensions arose from income concentration, unemployment, lack of opportunities, and from the intrusion of foreign interests. Social revolutions were attempted but frustrated in Guatemala, Bolivia and Chile (map 1), underlining the obstacles to change in economies too narrowly based to sustain welfare programmes, where local elites were prepared to collaborate with the United States.

Cuba after 1959 attempted to achieve social change, economic growth and freedom from the United States simultaneously; but although its revolution led to greater social equality and some improvement in the lot of rural workers, it also brought a repressive regime and dependence on the Soviet Union. Moreover its attempts to spread revolution in Central and South America all failed.

In the face of revolutionary change, with some support from the upper and middle classes, the military seized power in many areas and combined political repression with economic liberalization. But by the late 1980s their policies too had largely failed and, in

A government soldier in Peru (below), guards against attacks by the Shining Path guerrillas. The Shining Path (Sendero Luminoso) was founded in 1980 by Abimael Guzmán, a philosophy professor. It adopted a mixture of Maoist political and military tactics and gained control of large areas of the central Andean highlands in the early 1990s. After Guzmán's capture in 1992, the movement fragmented and the level of its attacks diminished sharply.

2 Economic development

direct US investment in Latin America
(figures in millions of US dollars)

1929 1943 1960 1979 1995

chief exports of Latin America
1955–2005

coffee chief exports 1955

coffee chief exports 2005

▲ represents over 50 per cent of
total exports

● represents over 25 per cent of
total exports

5000%
1989 hyperinflation peaks
(annualized percentage rates)

▲ coffee
oil
crude petroleum
coffee

● manufactured products
cocaine

▲ bananas
coffee
● crude petroleum
bananas

● cotton
sugar
meat/fish meal
natural gas
zinc

▲ tin
tungsten
● natural gas
zinc

▲ copper
nitrates
● copper
food stuffs
forestry

coffee ▲
cocoa
manufactured
products
coffee ▲

cotton
meat
raw cotton ●
soya beans ●

wool ▲
meat
meat
wool

wheat ●
meat
cereals and soya
petroleum

● oil
iron ore
● crude petroleum
aluminium

VENEZUELA
COLOMBIA
GUYANA
FRENCH GUIANA
SURINAM
ECUADOR
B R A Z I L
PERU
2500%
1989
BOLIVIA
11,750%
1985
PARAGUAY
CHILE
URUGUAY
ARGENTINA
5000%
1989

2500%
1983

232 373 2569 2206 3372 23,590

7514

194 233 953

5510

423 328 738 291

7962

2162

332 380 472

UNITED STATES OF AMERICA
US intervention
Dominican Republic 1916–24 1965–6
Grenada 1983
Cuba 1921–23, 1933, 1961
Haiti 1915–34, 1944, 1994
Panama 1903–18, 1989
Nicaragua 1912–33
Guatemala 1954
Mexico 1914

the face of economic recession and popular protest, their power gradually weakened. Instead, democratic government resumed in several states of the subcontinent. In 1992 Mexico signed a free trade agreement (NAFTA) with Canada and the United States, creating the world's largest integrated trading bloc. Yet serious economic crises in Mexico in 1994–5 and in Argentina in 2001–2 highlighted the continued vulnerability of even the largest Latin American economies.

MEXICO 5,000
Mexico City
Puebla • Veracruz

☐ Mexican revolution 1910–40
◇ Zapatista revolt, 1994

Havana
CUBA 125,000 M

1,400 **DOMINICAN REP.**

PUERTO RICO (USA)

☐ Cuban revolution 1959

BELIZE
750 M
GUAT.
Guatemala City
HONDURAS 300
Tegucigalpa
EL SALVADOR
NICARAGUA 100 M
Managua
125 M
San José
COSTA RICA 1,000 M
Cartagena

Cuban-inspired guerrilla movements 1959–68
HAITI n/a M
Caribbean Sea
GRENADA
Port of Spain
Caracas
VENEZUELA 8,000 M
Georgetown

☐ Guatemalan revolution 1944–54

▽ ◇ Military Junta 1979

☐ ○ Sandinista revolution 1979–90; democratization 1990

○ Figueres 1948

○ Liberal-Conservative Pact, 1957

PANAMA 500 M
Panama City
Bogotá
COLOMBIA 11,000 M/P

○ Rómulo Betancourt 1945–48, 1959–64; Carlos Andrés Pérez 1974–9
◇ Rafael Caldera 1969–74; Luis Herrera Campins 1979; Jaime Lusinchi 1984
☆ Hugo Chavez 1998–

GUYANA 100 M
Paramaribo
Cayenne
SUR. **FR. GUIANA**
Macapá
Amazon
Belém

☆ Getulio Vargas 1930–45; 1950–4
João Goulart 1961–4
▽ Modernizing militarism 1964

Quito
ECUADOR 1,200 M/P
Guayaquil
Piura

Civilian rule 1985; democratization 1986

Manaus

Fortaleza

▽ Intermittent militarism to 1978
○ Election of reformist government 1978

Trujillo
3,500 M/P
PERU
Huánuco
Callao
Cuzco
Lima

B R A Z I L 7,000 M/P

Recife

☆ Radical militarism 1968
Sendero Luminoso from 1980
○ Return to civil rule 1980
☆ Fujimori 1990–2000

Salvador (Bahía)

☐ Bolivian revolution 1952–64
☐ Che Guevara (killed 1967)
▽ Military 1980; democratization 1982

La Paz
BOLIVIA
Sucre
3,200 M/P
Arequipa

• Brasília
• Belo Horizonte
Rio de Janeiro
São Paulo
Santos

◇ Eduardo Frei 1964–70
☐ Salvador Allende (Popular Unity) 1970–3
▽ Pinochet 1973–88
○ Democratization 1989

PARAGUAY
Asunción

▽ Military dictatorship Stroessner 1954 Rodriguez 1989

Antofagasta
Copiapó
Tucumán
120,000 M
Córdoba Santa Fé
Uruguay
Florianópolis
Porto Alegre
Rio Grande

1 Latin America since 1945

political change in Latin America since 1945

Valparaíso
Mendoza
Santiago
Buenos Aires
Concepción
ARGENTINA 70,000 M
Valdivia
Bahía Blanca
Osorno
Rawson

Fray Bentos
URUGUAY 22,000 M
Montevideo

○ Batllismo 1903–33
▽ Military 1973
◇ Tupamaros
Civilian rule 1985; democratization 1986
◇ Montoneros

☐ **Social revolution** Fundamental change (attempted or achieved) in economic and social structure by nationalist or Marxist movements

○ **Reformism** Moderate socio-economic change or modernization for democratic or other process

☆ **Populism** Interventionist state based on multi-class alliance for policy of development

◇ **Christian Democracy** Radical socio-economic change by Christian Democratic parties

▽ **Unreformed militarism** Military dictatorship of the right without social or modernizing programme

◇ **Indigenous guerrilla movements** Urban guerrillas from late 1960s following failure of Cuban-inspired rural guerrillas

☆ Juan Domingo Perón 1943–55, 1973–4
▽ Military 1976–83
○ Democratization and civilian rule 1983

Comodoro Rivadavia
Santa Cruz
Stanley
Tierra del Fuego

Falkland Islands (Islas Malvinas) occupied by Argentina 1982; occupation ended by UK Task Force June 1982

communism in Latin America, 1974

70,000 communist party membership

M/P loyalty (Moscow/Peking)

communist party status

☐ in power
☐ legal opposition
☐ illegal

159

Africa since 1945

INTERNET LINKS

www.fordham.edu/halsall/
mod/modsbook53.html
Online resources on Africa
post 1945

After World War II, although some French and British liberals sympathetic to African claims for advancement initiated programmes of social improvement and political reform, the need to exploit every asset in order to assist metropolitan recovery led to attempts to reassert colonial control. Nevertheless in the 1950s both Britain and France began to transfer responsibility to elected governments in their West African colonies.

In Muslim North Africa, longer-established nationalist movements received great stimulus from the overthrow of the Egyptian monarchy in 1952 and the rise to power of Gamal Abdel Nasser. In 1956 an Anglo-French-Israeli invasion failed to topple him. Meanwhile France granted independence to Tunisia and Morocco but tried to incorporate Algeria, the colony with the largest white population, into metropolitan France. This sparked a civil war that lasted until France reluctantly granted independence in 1962.

Elsewhere, white settlers strove to maintain their ascendancy. In South Africa, a Nationalist government dedicated to policies of racial separation ('apartheid') came to power; in Kenya, British troops arrived to suppress the Mau-Mau insurrection directed against the settlers; in Central Africa, a federation of Nyasaland and Rhodesia aimed to preserve white dominance. But in 1963 Kenya achieved independence and the Federation collapsed. Southern Rhodesia's white settlers created their own independent state in 1965, but had to accept black majority rule in 1980. Portugal retained its colonies longest, but in all of them guerrilla warfare eventually led to ignominious withdrawal in 1974-5.

Most of the newly independent African states possessed borders drawn by European governments in the 19th century with insufficient attention to ethnic rivalries. Soon after independence, those rivalries began to tear them apart. In 1960, tribal and regional factions in Zaire (formerly the Belgian Congo) led to demands for a federal constitution and, when these were refused, the army mutinied and the mineral rich province of Katanga seceded. United Nations intervention reunited the country in 1963, but two years later the

1976 Western Sahara jointly occupied by Morocco and Mauritania; Polisario guerrilla resistance backed by Algeria
1991 cease-fire between Morocco and Polisario
W. SAHA

1976-79 war with Polisario
1978 military rule
1991 multi-party elections
MAURITA

1968 civilian government overthrown
1991 Moussa Traoré government deposed
Senega

1991 RUF launches civil war
1992 military coup
1996 civilian rule restored under Ahmad Tejan Kabbah
1997 military overthrow Kabbah
1998 Kabbah restored
1999 rebels almost capture Freetown
2001 foreign intervention and ceasefire
SENEGAL
GA.
GU.

1989 outbreak of civil war
1993 pan-African peace-keeping force (Ecomog) intervenes to halt civil war
2002 French intervention to halt further civil war
GUIN

1957 first Black African country to gain independence
1967-85 series of military coups
1992 and 1996 Rawlings wins presidential elections
SIERRA LEONE

1967-70 Nigerian civil war
1981 civilian rule restored
1984, 1985, 1993 military coups
1993 elections declared void; riots;interim government ousted by
1999 civilian ruled restored
LI

1966 military takeover led by Col. Bokassa, crowned emperor 19
1980 republic restored
1981 military coup   1998 UN peace-keeping mission

army seized power and retained it for 34 years. Similarly, in Nigeria the secession of Biafra in 1967 led to a three-year civil war that restored central control, but likewise delivered power to the army. Elsewhere, ethnic violence caused enormous casualties – in the small state of Rwanda, Hutu-Tutsi violence left over 500,000 dead in 1994 – while repeated droughts (compounded by government inefficiency and corruption) caused famine and massive refugee problems in many areas of East Africa. In Algeria, from 1990 Islamic Fundamentalism challenged government control.

By the 1980s, white supremacy survived only in South Africa where the nationalist regime sought to retain its grip by draconian internal repression, by sending troops against guerrillas in neighbouring states, and by granting spurious independence to some black settlement areas set up under apartheid. Eventually, however, economic crisis and international isolation forced concessions. In 1990, the nationalists released Nelson Mandela, imprisoned leader of the banned African National Congress, and within four years the ANC's victory in the first multiracial elections in South Africa's history swept away white rule. Despite the problems of healing decades of racial tension, the ANC created a more stable political system than under white rule and preserved the most successful economy on the continent. Mandela retired in 1999. Meanwhile in Zimbabwe (formerly Rhodesia) serious racial conflict broke out.

Nelson Mandela *(right)* joined the African National Congress in 1944. In 1961, frustrated at the failure of civil disobedience to undermine apartheid, he adopted the idea of armed struggle. In 1962 he was sentenced to life imprisonment. Released in 1990, aged 72, he became leader of the ANC and, in 1994, South Africa's first president elected by universal franchise. He retired from the presidency in 1999.

1 Africa: post-independence wars and revolutions

- ✦ civil war
- → invasion
- ✊ guerrilla activity
- ✴ border dispute

MOROCCO
'56 independence

TUNISIA
1956 independence
1984 major rioting
1987 Bourguiba ousted

ALGERIA
1962 independence
1960s border conflicts
with Morocco
1965 Ben Bella deposed
by Col. Boumedienne
1990 election of Islamic
fundamentalist-dominated
chamber of deputies
1991 election results nullified;
anti-government terrorist
campaign by Islamic
Fundamentalists

LIBYA
1969 King Idris deposed; replaced
by military junta under Col. Gadhafi
1986 US bomb Tripoli in retaliation
for terrorist attacks
1992-2003 UN sanctions over Libyan
involvement in Lockerbie bomb
2004 UN invited to inspect nuclear
programme

EGYPT
1952 King Farouk deposed by army
officers led by Neguib
1954-70 Nasser president
1956 Suez crisis
1967, 1973 wars with Israel
1981 Mubarak president on
assassination of Sadat
1991 forces join US-led war against
Iraqi occupation of Kuwait

SUDAN
1963-72 civil war
1969 General Numeiry takes
power in military coup,
intermittent civil war in
South since independence
1984 severe famine
1985 Numeiry overthrown
(civil war continues)
1989 military coup; National
Islamic Front in effective control
1994-5 ceasefire between
feuding southern anti-
government forces
1998 US air attack on
supposed terrorist target
2003 Darfur crisis begins
2006 Darfur Peace Agreement
(branded a failure)

CHAD
1960 civil war;
FROLINAT guerrillas
supported by Libya
1973, 1981 Libyan invasion
and withdrawal
1984 border war with Libya

ERITREA
1952 federated with Ethiopia 1962 Union
1961-91 armed resistance to Ethiopian
rule in both Eritrea and Tigre
1991 Eritrean and Tigrean
forces victorious
1993 independence
1998-2000 border war with
Ethiopia
2001 UN peace-
keeping force

ETHIOPIA
1961- war against Eritrea secessionists
1974 Emperor Haile Selassie
overthrown by army junta
1984-88 severe famine, aid from West
1991 Mengistu's Communist
regime overthrown after civil war
1998-2000 war with Eritrea

SOMALIA
1964, 1970 border disputes
with Ethiopia and Kenya
1976-78 occupation of Ogaden
and war with Ethiopia
1993 UN military intervention
to halt civil war and famine
1993 UN withdraw
2002 ceasefire agreed
2006-7 Ethiopian military intervention to
dislodge advent of Islamist regime in Mogadishu

KENYA
1970s border
disputes with
Uganda and Somalia

1965 civil war, massacre of Tutsi
(in Rwanda and Burundi)
1994 tribal violence/civil war;
exodus of refugees to Rwandan
borders. Mass killings of Tutsi
civilians; UN large scale assistance
1997-2002 Hutu militias and
Rwanda intervene in DRC

UGANDA
1966 Obote expels Kabaka (King) of Buganda
1970 border dispute with Kenya
1971 Obote overthrown by Amin; Asians expelled;
large-scale repression
1979 invaded by Tanzania, Amin overthrown;
Obote restored (1980), overthrown (Jan 1986)
1986 Yoweri Museveni president

DEMOCRATIC REPUBLIC OF CONGO (ZAIRE)
1960-69 civil war
1978 invasion of Shaba province by anti-Mobutu
dissidents, repelled with French assistance
1997 Mobuto overthrown by rebel movement led by
Laurent Kabila
1997-2000 continued civil war
2001 Kabila assassinated

BURUNDI
1962 independence followed by
civil war/tribal violence,
massive refugee movement to
neighbouring countries
1993-96 civil war

ANGOLA
1975- Marxist MPLA government in conflict
with UNITA guerrillas aided by South Africa
1991 peace agreement between MPLA and
UNITA breaks down after elections: civil war renewed
1992 renewed fighting
1994 agreement between UNITA and government
1998-9 fighting between UNITA and
government war restarts
2002 death of James Savimbi of
UNITA opens way to peace

ZAMBIA
support for black nationalists
in Angola, Namibia and Rhodesia
1991 Kaunda defeated in democratic election
1992-2001 President Chiluba in power;
liberalized economy results in high inflation

NAMIBIA
South African presence resisted by
SWAPO to 1990
1991 fully independent from South Africa

MADAGASCAR
1972 military
takeover
2001-2 disputed
election led to civil war

MOZAMBIQUE
1975-1993 civil war between Frelimo
government and Renamo guerrillas
1980- South African intervention
in support of Renamo
1994 and 1999 multi-party elections
following Renamo-Frelimo peace accord
2000 flooding in south and central region

ZIMBABWE
1965-80 Rhodesia under white-minority rule
1980 black majority rule established;
increasing steps towards one-party state
1988 Robert Mugabe declared executive president
2000 Mugabe's resettlement of "war veterans"
on white owned land causes serious unrest
2007 Mugabe arrests opposition leaders

REPUBLIC OF SOUTH AFRICA
1948 implementation of apartheid
1975 invasion of Angola
1976 mounting black urban unrest
1976-81 African homelands (Bantustans) established in Transkei,
Bophuthatswana and Ciskei
1984 new constitution, limited representation for Indians and coloureds
1985-87 growing African resistance and civil unrest
1986 commando raids on neighbouring countries
1990 Mandela released President de Klerk starts to dismantle
apartheid
1993 multiracial council paves way to free elections
1994 election victory for ANC; Mandela president
1996 National party leaves governing coalition
1999 Mandela steps down as president
1999 and 2004 ANC win further elections; Thabo Mbeki president

INTERNET LINKS

www.yale.edu/cgp
The Cambodian Genocide
Program's website

The history of southern Asia since independence has been dominated by three factors. First, the seizure of power by military leaders (Pakistan 1958, 1977 and 1999, Indonesia 1967), with the aim – rarely successful – of abolishing corruption and stabilizing the economy; second, the resurgence of long-standing regional, tribal and religious conflicts (Naga and Sikh unrest in India; nationalist uprisings among the Mons, Shans and other 'hill people' in Thailand and Burma); finally, intervention by the Great Powers (China and the United States in Vietnam).

Wars between states also characterized certain areas. The partition of the Indian subcontinent in 1947 left numerous points of friction between the new states of India and Pakistan (notably Kashmir, Punjab and Bengal) which erupted into war in 1965 and again in 1971 (after the secession of East Pakistan to form the separate state of Bangladesh). The potential for war became more serious after both countries developed nuclear arms in 1998, and serious clashes over Kashmir in 2002 carried the threat of nuclear confrontation. Indian forces also expelled the Portuguese from their coastal enclaves (1961), fought China over a frontier dispute (1962), and intervened in Sri Lanka to protect the Hindu Tamil minority (1986-90). Civil wars, however, proved far more common (map 1). Malaya suffered a communist insurrection (1948-60), led by ethnic Chinese; the Philippines experienced rebellions by both communists and Muslims from the 1960s; Cambodia was devastated by the civil war between the communist Khmer Rouge and its non-communist opponents; Tamils and Singhalese fought in Sri Lanka (1983-2002).

The most savage conflict, however, occurred in Vietnam (map 2). After the Japanese collapse in 1945 Ho Chi Minh established a communist regime in Hanoi while the French recreated their colonial empire in the south. In 1946 armed conflict began, continuing until a humiliating defeat at Dien Bien Phu in 1954 led the French to withdraw. Although this left Cambodia and Laos as independent states, it did not create a unified Vietnam: at the Geneva Peace Conference in 1954 Ho accepted a 'temporary' partition of the country at the 17th parallel until nationwide elections, mandated for 1956, took place. However an anti-commu-

nist regime in the south, backed by America, refused to hold elections. In 1959 Ho therefore attacked, and the US immediately provided munitions and advisers to the south, with regular troops and air strikes after 1965. Despite saturation bombing and the commitment of 500,000 US ground troops, the communists (supported by both Russia and China) held their own and launched a coordinated insurrection in numerous southern cities early in 1968 (the 'Tet offensive'). Negotiations between Hanoi and Washington began soon afterwards and in 1973 American forces withdrew. Although the US continued to supply the south on a massive scale, when the communists invaded in 1975 the south's army collapsed. Vietnam was now unified, under Hanoi, although its economy was ruined and its invasion of Cambodia in 1978 led to ostracism by the West until it withdrew in 1987.

Elsewhere in Asia, rapid development occurred. Following the path of Japan (page 152), Taiwan, Malaysia, Singapore, Thailand and eventually Indonesia achieved rapid rates of growth from the late 1960s. Even during the world recession of the

2 Indo-China 1966–8

areas of control, early 1966:

- controlled by the Vietcong
- under Vietcong influence
- controlled by the Government
- under Government influence
- heavily contested area
- ✴ 'Tet' offensive, 1968

7th US fleet 1964

NORTH VIETNAM

LAOS

Hue · Phu Bai

Da Nang

Ho Chi Minh trail

Chu Lai

Qui Nhon

SOUTH VIETNAM

CAMBODIA

Saigon

Mekong

South China Sea

Indira Gandhi daughter of India's first premier, Nehru, was the country's prime minister from 1972 to 1977 and from 1980 to 1985. She ruled over an India torn by ethnic and religious conflict. Between 1975 and 1977 she imposed a state of emergency following her conviction for electoral malpractice. In 1985 she was assassinated by one of her Sikh bodyguards.

58 military coup by Ayub Khan
55 border clashes with India in Rann of Kutch
55 war with India over Kashmir
'1 war with India over Bangladesh
'2 ceasefire lines established; 1977 military coup by Zia ul-Haq
88 democratic elections;. Benazir Bhutto prime minister
osed 1990); 1993 Benazir Bhutto returns
prime minister (deposed 1996)
98 nuclear tests conducted
99 military under
eneral Musharraf
verthrows
overnment of
awaz Sharif

1971 secession from
Pakistan; civil war
followed in 1975 by
murder of Sheikh Mujib
and military control

1954 French withdrawal; civil war
1956–73 US backed South Vietnam and the
communist-backed North engage in conflict
1973 US withdraws all forces
1976 North and South Vietnam
reunified under Viet-Minh rule
1978 invasion of Cambodia
and border clashes with China
1979 war with China
2000 stock market founded

NORTH KOREA

SOUTH KOREA

JAPAN

seat of Chinese Nationalist
government since 1949
1958 territorial dispute with
China over Quemoy and Matsu
1996 China attempts military intimidations
as Taiwan holds first free elections;
2000 and 2004 Chen Shui-bian
elected president

CHINA

TIBET

NEPAL

PAKISTAN

INDIA

spasmodic unrest among Nagas,
Sikhs and Tamils
1961 India occupies Portuguese
enclaves
1962 Sino-Indian border war
1975–7 state of emergency proclaimed
1984 Sikh separatist uprising
suppressed; Indira Gandhi
assassinated
1991 Rajiv Gandhi assassinated
1998 nuclear tests conducted
2002 serious confrontation with
Pakistan over Kashmir

BANGLADESH

BURMA

LAOS

VIETNAM

TAIWAN

1953–73 civil war
1975 monarchy abolished;
Pathet Lao seizes power

Communist and Muslim insurgency since
1968, eruption into civil war 1972–8
1986 Marcos regime ousted following
general election. Aquino president
1992 Ramos succeeds as president
2001 President Estrada forced to step down
by popular protests

THAILAND

guerrilla activity since
independence (1948)
1958, 1962 military coups
1974 Socialist People's
Republic inaugurated
May 1990 pro-democracy
protests lend to free elections;
military refuse to recognise result
1990– opposition leader
Aung San Suu Kyi and
her pro-democracy movement
suppressed by military

CAMBODIA

PHILIPPINES

Mindanao

1947 military takeover,
guerrilla activity since 1960
1976 border clashes with Cambodia
1976 and 1987 border
clashes with Laos
1992 "Black May" uprising
against military rule
2002 "War on Drugs", over 1000 shot dead

SRI LANKA

58, 1961 fighting between Sinhalese and Tamils
71 government assumes emergency powers after rural guerrilla uprisings;
83 intercommunal rioting
86–90 Indian peacekeeping force intervenes to protect Tamils
y 1993 President Ranasinghe killed in rebel Tamil attack
02 ceasefire; Norwegian sponsored peace talks

MALAYSIA

1970 monarchy abolished
1970–4 civil war; victory of Khmer Rouge
who massacre millions of civilians
1978 Vietnamese invasion overthrows Khmer Rouge
1989 Vietnamese forces withdraw
1991 peace agreement leads to May 1993 elections,
boycotted by Khmer Rouge which carries on civil war

Aceh

INDONESIA

Irian Jaya

1967 Sukarno ousted by military coup;
suppression of Communists
1976– resistance to Indonesian rule in E. Timor
1977–99 secessionist rising in Irian Jaya
1989– GAM independence movement in Aceh
fights guerilla campaign against government
1998 President Suharto steps down in face of rising protests
1999–2001 intercommunal violence in the Moluccas
1999 UN peace-keeping force enters East Timor
after violence following vote in referendum for
independence from Indonesia
2002 East Timor independent

East Timor

1948–60 'The Emergency'- civil war
with communist guerrillas
1975–8 Communist guerrilla activity
1981-2003 Prime Minister Mahathir Mohamad
1998 demonstrations against
Mahathir Mohamad

1 Post-independence wars and revolutions

★ civil war   → invasion   ✊ guerrilla activity   ✳ border dispute

1980s, each experienced an annual growth rate of well over 5 per cent. Various factors were responsible: all except Singapore possessed large pools of cheap labour; all created a substantial industrial base oriented towards export markets throughout Asia, Europe and North America; all the governments sought to attract substantial foreign investment through tax incentives and infrastructural development. A major part of that investment came from Japan. Finally, political stability – Lee in Singapore; Mahathir in Malaysia; Suharto in Indonesia – underpinned the economic strategy of industrial development and helped to attract foreign investment.

All these economies suffered in the economic turmoil which hit east Asia in 1997, when a currency crisis triggered a general crisis of confidence in the Asian economic model. Indonesia suffered a 75 per cent devaluation of the rupiah, again exacerbated by a major political crisis, as the 35-year old Suharto regime finally fell before nationwide protests. In general the region's economies recovered far faster than expected, although Indonesia experienced widespread civil and ethnic unrest which threatened to destabilize the whole country. In 2004 a tsunami (caused by a massive earthquake) caused over 150,000 deaths and catastrophic damage in coastal regions around the Indian Ocean (map 3).

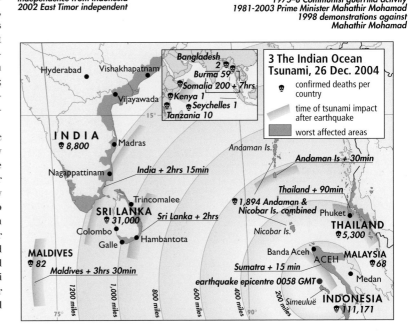

3 The Indian Ocean Tsunami, 26 Dec. 2004

☠ confirmed deaths per country

time of tsunami impact after earthquake

worst affected areas

Hyderabad
Vishakhapatnam
Vijayawada

Bangladesh 2
Burma 59
Somalia 200 + 7hrs
Kenya 1
Seychelles 1
Tanzania 10

INDIA
☠ 8,800
Madras

Nagappattinam

Andaman Is.

India + 2hrs 15min

Andaman Is + 30min

Thailand + 90min

☠ 1,894 Andaman &
Nicobar Is. combined

Phuket

Trincomalee

SRI LANKA
☠ 31,000

Sri Lanka + 2hrs

Nicobar Is.

THAILAND
☠ 5,300

Colombo
Galle
Hambantota

MALDIVES
☠ 82

Maldives + 3hrs 30min

Banda Aceh

ACEH

MALAYSIA
☠ 68

Sumatra + 15 min

Medan

earthquake epicentre 0058 GMT

Simeulue

INDONESIA
☠ 111,171

1200 miles   1,000 miles   800 miles   600 miles   400 miles   200 miles

15°

75°

90°

INTERNET LINKS

www.learningcurve.gov.uk/
coldwar
Online exhibition on the
Cold War

1947–89
The Cold War

1947 Greek Civil War: Truman Doctrine announced

1948–9 Berlin airlift

1949 NATO formed: Soviet Union detonates its first nuclear bomb

1950–3 Korean War

1955 Warsaw Pact formed

1962 Cuban missile crisis

1964–73 US intervenes militarily in Vietnam

1979 Soviet Union invades Afghanistan

1987 INF Treaty; phased elimination of intermediate range nuclear weapons

1991 Collapse of USSR; Cold War ends

The defeat of Germany, Italy and Japan and the weakening of Britain and France in World War II left the USA and USSR as the only 'superpowers'. Their ideological and political confrontation expressed itself as the Cold War. Conflict between the two had already appeared before the final victory: The Western Allies had already agreed (reluctantly) at Yalta (February 1945) to allow Soviet control of eastern Europe after the end of the war. By 1949 Stalin had developed an atomic bomb, thus ending the US monopoly of nuclear weapons. In reply, the USA built up the defence of western Europe with the formation of the North Atlantic Treaty Organization (NATO) in 1949 (page 146). In 1952 the US tested a thermo-nuclear (hydrogen) bomb; Russia followed suit in 1953.

Although it started as a conflict over central Europe, the Cold War soon developed into a global confrontation. The US saw the Korean War (1950-3: page 152) as evidence of a world-wide communist conspiracy, and American policy now became the 'containment' of Communism by a series of encircling alliances. NATO was followed by the South-East Asia Treaty Organization (SEATO) in 1954 and the Baghdad Pact (1955); the US maintained over 1400 foreign bases, including 275 bases for nuclear bombers, in 31 countries around the Soviet perimeter (map 1). As long as nuclear devices could only be delivered by aircraft, possession of these bases conferred an enormous advantage on the US. But when in the early 1960s both sides began to deploy ballistic nuclear missiles

US inspectors at a Soviet nuclear weapons site, 20 kilometres from Saratov *(below)*. Under the terms of the disarmament agreement of 1987 both sides agreed to the decommissioning of a large proportion of their nuclear stockpiles and to a system of inspections.

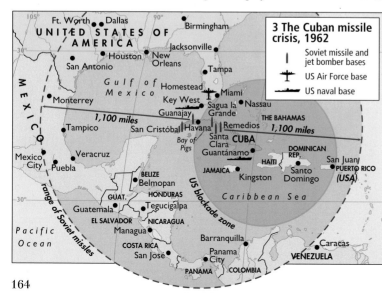

3 The Cuban missile crisis, 1962

| Soviet missile and jet bomber bases |
| US Air Force base |
| US naval base |

1 The age of bipolarity

Map labels:
JAPAN · S. KOREA · KOREA 1950–53 · Okinawa · US 7th fleet · TAIWAN Quemoy, Matsu 1954–55, 1958 · PHILIPPINES · SOUTH VIETNAM 1945–54, 1957–73 · MALAYSIA · THAILAND · SOVIET · SOVIET UNION · MONGOLIA · CHINA left Soviet bloc, 1960 · Arctic Ocean · EAST PAKISTAN · INDIA · PAKISTAN · AFGHANISTAN · IRAN · Indian Ocean · NORWAY · DENMARK · E. GERMANY · GERMANY · HOLLAND · BELGIUM · UNITED KINGDOM · FRANCE · POLAND · CZECH. · HUNGARY · ROMANIA · YUGO. 1948–53 · ALBANIA · BULGARIA · ITALY · GREECE 1946–9 · TURKEY 1945–7 · 1958 · IRAQ · SAUDI ARABIA · LEBANON 1958 · US 6th fleet · Suez, 1956 · EGYPT · LIBYA · SPAIN · PORTUGAL

Legend:

- USA and allies, 1958
- USSR and allies, 1958
- Soviet ICBM bases (7000 mile range)
- other Soviet missile sites, 1961
- principal Soviet military airfields
- US ICBM bases (5000 mile range)
- US heavy bomber bases (capable of reaching USSR with airborne refuelling)
- US nuclear and other major bases (Oct. 1962)
- strategic US fleets
- points of conflict in the Cold War
- uprisings in the Communist world

Czechoslovakia
- 1948
- 1968

East Germany
- Berlin 1948–9, 1958–62
- Berlin 1953

Estonia (E)
- 1944–55

Hungary
- 1956

Poland
- 1945–8, 1956

Lithuania (L)
- 1945–7

Ukraine (U)
- 1945–50

2 The nuclear balance, 1955–80

USSR intercontinental (bombers, land missiles, sea missiles, warheads)
8,000 · 6,000 · 4,000 · 2,000 · 0
1955 · 1960 · 1965 · 1970 · 1975 · 1980

USA intercontinental (bombers, land missiles, sea missiles, warheads)
1955 · 1960 · 1965 · 1970 · 1975 · 1980

USSR regional (bombers, missiles, warheads)
3,000 · 2,000 · 1,000 · 0
1955 · 1960 · 1965 · 1970 · 1975 · 1980

USA regional (bombers, missiles)
1955 · 1960 · 1965 · 1970 · 1975 · 1980

---

capable of being launched from land silos and submarines, the odds altered: now, in the event of war, each of the two superpowers could attack the other's cities directly (chart 2).

In October 1962, this scenario was almost put to the test when, following an unsuccessful US attempt to unseat the communist regime, the USSR established nuclear missile sites in Cuba. President Kennedy proclaimed a 'quarantine' of the island and threatened that, if the missiles were fired, the US would immediately retaliate against the USSR. The Russians then agreed to their removal (map 3). In return, Kennedy agreed to remove some of the US missile sites from Turkey.

This crisis, with its real threat of nuclear holocaust, proved a turning point in the Cold War. Already both monolithic blocs had begun to show signs of strain, most seriously on the Soviet side: Hungary and Poland rebelled in 1956, and from 1960 China began to quarrel openly over territory and ideology. In western Europe, France rejected American political leadership after 1958 and left NATO. A desire to limit the spread of nuclear weapons led to the conclusion of a partial test-ban treaty in 1963 and a nuclear non-proliferation treaty in 1968, but not all nuclear or potential nuclear powers signed these agreements (notably France, China and India) while others (such as Iraq) later reneged on their commitment. The Cold War therefore continued and the superpowers created huge nuclear arsenals.

In the event, the economic and political difficulties of the USSR increased to the point where the Soviet leader Mikhail Gorbachev (1985-91) felt that only a dramatic reduction in the crushing burden of military expenditure could bring relief (page 168). First the Soviets withdrew their forces from eastern Europe (1989), then NATO and the Warsaw Pact declared that the other was no longer an enemy (1990), and finally the USSR itself began to disintegrate (1991). Further agreements on the reduction of nuclear and conventional forces soon followed, although the fate of the vast arsenal accumulated by the former USSR gave cause for concern.

Western Europe; separatism and nationalism

http://ec.europa.eu/euro/
entry.html —
Detailed information on
the euro

INTERNET LINKS

1973 Oil crisis

1974 Salazar dies: democracy restored to Portugal

1975 Franco dies: democracy restored to Spain

1980–1 Solidarity campaign begins in Poland

1985 Gorbachev becomes Soviet leader; EEC agrees to create a single market

1989 Communist bloc in eastern Europe disintegrates

1990 Reunification of Germany

1991 Maastricht Treaty signed

1995 European Union formed

1998 Good Friday Accord ends sectarian violence in Northern Ireland

1999 Single European currency (the Euro) launched

2004 EU expands to include 25 members

2006 Major rioting in French cities

2007 Romania and Bulgaria admitted to EU

2007 British army withdraws from Northern Ireland after 28 years

In 1973 the oil-producing states almost trebled the cost of oil, triggering worldwide price inflation. In Europe, the crisis coincided with a general slowdown in productivity and profit growth and mounting unemployment, producing widespread labour unrest. Behind the Iron Curtain, rising oil prices caused economic performance to stagnate or decline.

In western Europe, the crisis encouraged the trend to greater economic integration. By the late 1960s, the original six members of the EEC (European Economic Community) had emerged as the economic vanguard of the continent. In 1973 Britain, Ireland and Denmark joined, followed in 1981 by Greece, in 1986 by Spain and Portugal, and in 1995 by Austria, Finland and Sweden. By the Maastricht Treaty (1991), members agreed to form a single free-trade market (renamed the EU, or European Union, in 1995) and most also agreed to introduce a single currency, the Euro, by 1999. Eight more countries joined the EU (though not the Eurozone) in 2004, and two more in 2007, bringing the total of member states to 27 (map 1 and page 175).

The combined effects of the economic slowdown after 1973 and the realization that clinging to their pre-war authoritarian governments would push them to the margins of Europe helped reintroduce democracy to Portugal (1974) and Spain (1975). Greece also embraced democracy in 1974. But these changes paled in comparison with events in eastern Europe in the late 1980s, where the disintegration of the Soviet Union and the fall of communism in every one of its satellite states produced in its wake no less than 15 new countries (page 168). The nationalist tensions released also led to civil wars in the former Yugoslavia (page 170).

Nationalist tensions likewise continued in western Europe. Many areas achieved a measure of devolution, often on linguistic grounds (as in Belgium), while Basque separatists in Spain and Irish nationalists in Ulster used terror to try and gain autonomy. They failed, and tentative political agreements were reached in both areas in 1998, though tensions survived (map 2).

2 Western Europe: separatism and nationalism since 1945

——— territorial autonomy based on ethnic group, with date of autonomy	✓ devolution approved by referendum, with date
——— separate administration/ autonomy for other reasons	✊ linguistic minorities or other communities whose members have used violence in pursuit of greater autonomy or other change of political status, with areas inhabited
✗ devolution rejected by referendum, with date	● ethnic or other communal based party delegated to national parliament in 1985

NORWAY
SWEDEN
FINLAND
Trondhjem
Bergen
Oslo
Swedes
Turku
Åland Is.
Swedes
Stockholm
Helsinki
Porkkala
Gothenburg
Århus
Copenhagen
Malmö
DENMARK

The success of the EU in modernizing and rationalizing European agriculture produced regular food gluts in he 1970s and 1980s. Here *(right)* Sicilian oranges have been turned, quite literally, into a food mountain. The sheer cost of maintaining farm incomes put a great strain on the European Union's budget, raising periodic calls for reform of the Common Agricultural Policy, especially urgent from the late 1990s, with the prospect of further enlargement to the east.

.H.
terdam
Hamburg
Bremen
emings
Bonn
Germans
GERMANY
Berlin
Hanover
Leipzig
Elbe
Dresden
POLAND
UX.
bourg
Rhine
strongly autonomous regions
CZECH REPUBLIC
Stuttgart
J1974
Munich
Danube
Vienna
ardinia
Zurich
LIECH.
SWITZ.
Germans
BOLZANO
strongly autonomous regions
AUSTRIA
HU
FRIULI-VENEZ
Milan
Venice
Trieste
GIULIA
Friulians, Slovene
1963
TRENTINO-ALTO ADIGE
Germans, Ladins, 1948
Verona
rin
Genoa
Bologna
CROATIA
NACO
Florence
SAN MARINO
Perugia
ITALY
Corsica
orsicans
talians)
Rome
Naples
Bari
ardinia
rds 1948
Taranto
Cagliari

1 The expansion of the European Union, 1981–2007

members of the EEC, Jan. 1981
joined Jan. 1986
admitted Oct. 1990
joined Jan. 1995
joined May 2004
joined Jan. 2007
other countries applying for membership
● countries in Euro area (information current 2007)

The European Economic Area (EEA)
members of the EEA, June 1996

ICELAND
Norwegian Sea
ATLANTIC OCEAN
Faeroe Islands
NORWAY
SWEDEN
FINLAND
ESTONIA
LATVIA
North Sea
DENMARK
LITHUANIA
RUS. FED.
IRELAND
UNITED KINGDOM
NETHER-LANDS
GERMANY
POLAND
BELARUS
BELGIUM
LUX.
CZECH REP.
SLOVAKIA
UKRAINE
MOLDOVA
FRANCE
LIECT.
AUSTRIA
HUNGARY
SWITZ.
SLOVENIA
CROATIA
ROMANIA
GEORGIA
ARMENIA
Bay of Biscay
MONACO
SAN MARINO
ANDORRA
BOS.-HERZ.
YUGO.
BULGARIA
Black Sea
TURKEY
customs union with EU effective from 1 Jan. 1996; application to EU recognised, Feb. 2003
applied 2003
PORTUGAL
SPAIN
Corsica
ITALY
Sardinia
ALBANIA
MAC.
GREECE
SYRIA
Balearic Is.
GIBRALTAR
Sicily
MALTA
Crete
CYPRUS
IRAQ
MOROCCO
ALGERIA
TUNISIA
Mediterranean Sea
JORDAN

MACEDONIA (F.Y.R.O.M.)
BULGARIA
Edirne
Istanbul
ALBANIA
Salonica
Mt. Athos
Ankara
40
Janina
TURKEY
GREECE
Izmir
Mediterranean
Palermo
Messina
Sicily 1946
Catania
Adana
Patras
Athens
Turkish Federated State of Cyprus, estb. 1975; independent "Turkish Rep. of Northern Cyprus" from 1983
J1975
Cyprus
Nicosia
ethnic distribution before 1974
Turks
Greeks
Sea
Crete

INTERNET LINKS

http://soviethistory.org/index.
php?action=L2&SubjectID=
1991end&Year=1991 —
The dissolution of the USSR

The collapse of Communism since 1985

The collapse of the communist regimes of Eastern Europe arose directly from the changes implemented Mikhail Gorbachev, leader of the USSR (page 148). Regarding the other communist states as a drain on Soviet resources, he encouraged them to pursue economic and political reform. This policy change came at a difficult time for the Eastern bloc states, whose economic development had been adversely affected by recession in the West and by reductions in trade and aid resulting from renewed Cold War pressures. Economic modernization slowed, and provoked growing popular unrest, particularly in Poland, where a military dictatorship had arisen in 1981 to suppress the democracy movement and forestall possible Soviet military intervention.

Although few showed enthusiasm for the old regimes, popular opposition remained muted until Gorbachev pressured his communist partners to grasp the nettle of reform. Without Soviet backing, the regimes crumbled one by one: Hungary legalized opposition parties in January 1989; Poland established the first non-communist government since 1948 the following August; demonstrations ended communist rule in Czechoslovakia, East Germany and Bulgaria in November. Violence occurred only in Romania, where an army firing squad shot the fallen dictator Nicolae Ceauçescu in December (map 1).

Throughout the Eastern bloc, elections now brought to power coalition governments committed to democratic reform and economic liberalization. In the course of 1990, East Germany voted first for currency union and then for full integration with West Germany, ending the partition imposed after World War II; but other former communist countries, exposed to market pressures, soon plunged into economic decline. High unemployment and rural poverty contributed to the revival of the deep-rooted ethnic and religious conflicts that the communist regimes had papered over for 40 years. In 1993, tensions between Czechs and Slovaks produced the partition of Czechoslovakia.

Meanwhile, in the USSR, nationalist unrest grew as the Russian-dominated republics of the USSR sensed an opportunity to gain independence. The president of the Russian Republic, Boris Yeltsin, urged Gorbachev to give the Soviet republics more independence. In August 1991, a group of hard-line communists attempted a coup and, although Yeltsin suppressed the revolt, the non-Russian republics soon declared their independence. When the Ukraine staged a referendum in December 1991 that resulted in an overwhelming vote for independence, Gorbachev bowed to reality. The USSR was dissolved on 31 December, to be replaced by a Commonwealth of Independent States, co-operating on military and economic issues but no longer controlled from Moscow.

With no country left to rule, Gorbachev slipped into obscurity. Russia embraced a form of presidential democracy, with Yeltsin as its first president. In 1993, hard-line parliamentary delegates hostile to further reform tried to depose Yeltsin, but he crushed them too. Re-elected as president in 1996, Yeltsin stepped down in 1999 and power passed peacefully to Vladimir Putin. Meanwhile some republics (Belarus, Uzbekistan, Kazakhstan, Turkmenistan) maintained reformed communist governments while others adopted some form of democracy – although, as in as Ukraine in 2004, fraud marred several elections. In Russia itself the constituent republics established greater autonomy (map 2) while Chechenia sought to break away from Russia by force (page 170).

Sep. 1989: mass exodus of political refugees reach the West via Hungary; Communist leadership in crisis
Oct.–Nov. 1989: widespread demonstrations against leadership
9 Nov. 1989: Berlin Wall breached
Mar. 1990: free elections
July 1990: currency union with West Germany
Oct. 1990: reunified with West Germany

from 1980: Solidarity opposition to communis
June 1989: partially fre elections
Aug. 1989: Solidarity-le government takes office
Jan. 1990: Communist Party dissolved
Oct. 1991: free election

Dec. 1989: economic war between Belgrade government and Slovenia
Apr. 1990: free elections
June 1991: independence declared; Yugoslav army attempts to regain control of Slovenia
July 1991: Brioni Agreement ends fighting in Slovenia; Yugoslav army withdraws

Apr.–May 1990: free elections
Dec. 1990: Serb-inhabited areas declare independence
June 1991: independence declared; fighting in Slovenia spreads to Croatia as Serbs attempt to extend territory in Croatia and Bosnia

1987: mass strikes against wage freeze and falling living standards; growing Serb militancy against minorities
July 1990: provincial autonomies abolished
1990–1: increasing tension between Belgrade government and Slovenia and Croatia

Jan.–May 1990: democratic reforms initiated by leadership
Mar. 1991: free elections

SWEDEN
DENMARK
NETHERLANDS
BELGIUM
GERMANY
Berlin
Bonn
POLA
Prague
CZECHOSLOVAKI
SWITZ.
AUSTRIA
Bratislava
Budapest
HUNGAR
SLOVENIA
Zagreb
CROATIA
Belgrade
Sarajevo
YUGOSLAV
ITALY
KOSO
Tirana
ALBANIA

2 The Russian Federation, since 1991

- the Russian Federation
- constituent republics within the Russian Federation, Mar. 1992
- independence declared, Nov. 1991; at war with Russia from Dec. 1994 to 1996 and from Aug. 1999

The Commonwealth of Independent States (CIS)

- entered close political and economic union with Russia, 2 Apr. 1996
- entered close economic union with Russia, 30 Mar. 1996
- other members of the CIS
- **60%** percentage of Russians in other members of the Russian Federation
- **AD** autonomous district
- **AO** autonomous oblast

Map 2 labels

Arctic Ocean
FINLAND
Murmansk
POLAND
BELARUS
St Petersburg
KARELIA 74%
MOLDOVA
UKRAINE
Moscow
NENETS
CHUVASHIA 27%
KOMI 58%
YAMALO-NENETS AD
TAYMYR AD
CHUKCHI AD
KORYAK AD
RUSSIAN FEDERATION
MARIYEL 47%
MORDOVIA 61%
stov-Don
Volgograd
TATARSTAN 43%
KOMI 59
KOMI-PERMYAK
KHANTY-MANSI AD
UDMURTIA 59%
Yekaterinburg
EVENKI AD
SAKHA (YAKUTIYA) 50%
Sea of Okhotsk
KALMYKIA 38%
GIA
b d
BASHKORTOSTAN
DAGESTAN 9%
AZER.
Caspian Sea
KAZAKHSTAN
Omsk
Novosibirsk
KHAKASSIA
ALTAY 79%
UST-ORDA BURYAT AD
BURYATIA 70%
AGA BURYAT AD
JEWISH AO
Khabarovsk
TURKMENISTAN
UZBEKISTAN
TYVA 32%
60%
Chita
Irkutsk
AN
KYRGYZSTAN
AFGHANISTAN TAJIKISTAN
MONGOLIA
CHINA
Vladivostok

a KARACHAY-CHERKESSIA 42%
b KABARDINO-BALKARIA 39%
c NORTH-OSSETIA 30%
d INGUSHETIA (from June 1992) } 23% combined
e CHECHENIA

Lower map labels and annotations

Sea
Tallinn
ESTONIA
Mar. 1990: Congress of Estonia formed, declares Soviet rule illegal
Mar. 1991: referendum endorses independence
Aug. 1991: independence declared
Sep. 1991: independence recognized by USSR

Riga LATVIA
1989: mass anti-Communist demonstrations
Mar. 1991: referendum endorses independence
Aug. 1991: independence declared
Sep. 1991: independence recognized by USSR

LITHUANIA
Vilnius
N FED.
1989: mass anti-Communist demonstrations
Mar. 1991: independence declared
Apr.–June 1990: economic embargo imposed by USSR
Sep. 1991: independence recognized by USSR

Minsk
BELARUS
June 1989: Popular Front founded
Aug. 1991: independence declared
Dec. 1991: founder member of Commonwealth of Independent States

Moscow

RUSSIAN FEDERATION

Mar. 1985: Mikhail Gorbachev becomes leader of Communist Party; initiates perestroika and glasnost, loosens Soviet control of satellite states
June 1991: Boris Yeltsin elected president of Russian Federation
Aug. 1991: hard-line Communist coup against Gorbachev fails
Nov. 1991: Communist Party declared illegal
Dec. 1991: USSR dissolved

aw
m 1988: anti-government nstrations
v. 1989: mass demonstrations
Communist rule
1990: new constitution
pted; becomes a federation
1990: free elections

m 1987: Communist
ime relaxes
trol
1989: allows
t Germans to
vel to the West
1990: Communist
e ends peacefully
r.–Apr. 1990: free
tions

Kiev
UKRAINE
1989: opposition mass-movements emerge
Aug. 1991: independence declared
Dec. 1991: referendum endorses independence; founder member of Commonwealth of Independent States

TRANSNISTRIA
June 1989: Popular Front wins 75% of votes in election
Aug. 1991: independence declared

GAGAUZIA

MOLDOVA

OMANIA
ucharest
Dec. 1989: mass demonstrations lead to armed uprisings and overthrow of Ceausescu regime
June 1991: free elections
Nov. 1991: new constitution adopted

ULGARIA
Nov. 1989: President Zhivkov removed from office
June 1990: free elections
July 1991: fresh elections following adoption of new constitution

Nov. 1988: mass demonstrations against Russification
Mar. 1991: referendum endorses independence
Apr. 1991: independence declared

Sep. 1989: economic embargo imposed by Azerbaijan
Sep. 1991: referendum endorses independence; independence declared

Nov. 1991: independence declared

Jan. 1990: state of emergency declared; Soviet troops intervene
Oct. 1991: independence declared

CHECHENIA
Grozny
GEORGIA
Sep. 1991: independence declared

AZERBAIJAN
ARMENIA
NAGORNO-KARABAKH

Photo caption

In 2004 Ukraine held bitterly disputed presidential elections in which a candidate loyal to Moscow faced a challenger who favoured closer ties with the west: Viktor Yushchenko *(above)*. Government agents apparently attempted to poison Yushchenko (hence his scarred face) but he survived to win and, after massive public demonstrations, became president. Despite opposition, Yushchenko's 'Orange Revolution' party and its allies retained power in bitterly contested elections in 2007.

1 The collapse of communism, 1985–91

- Soviet-dominated eastern Europe to 1989
- Soviet Union to 1991
- Yugoslavia to 1991
- united with the Federal Republic of Germany, 1990
- independent, 1991
- other former communist states, 1991
- de facto independent states, late 1991, on former territory of the Soviet Union, internationally unrecognized
- overrun by Yugoslav army, July–Dec. 1991
- borders, 1991

Civil wars in the communist successor states

The greatest casualty of the collapse of the communist bloc was Yugoslavia. Its six constituent republics (Serbia, Croatia, Macedonia, Bosnia-Herzegovina, Slovenia and Montenegro) were held together by an over-arching communist apparatus and the personal authority of Josip Broz Tito, the founder of communist Yugoslavia. Internal divisions appeared soon after his death in 1980, triggered by the rise of aggressive nationalism. In 1987, following the choice of Slobodan Milosevic as leader of Serbia, tensions between the republics grew stronger. Milosevic at once suppressed the Albanian minority in Kosovo, and set out to expand Serbia's influence throughout the federation.

In 1990 multi-party elections brought nationalists to the fore in Slovenia and Croatia and paved the way for their simultaneous declaration of independence in 1991. This provoked a vicious seven-month war when Serb forces intervened, allegedly to protect the ethnic Serb minority in Croatia. Another savage civil war broke out in Bosnia-Herzegovina, where Bosnian Muslims (44% of the population) and Croats (17%) demanded independence despite bitter opposition from the Bosnian Serbs (31%). Each ethnic group sought to 'cleanse' the areas under its control of all opponents until by 1993 the Serbs controlled around 70 per cent of Bosnia and besieged Sarajevo, held by the Muslim-led government. The war caused the

1 The Yugoslav civil war, 1991–5

- Croatia, June 1991
- Bosnia-Herzegovina Mar. 1992
- secured by Yugoslav army and Bosnian Serb forces by Dec. 1992
- controlled by Bosnian Croat forces, Dec. 1992
- under Bosnian government control , Dec. 1992
- → Croatian advances, Jan. 1993
- → Federation of Bosnia and Herzegovina advances, Oct.–Nov. 1994
- ‑‑‑▶ Croatian and Federation of Bosnia and Herzegovina advances, spring 1995
- → Bosnian Serb advances, summer 1995
- Croatian and Federation of Bosnia and Herzegovina advances, Aug.–Oct. 1995
- overwhelmingly or largely Muslim, 1991; no significant Muslim presence by 1996
- Autonomous Province of Western Bosnia, Sep. 1993–Aug. 1994
- remained under Serb control by Dayton Agreement Nov.1995
- returned to Croatian control in Jan. 1998 under Erdut agreement of Nov. 1995
- overrun by Yugoslav army and Croatian Serb forces by Dec. 19
- UN-designated 'safe areas'

death of at least 100,000 and displaced half of the region's 4 million inhabitants. In 1995 a renewed Serb offensive provoked NATO intervention, leading to an uneasy peace (the Dayton Accords) which left Bosnia divided between the three ethnic groups and utterly devastated by four years of war (map 1).

3 The Caucasus, since 1988

- notional extent of Georgia at independence
- advance of pro-Gamsa-khurdia forces, Oct. 1993
- Georgian advance into Abkhazia, Aug. 1992
- areas of Georgia under Abkhazian control, Oct. 1993
- evacuated by Georgia, Oct. 199
- notional extent of Azerbaijan at independence
- Armenia at independence
- limit of Armenian control, May 1992
- Azerbaijani advance into Karabakh, Oct. 1992
- secured by Armenia and Karabakh by Nov. 1993
- Chechnya-Ingushetia at independence
- seceded from Chechnya, joined Russian Fed. Mar. 1992
- claimed by Ingushetia, 1992
- Russian advance into Chechnya by May 1995
- mass movements of refugees
- autonomous within Russian Federation

Nov. 1991: independence declared
Dec. 1994: Russian troops invade; Grozny largely destroyed;
May 1996: Russian-Chechen ceasefire; Russian troops withdraw
Aug. 1999: renewed Russian invasion and occupation of most Chechnya
2000-7: violent insurgency
2007: Ramzan Kadyrov becomes President

June 1995: attacked by Chechen forces

Oct. 1992: clashes between Ossetians and Ingush; Russian troops intervene
Jul. 1995: North Ossetia and Ingushetia sign joint peace protocol

Nov. 1996: Balkar Republic proclaimed

1989: clashes between Ossetians and Georgians
Dec. 1991 breaks from Georgia in favour of Russian Federation
Jan.–May 1992: clashes with Georgian troops; North Ossetians assist South (Apr. 1992)

Apr. 1991: independence declared
Dec. 1991: President Gamsakhurdia overthrown
1992: Eduard Shevardnadze becomes chairman of State Council
1993: Georgia joins CIS
Nov. 1995: Shevardnadze elected president

1990: clashes between Abkhazians and Georgians
July 1992: asserts independence from Georgia; Georgian and Russian troops intervene, North Caucasian Muslims assist Abkhazians (Aug. 1992)
May 1994: ceasefire; Russian peace-keeping troops deployed
1998: 40,000 ethnic Georgians expelled from Gali district

Jan. 1990: rioting in Baku; Soviet troops intervene
Oct. 1991: independence declared
Sep. 1992: unsuccessful attempts to subjugate Nagorno-Karabakh and Armenia (to May 1994)

Jan. 1990: independence declared

Sep. 1991: independence declared; Azerbaijani forces intervene; Armenian-supported Karabakh forces clash with Azeris; Armenian invasion of Azerbaijan follows
May 1994: ceasefire

2 The war in Kosovo

- → flight of Kosovan Albanian refugees, Mar.–May 1999
- ✴ towns bombed by NATO forces, Mar.–June 1999
- ▨ KLA strongholds
- ⊕ sites of religous significance to Serbs
- --- NATO zone of occupatic with nationality of occupying force
- → NATO bombing raid
- ☠ major massacres

Map labels: SERBIA, Novi Pazar, 50,000 Serbs, Leposavic, 5km demilitarized zone established 1999, MONTENEGRO, refugees 61,700, Kosovska Mitrovica, Podujevo, Istok, Pec, patriarchate of Pec, Decani, Kosovo Polje 1389, Pristina, Gracanica, Vranje, KOSOVO, Gnjilane, main routes for weapons to KLA, ALBANIA, Urosevac, Prizren, Kukes, refugees 405,360, church of Bogorodica Ljeviska, Albanian guerilla – Macedonian government clashes 2001, MACEDONIA (F.Y.R.O.M.), refugees 197,870, Skopje

Inset map: HUNGARY, ROMANIA, CROATIA, Novi Sad, BOSNIA, Belgrade, HERZE-GOVINA, Kragujevac, SERBIA, Nis, MONTENEGRO, KOSOVO, Podgorica, Pristina, ALBANIA, Skopje, MACEDONIA

Bosnia map labels: SLOVENIA, HUNGARY, Zagreb, Drava, Barania, CROATIA, Sisak, Osijek, Glina, Okucani, Vukovar, Sava, Bihac, Prijedor, Oraje, Bosanka Krupa, Banja Luka, Bosna, Brcko, Sanski Most, Doboj, UN, Kljuc, BOSNIA-, Maglaj, Tuzla, Vrbas, Zepce, Mrkonjic-Grad, Jajce, Travnik, Zenica, Vitez, Olovo, Donji Vakuf, Bugojno, Srebrenica, UN, Kupres, Gornji Vakuf, Kiseljak, Sarajevo, Zepa, Glamoc, Dinaric Alps, Prozor, Pale, Visegrad, Knin, Livno, Jablanica, Gorazde, DALMATIA, HERZEGOVINA, Mostar, slenica, Brac, Hvar, Split, YUGOSLAVIA, Korcula, Dubrovnik

In 1998, conflict escalated in Serbia's province of Kosovo. Talks brokered by international mediators offered the Kosovo Albanians full autonomy within Serbia, but Milosevic objected. NATO responded with air strikes against Yugoslavia to force Belgrade to sign the peace agreement and to stop the repression of Kosovo Albanians. The Serbian security forces instead accelerated a programme of 'ethnic cleansing' against Kosovo Albanians. After more than two months of NATO bombing, Milosevic agreed to a peace plan that incorporated most of NATO's demands and a NATO-led peace implementation force entered the province (map 2).

Tensions within the Yugoslav Federation continued as the pro-western government of Montenegro sought to assert its independence from Belgrade until December 2000, when protests against election fraud drove Milosevic from office. His successor, Vojislav Kostunica, made overtures to the West and promised a return to democratic rule, and in 2001 delivered Milosevic to The Hague for trial by the International Criminal Tribunal for the former Yugoslavia.

The break-up of the Soviet Union, too, saw widespread ethnic and political conflict, particularly in the Caucasus region (map 3). Armenia and Azerbaijan fought over the Christian Armenian enclave of Nagorno-Karabak; Georgia fought to keep South Ossetia within her boundaries and to prevent the independence of Abkhazia. The worst conflict occurred in Chechenia, which Russian forces invaded in 1994 and 1999 to prevent secession. Russia suffered heavy casualties in both operations and, despite occupying virtually the whole province, could not stifle a vigorous Chechen guerrilla resistance or, after 2002, prevent guerrilla attacks in Russia itself.

In July 2007 Bosnian workers prepared new graves for the bodies of 465 Muslims killed by Bosnian-Serbs during the 1992–1995 war in Bosnia-Herzegovina and subsequently excavated from mass-graves (*left*). Bosnian Serb troops and police massacred some 8,000 Bosnian Muslim men after capturing Srebrenica on 11 July, 1995. In 1997 the UN established an International Criminal Tribunal for the former Yugoslavia which tried, convicted and imprisoned many perpetrators.

The 21st-century world

INTERNET LINKS

www.un.org/esa/population/
publications/AIDSimpact/
AIDSWebAnnounce.htm —
UN report on the
impact of AIDS

2001 Al-Qaeda attacks
New York and Washington

2002 Taliban overthrown
in Afghanistan; common
European currency; Bali
terrorist bombing; Indian-
Pakistani crisis over Kashmir

2003 US-led coalition
invades Iraq, topples regime
of Saddam Hussein and
starts civil war

2004 Huge increase in
Islamic terrorism in Middle
East; Madrid terrorist
bombings; Beslan school
massacre

2005 London transport
bombing

After the end of the Cold War (page 164), the super-powers began to disarm; economic development stabilized in most of the northern hemisphere; democracy spread; and armed conflicts between states decreased. Yet the absence of global confrontation did not prevent regional disputes, many of which dragged in the major powers as arbiters. In 1990, Iraq invaded Kuwait, only to be expelled by US-led coalition forces in 1991. Thereafter, tensions persisted until in 2003 a smaller US-led coalition occupied Iraq and sought to introduce democracy. In Chechenia, Russian forces fought a grim civil war against separatists, which left the region desolate and produced Chechen terrorist attacks in Russia. The largest war of all involved the states that

emerged from the collapse of former Yugoslavia in 1991 (page 170).

Religious differences exacerbated many of these conflicts. Radical movements developed throughout the Islamic world, including the large Muslim communities now living and working in the West. The failure of western-style modernization encouraged many young Muslims to exalt traditional values, and to seek to destroy western 'imperialism', both by driving it out of Islamic countries, and by attacking it in its heartland. This led to civil war between Fundamentalists and Modernizers in several Muslim countries (Afghanistan, Algeria and Iran); and to attacks by terrorist groups

2 World population at the millennium

**Family size and
population growth**

- ◼ very rapid growth
  (more than 5 children per family)
- ◼ intermediate growth
  (2.1–5 children per family)
- ◻ slow growth (fewer than
  2.1 children per family)

**Fastest-growing
populations** (% per annum)

- 4.5% 2000–5
- 4.0% 2045–50 (projection)
- 48.6 % of population under 15

Slowest-growing populations
(% per annum)

- -4.5% 2000–5
- -4.0% 2045–50 (projection)

JAPAN 9 — countries with population of 50 milli... or more in 2000, in ranking order

JAPAN (15) — countries with population of 50 milli... more in 2050 (projection), in ranking...

JAPAN -13.6 — countries with projected population decrease 2000–50, with percentage

Tokyo 26.4 — cities with populations over 10 millio... in 2000 (with population)

Tokyo (27.2) — cities with populations over 10 millio... in 2050 (with projected population)

172

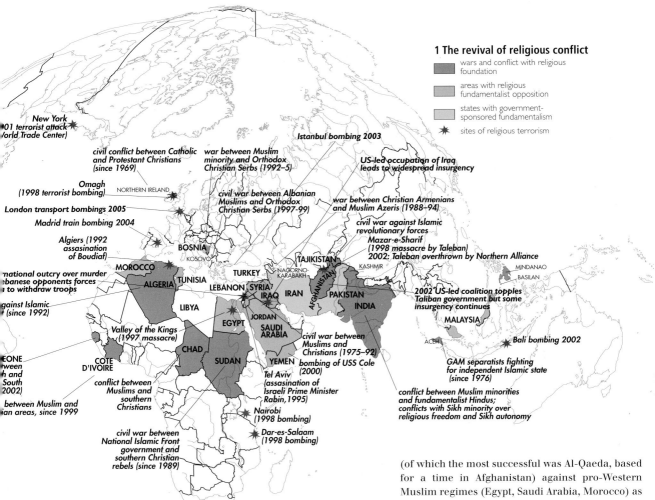

1 The revival of religious conflict

- wars and conflict with religious foundation
- areas with religious fundamentalist opposition
- states with government-sponsored fundamentalism
- ★ sites of religious terrorism

New York
01 terrorist attack
/orld Trade Center)

civil conflict between Catholic and Protestant Christians (since 1969)

Omagh (1998 terrorist bombing)

NORTHERN IRELAND

London transport bombings 2005

Madrid train bombing 2004

Algiers (1992 assasination of Boudiaf)

national outcry over murder ebanese opponents forces to withdraw troops

against Islamic (since 1992)

war between Muslim minority and Orthodox Christian Serbs (1992–5)

civil war between Albanian Muslims and Orthodox Christian Serbs (1997-99)

Istanbul bombing 2003

US-led occupation of Iraq leads to widespread insurgency

war between Christian Armenians and Muslim Azeris (1988–94)

civil war against Islamic revolutionary forces

Mazar-e-Sharif (1998 massacre by Taleban) 2002: Taleban overthrown by Northern Alliance

BOSNIA

KOSOVO

MOROCCO

ALGERIA

TUNISIA

TURKEY

LEBANON

LIBYA

SYRIA
IRAQ

IRAN

TAJIKISTAN

NAGORNO-KARABAKH

AFGHANISTAN

KASHMIR

MINDANAO

BASILAN

PAKISTAN

INDIA

2002 US-led coalition topples Taliban government but some insurgency continues

MALAYSIA

Valley of the Kings (1997 massacre)

EGYPT

JORDAN
SAUDI ARABIA

ACEH

Bali bombing 2002

EONE
ween
h and
South
2002)

CHAD

COTE D'IVOIRE

SUDAN

YEMEN

civil war between Muslims and Christians (1975–92)

bombing of USS Cole (2000)

GAM separatists fighting for independent Islamic state (since 1976)

conflict between Muslims and southern Christians

Tel Aviv (assasination of Israeli Prime Minister Rabin, 1995)

Nairobi (1998 bombing)

conflict between Muslim minorities and fundamentalist Hindus; conflicts with Sikh minority over religious freedom and Sikh autonomy

between Muslim and ian areas, since 1999

Dar-es-Salaam (1998 bombing)

civil war between National Islamic Front government and southern Christian rebels (since 1989)

(of which the most successful was Al-Qaeda, based for a time in Afghanistan) against pro-Western Muslim regimes (Egypt, Saudi Arabia, Morocco) as well as against the United States (2001), Spain (2004) and Britain (2005). Religious differences also fuelled inter-communal violence in India, Indonesia, Northern Ireland and Yugoslavia, and inter-state conflicts between Iran and Iraq and between Israel and most of her Arab neighbours (map 1).

Some of the tensions in the Middle East and in south and southeast Asia arose from rapid population growth. In these areas, people under 25 sometimes made up half the total population. Indeed students and schoolchildren played a conspicuous part in protests in India, Indonesia, Burma and in Tiananmen Square in Beijing in 1989. Young South Africans, too, played a central part in achieving democracy in 1990–4. The image of the peasant-soldier typical of the liberation movements of the 1960s gave way to chilling images of pre-teenage boys with modern weapons in their hands.

Many other critical issues remained. Extreme weather events (such as prolonged droughts and catastrophic floods), acid rain, and 'global warming' all caused alarm. Above all, population growth threatened to destabilize the world system because, although in the late 1990s the growth began to slow, famine and impoverishment afflicted many overpopulated developing states (map 2). Few people entered the new millennium with complete confidence.

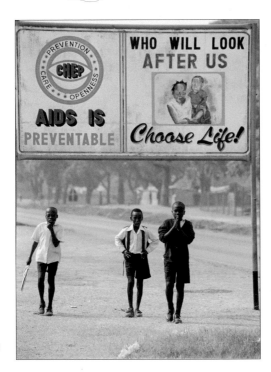

NEW ZEALAND

Since 1981, AIDS (Auto-immune Deficiency Syndrome) has killed 19 million people world-wide, over 11 million of them in Sub-Saharan Africa, where in 2004 almost 6,000 people died every day from the disease. Over 34 million more people currently suffer from AIDS (or HIV, the virus that leads to AIDS), two-thirds of them in Sub-Saharan Africa where the death of young adults from the disease has left over 12 million orphans. Even those who do not already have the disease face a grim future.

INTERNET LINKS

www.imf.org/external/np/
exr/ib/2000/041200.htm
The IMF's views on
globalization

The global economy

By the early 21st century electronic communication and world-wide investment and marketing had created a genuinely global economy. Giant transnational companies dominated finance and production. However, world economic development still depended in part on the central management of key economic factors by groups of states, and on collaboration between them. Representatives of the largest industrial economies met regularly as the Group of Seven to co-ordinate financial and trade policies. Additionally, regional agreements sought to expand trade between small groups of states.

1987 Single European Act for full economic union

1991 Russia begins programme of economic reforms

1991 World Wide Web (WWW) launched

1992 Maastricht Treaty

1994 Mexico joins North American Free Trade Area (NAFTA)

1995 EEC becomes the European Union

1997-8 Financial crisis rocks east Asian economies

1998 Russian financial crisis

1999 European single currency (the 'euro') introduced

2007 Collapse of US sub-prime mortgage market adversely affects stock and credit markets

2 The world's top trading nations, 2003

merchandise exports
% world total

Germany, United States, China, Japan, France, UK, Netherlands, Italy, Canada, Belgium

millions US$
% of world total

3 Regional distribution of wealth to population

total world GDP 2003: US$ 36,356,240 million (regional percentage of total in Rom·
total world population, 2004: 6.39 billion (regional figures in bracke

N.America 33.9% (326,000,000)
Europe 33.4% (728,000,000)
Asia 25.9% (3,875,000,000)
S. America 3.6% (549,000,000)
Africa 1.6% (885,000,000)
Oceania 1.6% (33,000,000)

European Union (EU)

US$69,800
LUXEMBOURG

US$42,364

NORWAY SWEDEN FINLAND

US$34,740 DENMARK

EST.
LATVIA
LITHUANIA

UK

IRELAND

US$40,610

US$2,006 bn

NETH.)
BEL.

Paris
OECD
FRANCE

GERMANY

US$2,436 bn

POLAND

CZ.R.

Vienna SLA.
AUSTRIA
HUNGARY

ROMANIA

Basle
SWITZ.

OPEC

US$1,835 bn

SL.

ITALY

SAN MARINO

BULGARIA

SPAIN

US$32,571

GREECE

US$1,713 bn

*Bank for Int'l
Settlements*

PORTUGAL

US$33,432

MALTA

CYPRUS

,479
ONG

ONESIA

NEW
ZEALAND

AUSTRALIA

he world economy and economic groupings

- North American Free Trade Association (NAFTA)
- Common Market of the Southern Cone (Mercosur)
- Central American Common Market (CACM)
- Economic Community of West African States (ECOWAS)
- Organization for Economic Co-operation and Development (OECD)
- Organization for Petroleum Exporting Countries (OPEC)
- Southern African Development Community (SADC) (note: Seychelles and Mauritius are members)
- Association of South East Asian Nations (ASEAN)
- Organization of American States (OAS)
- African Union
- 10 largest economies, in US$ bn (2005)
- 10 largest GDP per capita (2005 PPP adjusted)
- 10 smallest GDP per capita (2005 PPP adjusted)

The most successful of these groupings was the European Union, which grew from the original six members of the EEC in 1957 to embrace 27 states by 2007 (page 166). Gradual economic integration culminated in 1999 with the introduction of a single currency, the euro, and the abolition of national currencies within the Eurozone in 2002. Economic groups elsewhere formed looser associations aiming to enhance regional economic integration. In 1994, for example, the USA, Canada and Mexico joined in the North American Free Trade Association (NAFTA) (map 1 and inset).

The world's top ten trading nations in 2003 provided almost two-thirds of the world's imports and exports (chart 2). A high proportion of that trade took place between the top traders, rather than trade between the developed and developing world; and an increasing proportion occurred within free-trade blocs. The fruits of the global economic success were spread very unevenly. In 2003, Europe possessed one-third of the world's wealth and North America possessed another third (chart 3). Sustained expansion in Asia, Europe and the United States contrasted with economic decline in Africa, Latin America and the former Soviet bloc. The Russian economy in particular faced serious crisis by 1998 as the rush for capitalism failed to generate the wealth to sustain employment and welfare at the level achieved under communism. Even in east Asia, which grew faster than anywhere else in the world from the 1960s to the mid-1990s, the boom turned sour in 1997. Burdened with debt, high population growth and excessive dependence on a cluster of manufacturing exports, the new Asian economies generated a financial crisis that threatened the health of the whole global economy.

Outside the growth areas, there was persistent reliance on aid and investment from the developed world, much of it supplied by the International Monetary Fund (IMF) or the Organization for Economic Co-operation and Development (OECD). The per capita Gross Domestic Product (GDP) of the poorest states in the early 21st century was less than $300, while per capita GDP in the USA was almost $27,000. For many sub-Saharan African states, aid represented more than half of the value of total GDP. Since this pattern of aid-dependence altered little, the gulf between the poverty of the developing world and the vast wealth of the developed industrial core remained one of the unresolved issues of global economics.

A Euro coin (above). Gradual economic integration within the European Union culminated in the introduction of a single currency, the Euro, on 1 January 1999. Initially the Euro showed unexpected weakness against the dollar, but it rallied soon after Euro notes and coins became legal tender on 1 January 2002. National currencies within the Eurozone (which did not include the United Kingdom or Denmark, or the ten new states that joined in 2004–7) ceased to exist.

The global environment

Until the 20th century, natural changes largely determined the environment. Now, industrialization, modern communications and mass consumption have combined to produce damaging man-made environmental change. Ecological disasters have become urgent global problems.

The onset of large-scale population growth and industrialization in the 19th century (page 100), stimulated a parallel rapid increase in man-made damage to the world's environment. Before 1945, this damage was largely localized, though very visible; the spread of industry worldwide after 1945 produced new threats to the environment which, if less visible, were nonetheless more deadly. Acid rain from waste in the atmosphere destroyed forests and eroded buildings. Pollutants in rivers and seas poisoned wildlife (map 1).

High levels of carbon dioxide released from the burning of fossil fuels raised global temperatures, while other chemicals began to weaken the ozone layer in the earth's atmosphere. Between 1800 and 1900 the level of carbon dioxide in the atmosphere increased by only 4 per cent; in the 20th century it increased by 23 per cent, with most of the change

into the atmosphere which blocked the natural loss of heat and created the so-called 'greenhouse effect', leading to a global rise in temperatures (map 2).

The search for alternative sources of energy produced other types of disaster, however. In 1986, a nuclear reactor at Chernobyl in the Ukraine exploded, spreading a cloud of radioactive waste around the world (map 3). This catastrophe was but the most spectacular of many accidents in the production of nuclear power, eventually causing a reduction in its use.

Environmental issues became a central concern and state action produced some positive results. In Brazil, deforestation fell from a rate of 21,000 square kilometres in 1988 to only 1000 square kilometres by 1993. At Rio de Janeiro in 1992 an assembly of world leaders agreed to reduce harmful pollutants and emissions, a decision reaffirmed at a further meeting in Kyoto in 1997. By 2005, when the Kyoto protocols took effect, although 141 governments had promised to reduce emissions by 5% within seven years the world's worst polluter, the US, refused to sign up (President George W Bush even denied that global warming existed) and developing economies were exempt (including India and China, whose emissions were also high). The global temperature therefore continued to rise, bringing with it an increase in extreme climatic events such as Hurricane Katrina, which in 2005 rendered 300,000 homes uninhabitable and flooded over 16 million acres of the US Gulf Coast.

3 Radioactive fall-out from the Chernobyl accident, 1986

∴ pattern of fall-out

occurring since the 1950s. This raised world temperatures significantly: eight of the warmest summers on record occurred between 1997 and 2007.

Global warming stemmed in part from a massive increase in energy consumption, most of which consisted of fossil fuels (oil, coal and natural gas). Between 1970 and 1990 energy consumption grew by 60 per cent, despite efforts to find more efficient ways of generating power and to reduce emissions. Fossil fuels released a range of chemicals

1 The crisis of the environment

deforestation: rainforests under threat

- tropical rainforest
- edge of rainforest undergoing the most rapid deforestation
- ★ threatened area with large concentrations of endangered species

ocean and river pollution: oil slicks and tar balls

- high occurrence
- low occurrence

oceanic pollution

- frequent and severe
- partial and intermittent
- major oil tanker disaster
- oil rig blowout
- natural seepage

river pollution

- severe
- background

Map 1 labels

Exxon Valdez 1989

CANADA
UNITED STATES
ICELAND

North Atlantic Ocean

Braer 1993
IRELAND
UK
Sea Empress 1995
Amoco Cadiz 1978
Prestige 2002
Aegean Sea 1992
Jakob Maersk 1975
Sea Spirit 1990
Ellen Conway 1976
Shark 5 1989

NORWAY SWEDEN FINLAND
RUSSIAN FEDERATION
FRANCE GERMANY POLAND
PORTUGAL SPAIN
UKRAINE
KAZAKHSTAN
Aral Sea
MONGOLIA
CHINA
NORTH KOREA
SOUTH KOREA
JAPAN
Nakhodka 1997
Yuyo Maru No.10 1974
TAIWAN
PHILIPPINES

Haven 1991
Independenta 1979
TUNISIA
GREECE
TURKEY
ALGERIA
MAURITANIA
SENEGAL
MALI
GUINEA
LIBERIA
WEST AFRICA forest almost completely gone
NIGERIA
AFRICA
CAMEROON
C. A. R.
GABON
DEM. REP. CONGO
ANGOLA
NAMIBIA
SOUTH AFRICA

SYRIA
IRAQ
IRAN
AFGHAN
PAKISTAN
SAUDI ARABIA
EGYPT
LIBYA
CHAD
SUDAN
ETHIOPIA
SOMALIA
KENYA
TANZANIA
MOZAMBIQUE
MADAGASCAR
YEMEN
OMAN
Assimi 1983
INDIAN SUB-CONTINENT
complete deforestation
INDIA
BURMA
THAILAND
VIETNAM
SRI LANKA
nearly 50% of rainforest destroyed
SOUTH EAST ASIA
Tadotsu 1978
PENINSULAR MALAYSIA
MALAYSIA
NORTH WEST BORNEO
INDONESIA

PAPUA NEW GUINEA
Tuvalu 2007, flood risk
QUEENSLAND
AUSTRALIA
NEW ZEALAND

Indian Ocean

ABT Summer 1991
Castillo de Bellver 1983
Wafra 1971
Katina P 1992

2 Global warming

- more humid than before
- drier than before
- principal farming regions
- ● flooding through rise in sea level
- 1°c increase in surface temperature

Map 2 labels

sharp fall in grain crop yields
melting ice-caps lead to heavy pack ice
c 1°C
c 3–4°C
short wet winters, long dry summers
sharp fall in grain crop yields
more destructive hurricanes
rise in sea level
failure of anchovy fisheries
increase in farming
millions made homeless by flooding
poor rice crop
c 0.3°C–0.5°C
rise in sea level

It is likely that the island nation of Tuvalu (*left*) will be the first country to disappear as a result of climate change. Rising sea levels in Funafuti Atoll, Tuvalu, are already putting the population of 10,000 at risk. During the highest tides, sea water is forced up through the porous coral atoll, flooding many low-lying areas. The salt water poisons the thin soil and makes growing crops very difficult, leaving the Tuvaluans dependent on expensive imports. Weather patterns are also altering: increased storm activity is creating wave erosion with many parts of the island suffering land loss and trees are washed into the sea as the island is undercut.

Index

1 HISTORICAL PLACE NAMES

Geographical names vary with time and with language, and there is some difficulty in treating them consistently in an historical atlas, especially for individual maps within whose time span the same place has been known by different names. We have aimed at the simplest possible approach to the names on the maps, using the index to weld together the variations.

On the maps forms of names will be found in the following hierarchy of preference:

a English conventional names or spellings, in the widest sense, for all principal places and features, e.g., Moscow, Vienna, Munich (including those that today might be considered obsolete when these are appropriate to the context, e.g., Leghorn).

b Names that are contemporary in terms of the maps concerned. There are here three broad categories:

i names in the ancient world, where the forms used are classical, e.g., Latin or latinized Greek, but extending also to Persian, Sanskrit, etc.

ii names in the post-medieval modern world, which are given in the form (though not necessarily the spelling) current at the time of the map (e.g., St. Petersburg before 1914, not Leningrad).

iii modern names where the spelling generally follows that of The Times Atlas of the World, though in the interests of simplicity there has been a general omission of diacritics in spellings derived by transliteration from non-roman scripts, e.g., Sana rather than Şanʿāʾ.

2 THE INDEX

Where a place is referred to by two or more different names in the course of the atlas, there will be a corresponding number of main entries in the index. The variant names in each case are given in brackets at the beginning of the entry, their different forms and origins being distinguished by such words as now, later, formerly and others included in the list of abbreviations (right).

'Bizerta (anc. Hippo Zarytus)' means that the page references to that city on maps dealing with periods when it was known as Bizerta follow that entry, but the page references pertaining to it in ancient times will be found under the entry for Hippo Zarytus. Places are located generally by reference to the country in which they lie (exceptionally by reference to island groups or sea areas), this being narrowed down where necessary by location as E(ast), C(entral), etc. The reference will normally be to the modern state in which the place now falls unless (a) there is a conventional or historical name which conveniently avoids the inevitably anachronistic ring of some modern names, e.g., Anatolia rather than Turkey, Mesopotamia rather than Iraq, or (b) the modern state is little known or not delineated on the map concerned, e.g., many places on the Africa plates can only be located as W, E, Africa, etc.

Reference is generally to page number/map number (e.g. 118/1) unless the subject is dealt with over the plate as a whole, when the references have been given sub-headings where possible, e.g., Civil War 129/4. Battles are indicted by the symbol ✗.

Though page references are generally kept in numerical order, since this corresponds for the most part with chronological order, they have been rearranged occasionally where the chronological sequence would be obviously wrong, or in the interests of grouping appropriate references under a single sub-heading.

3 ABBREVIATIONS

a/c also called	**form.** former(ly)	**obs.** obsolete
AD Autonomous District	**Fr.** French	**OT** Old Testament
Alb. Albanian	**f/s** formerly spelled	**Pers.** Persian
anc. ancient	**Ger.** German	**Pol.** Polish
AR Autonomous Region	**Gr.** Greek	**Port.** Portuguese
Ar. Arabic	**Heb.** Hebrew	**Rom.** Romanian
a/s also spelled	**Hung.** Hungarian	**Russ.** Russian
ASSR Autonomous Soviet	**Indon.** Indonesian	**S** South(ern)
Socialist Republic	**Ir.** Irish	**s/c** sometimes called
Bibl. Biblical	**Is.** Island	**Som.** Somali
Bulg. Bulgarian	**It.** Italian	**Sp.** Spanish
C Century (when preceded	**Jap.** Japanese	**S.Cr.** Serbo-Croat
by 17, 18, etc.)	**Kor.** Korean	**SSR** Soviet Socialist
C Central	**Lat.** Latin	Republic
Cat. Catalan	**Latv.** Latvian	**Sw.** Swedish
Chin. Chinese	**Lith.** Lithuanian	**Turk.** Turkish
Cz. Czech	**Mal.** Malay	**Ukr.** Ukrainian
Dan. Danish	**med.** medieval	**US(A)** United States (of
Dut. Dutch	**mod.** modern	America)
E East(ern)	**Mong.** Mongolian	**var.** variant
Eng. English	**N** North(ern)	**W** West(ern)
Est. Estonian	**n/c** now called	**Wel.** Welsh
f/c formerly called	**Nor.** Norwegian	**WW1** World War 1
Finn. Finnish	**n/s** now spelled	**WW2** World War 2
	NT New Testament	

Aachen (*Fr.* Aix-la-Chapelle *anc.* Aquisgranum) W Germany Frankish royal residence 53/1; WW1 86/2

Abkhazia autonomous region of Georgia 170/3

Abasgia region of the Caucasus 49/1

Abyssinia (*now* Ethiopia) 111/1

Achaea (*a/s* Achaia) Roman province 37/1

Acragas (*Lat.* Agrigentum *mod.* Agrigento) Sicily Greek colony 32/1

Addis Ababa Ethiopia Italian penetration 111/1

Aden S Arabia early town 81/1; Ottoman Empire 108/1; taken by British 118/1; British base 154/1

Aden Protectorate (*successively renamed* Protectorate of South Arabia, Federation of South Arabia, People's Republic of South Yemen, People's Democratic Republic of Yemen; *now part of* United Yemen)

Admiralty Islands S Pacific Japanese attack 142/1

Adowa N Ethiopia ✗111/1

Adrianople (*anc.* Adrianopolis *mod.* Edirne) W Turkey Byzantine Empire 49/1,2; Ottoman centre 71/1; occupied by Greece 136/1

Aegospotami (*Turk.* Karaova Suyu) NW Turkey ✗33/2

Aegyptus (*mod.* Egypt) Roman province 37/1

Afars and Issas, French Territory of (*form.* French Somaliland *now* Republic of Djibouti)

Afghanistan invaded by USSR 149/1, 163/1; civil war 157/3; Islamic fundamentalism 157/3

Africa early man 12/1, 14/2; cave art 15/1; agricultural origins 17/1; early cultures 27/2; early empires 58/1; slave trade 59/2; early European voyages of discovery 79/1; European expansion and trade 80-81; 18C European trade 103/2; European penetration 111/1; colonial empires 119/2; foreign investment 1914 127/1; Japanese imports 152/2; anti-colonial resistance 154/1; modern political developments 161/1; population growth 172/2; armament imports 173/1; economic groupings 174/2; economy 174/2 environment 177/1,2

Africa (*mod.* Tunisia and Libya) conversion to Christianity 34/1, 44/1; Roman province 36/1; Byzantine province 48/1

Aga Buryat AD S Siberia in Russian Federation 169/2

Aigun NE China treaty port 95/2

Ain Jalut Palestine ✗50/2

Aix (*or* Aix-en-Provence *anc.* Aquae Sextiae) S France archbishopric 53/1; *parlement* 83/2

Aachen (*Fr.* Aix-la-Chapelle *anc.* Aquisgranum) W Germany Frankish royal residence 53/1; WW1 86/2

Ajaria autonomous district of Georgia 170/3

Ajnadain Palestine ✗51/1

Aksum early empire of E Africa 27/2

Åland Islands (*Finn.* Ahvenanmaa) SW Finland neutralized 136/1

Alaska state of USA purchase from Russia 114/1

Albania Black Death 67/1; Ottoman province 108/1; principality 125/2, 137/2; annexed by Italy 145/1; Cold War 165/1; free elections 169/1; Kosovo crisis 171/2; Kosovan refugees 171/2

Albania ancient country of Caucasus 37/1

Albany (*form.* Fort Orange) NE USA seized by English 86/2

Alemannia SW Germany part of Frankish Empire 53/1

Aleppo (*anc.* Beroea *a/c* Yamkhad *Fr.* Alep *Ar.* Halab) Syria Mitannian city 22/3; centre of European trade 103/2

Alessandria N Italy Lombard League 55/2

Aleutian Islands W Alaska to USA 114/1; attacked by Japanese 142/1; retaken by Americans 143/2

Alexandria (*Ar.* Al Iskandariyah) Egypt taken by Alexander 32/3; spread of Christianity 34/1; Roman Empire 37/1; Christian centre 45/1; Arab conquest 51/1; trade 59/2; centre of European trade 103/2

Algeria Ottoman province 70/2; French invasion 111/1; French colonization 118/1; under Vichy control 140/1; independence 154/1; Islamic fundamentalism 157/3; political development 161/1

Algiers (*Fr.* Alger *Sp.* Argel *Ar.* Al Jaza'ir *anc.* Icosium) N Algeria Ottoman rule 70/2; Habsburg Empire 93/1; Allied landing WW2 141/2

Allenstein (*Pol.* Olsztyn) W Poland acquired by Germany after plebiscite 136/1

Almanza Spain ✗83/3

Almohads Muslim dynasty and empire of North Africa 58/1

Almoravids Muslim dynasty of Morocco 58/1

Alpes Cottiae Roman province, France/Italy 36/1

Alpes Maritimae Roman province, France/Italy 36/1

Alpes Poeninae Roman province, France/Italy 36/1

Alsace (*anc.* Alsatia *Ger.* Elsass) in German Empire 55/2; acquired by French 83/2; Habsburg Empire 93/1

Alsace-Lorraine (*Ger.* Elsass-Lothringen) region of E France annexed by German Empire 116/2; ceded to France 136/1

Altay C Asia republic of Russian Federation 169/2

America, Central (a/c Mesoamerica) agricultural origins 16/1; early peoples 25/1; early civilizations 24/2; Aztec Empire 72/2; colonial expansion 87/1; 18C Atlantic economy 81/1; economy 174/1

America, North early man 14/2; early cultures 25/1; early voyages of discovery 78/1; colonial expansion 87/1; industrialization 145/1; Japanese imports 153/2; population growth 172/2; armament exports 173/2; economic groupings 174/2; environment 177/1,2. See also Canada, United States

America, South early man 14/2; agricultural origins 16/1; early peoples and civilizations 25/1; Inca Empire 73/3; early voyages of discovery 78/1; colonial expansion 87/1; independence 113/1; modern politics 113/1; foreign investment 1914 126/2; Japanese imports 153/2; population growth 172/2; armament imports 173/1; economy 174/1; economic groupings 174/2; environment 177/1,2

American Samoa S Pacific 155/1 (inset)

Amoy (n/s Xiamen) S China treaty port 95/2; Japanese influence 95/2; occupied by Japanese 123/2

Amphipolis N Greece ✕33/2

Anatolia early agriculture 20/1; incipient urbanization 18/1; Hittites 22/3; Black Death 67/1; Ottoman conquest 71/1. See also Asia Minor

Ancyra (mod. Ankara obs. Eng. Angora) W Anatolia Roman empire 35/1; Byzantine Empire 44/1

Andalusia autonomous region of S Spain 166/2

Angkor Cambodia Buddhist site 35/1

Angles tribe of NW Europe, migrations 40/1

Anglo-Egyptian Sudan condominium 70/2; Ottoman territory under British control 108/1

Angola SW Africa source of slaves 59/2; Portuguese colonization 110-11; independence 154/1; political development 161/1; Cuban military intervention 149/1

Angora (anc. Ancyra mod. Ankara) W Anatolia ✕60/2

Anguilla island of West Indies independence 155/1 (inset)

Anhwei (a/s Anhui) province of E China Manchu expansion 94/1; economy 151/2

Annam N Indo-China under T'ang control 47/1; expansion and early trade 89/2

Antigua island of West Indies colony 112/1; independence 155/1 (inset)

Antioch (Lat. Antiochia mod. Antakya) NW Syria Roman Empire 37/1; archbishopric 45/1, 2; Byzantine rule 49/1

Antung (now Dandong) Manchuria treaty port 95/2

Antwerp (Fr. Anvers Dut. Antwerpen) Belgium town of Spanish Neth-erlands 92/2; WW1 132/2

Aquileia (med. Aglar) N Italy Byzantine Empire 37/1

Aquincum (mod. Budapest) Hungary Roman Empire 37/1

Aquitaine (anc. Aquitania mod. Guyenne) region of SW France Black Death 67/1

Aquitania (mod. Aquitaine later Guyenne) Roman province of Gaul 36/1; Visigothic territory conquered by Franks 52/1

Arabia maritime trading 20/1; spread of Judaism 34/1; centre of Islam 51/1; 18C European trade 103/2

Arabia Petraea Roman province of N Arabia 37/1

Arabs territorial losses to Byzantine Empire 49/1; independence from Ottomans 108/1; emigration from Israel 156/1

Arachosia (a/c Harauvatish) Afghanistan ancient province of Mauryan Empire 29/3

Aragon (Sp. Aragón) region of E Spain rural uprisings 67/1; Habsburg Empire 93/1

Arakan district of SW Burma Islamic states 64/2; British control 89/2

Archangel (Russ. Arkhangelsk) N Russia founded 83/1; Allied occupation 135/1

Arcole N Italy ✕99/2

Ardennes forest Belgium/France WW1 132/2

Arelate (mod. Arles) S France Roman Empire 36/1, 37/2

Argentina independence from Spain 113/1; political developments 159/1; industrialization and economy 126/1, 159/2

Arginusae islands of the Aegean ✕33/2

Arles medieval kingdom of S France 55/2

Armagnac region of SW France annexed to France 82/1

Armenia (anc. Urartu) country of Caucasus Roman province 37/1; Muslim conquest 51/1; Ottoman Empire 108/1; independence after WW1 136/1; independence 1991 169/1; invasion of Azerbaijan 170/2

Arras (anc. Nemetocenna) N France WW1 132/2

Arretium (mod. Arezzo) C Italy Etruscan city 32/1

Artaxata Armenia Roman Empire 37/1

Artois region of NE France Burgundian possession 82/1; province of France 83/2

Arzawans early people of Anatolia 22/3

Ashur (mod. Sharqat) Mesopotamia Assyrian Empire 22/3

Asia early man 12/1, 14/2; cave art 15/1; agricultural origins 17/1; first farmers 18-19; rise of civilization 20-21; Chinese expansion 39/1; tribal movements 41/1; early voyages of discovery 79/1, 81/1; Russian expansion 84/2; colonial empires 118/1, 119/2; foreign investment 1914 126/1; anti-colonial resistance 155/1; population growth 172/2; armament exports 173/1; economy 174/1; economic groupings 174/2; environment 177/1,2

Asia (Byzantine name Asiana) Roman province of Anatolia 37/1

Asia Minor conversion to Christianity 34/1, 45/1; Ottoman control 71/1. See also Anatolia

Asoka's Empire India 29/3

Aspern/Essling Austria ✕99/2

Assyria Empire 22/3; Roman province 37/1

Astrakhan S Russia occupied by Mongols 60/2; Tartar khanate 85/1; Bolshevik seizure 135/1

Athens (Lat. Athenae mod. Gr. Athinai) Greece Greek parent state 33/1; war with Sparta 33/2; invaded by Huns 40/1; Byzantine Empire 79/1; WW2 141/2

Augusta Treverorum (mod. Trier Eng. Treves) W Germany Roman Empire 36/1

Augusta Vindelicorum (mod. Augsburg) S Germany Roman Empire 36/1

Augustodunum (mod. Autun) C France Roman Empire 36/1

Austerlitz (mod. Slavkov) Czechoslovakia ✕99/2

Australia (originally called New Holland) early man 14/1; cave art 15/1; before the Europeans 26/1; settlement and development 106/1; emergence of Commonwealth 119/1; WW2 143/2; Pacific trade 152/2; economy 174/1

Australasia the eastern Frankish Empire 53/1

Austria (Ger. Österreich) German settlement 55/2; Black Death 67/1; attacked by Ottomans 70/2; War of the Spanish Succession 83/3; Habsburg Empire 93/1; opposition to Napoleon 99/2; annexed by Germany 137/2; Allied occupation zones 146/1; EU 167/1

Austro-Hungarian Empire (a/c Austria-Hungary) Industrial Revolution 101/2; European alliances 124/1; WW1 133/1; dismantled 136/1

Avanti early kingdom of C India 29/3

Avars (Chin. Juan-juan) ancient people of Asia and Europe 40-41; kingdom destroyed 53/1

Avignon (anc. Avenio) S France Papal enclave 83/2

Azerbaijan (anc. Atropatene) country of the Caucasus Mongol Empire 60/1; Muslim conquest 51/1; Ottoman conquest 70/2; acquired by Russia 85/1; independence after WW1 136/1; independence 1991 169/1; invaded by Armenia 170/3

Azores (Port. Açores) islands of N Atlantic Portuguese colony 119/2

Aztec Empire Mexico 72/2

Babylon Mesopotamia Sumerian city 23/1; taken by Alexander 32/3

Bactria ancient country of SW Asia 29/3, 32/3

Badajoz SW Spain ✕98/2

Baden country of S Germany unification 116/2

Badr W Arabia ✕ 51/1

Baetica S Spain Roman province 36/1

Baffin Island N Canada discovery 78/1

Baghdad Mesopotamia Mongol attack 60/1; Mongol conquest 60/2; under Ottoman rule 70/2

Bahamas islands of N Caribbean discovery 78/1; British colony 118/2; independence 155/1 (inset)

Bahrain (f/s Bahrein Ar. Al Bahrayn) island of Persian Gulf independence 154/1

Bailén S Spain ✕98/1

Baku (n/s Baki) Azerbaijan conquered by Ottomans 70/2; British occupation 135/1

Balagansk s/c Siberia founded 84/1

Balearic Islands W Mediterranean Byzantine Empire 48/1; attacked by Saracens 54/1; to Spain 83/3

Balkans alliances 125/2; rise of nationalism 171/2

Balkh (anc. Bactra a/c Zariaspa) Afghanistan Mongol attack 61/1; conquest 51/1

Baluchistan region of NW India district of Mughal Empire 63/1; tribal agency 97/3

Bandjarmasin (n/s Banjarmasin) S Borneo trade centre 64/2

Bangkok (Thai. Krung Thep) S Thailand captured by Japanese 142/1

Bangladesh (form. East Pakistan or East Bengal) 163/1

Bantam (form. Banten) Java early trade 64/2

Baqubah N Iraq oilfield 157/2

Bar region of NE France/W Germany Burgundian possession 82/1

Barbados island of West Indies British colony 112/1; independence 155/1 (inset)

Barcelona (anc. Barcino) NE Spain urban revolt 67/1

Bashkortostan (form. Bashkiria) W Russia republic of Russian Federation 169/2

Basque Country (Sp. País Vasco) autonomous region of N Spain 1979 166/2

Basque Republic N Spain autonomy 136/1

Basra (Ar. Al Başrah) Mesopotamia ✕51/1; Ottoman conquest 70/2; centre of European trade 103/2

Bassano N Italy ✕99/2

Basutoland (now Lesotho) S Africa British protectorate 119/2

Batavia (form. Sunda Kalapa, since 1949 Jakarta f/s Djakarta) Java centre of European trade 103/2; occupied by Japanese 142/1

Batum (n/s Batumi) Caucasus British occupation 135/1

Bautzen E Germany ✕99/2

Bavaria (Ger. Bayern) part of Frankish Empire 53/2; Reformation 91/1; German Empire 116/2

Bechuanaland (now Botswana) country of S Africa British protectorate 119/2

Beijing (f/s Peking) N China economy 1979-92 151/2

Belarus (a/c Belorussia) end of Communism 169/1

Belgian Congo (form. Congo Free State later Zaire now Democratic Republic of Congo) colony 111/1, 119/2; independence 154/1

Belgica Roman province of NE France 36/1

Belgium (*form.* Spanish Netherlands *or* Southern Netherlands) colonial empire 119/2; WW1 132/2; acquisition of Eupen and Malmédy 136/1; economic and social development 1929-39, 138/1; WW2 140/1; EEC and NATO 165/1, 167/1

Belgrade (*anc.* Singidunum *S. Cr.* Beograd) C Yugoslavia Ottoman conquest 71/1; WW2 140/1

Belize (*form.* British Honduras) independence 155/1 (inset)

Belorussia (*n/c* Belarus, *f/c* White Russia) independence after WW1 61/1

Benevento (*anc.* Beneventum) C Italy dukedom under Byzantine Empire 49/1

Bengal country of E India district of Mughal Empire 63/1; under British rule 96-97

Benghazi (*anc.* Berenice *Ar.* Banghazi) Libya Italian occupation 111/1; WW2 141/2

Bensington S England ✕53/1

Berbers attack Roman Africa 40/1; people of NW Africa 50/2

Berenice (*mod.* Benghazi) Libya city of Roman Empire 37/1

Berezina river W Russia ✕99/2

Berlin E Germany Allied occupation zones 147/2; united Germany 169/2

Besançon (*anc.* Vesontio) E France archbishopric 52/1; fort 83/2

Beshbalik W Mongolia Mongol attack 61/1

Bessarabia region of Romania/Russia acquired by Russia 85/1; Ottoman province 108/1; regained by Russia 135/1; lost to Romania 136/1

Bigorre region of SW France independent fief 82/1

Bihać Bosnia-Herzegovina civil war 171/1

Bithynia ancient country of NW Anatolia 33/1; Byzantine Empire 79/1

Bithynia and Pontus Anatolia Roman province 37/1

Bizerta (*anc.* Hippo Zarytus *Fr.* Bizerte *Ar.* Banzart) Tunisia Habsburg Empire 937/1; WW2 141/2

Black Death 67/1

Blenheim (*Ger.* Blindheim) W Germany ✕(called Höchstädt by French and Germans) 83/3

Boğazköy see Hattushash

Bohemia (*Ger.* Böhmen) W part of mod. Czechoslovakia kingdom within Holy Roman Empire 55/2; expansion 66/2; Reformation 92/1; Habsburg Empire 93/2; Austro-Hungarian Empire 136/1

Bolgar (*a/c* Bulgar) C Russia Mongol city 60/1

Bolivia country of S America independence 113/1; 20C revolutions 159/1; economy 159/2

Bombay W India British rule 96/2; industry 97/3; centre of European trade 103/2

Bona (*mod.* Annaba *Fr.* Bône) N Algeria acquired by Habsburgs 93/1

Bonin Islands (*a/c* Ogasawara Islands) N Pacific annexed by Japan 142/1

Borneo (*Indon.* Kalimantan) island of East Indies trade 89/2; Dutch and British colonization 118/1, 119/2; occupied by Japanese 142/1; retaken by Allies 143/2

Bornhöved N Germany ✕55/2

Bornu Nigeria early state 58/2

Borobudur C Java Buddhist site 35/1

Borodino W Russia ✕99/2

Bosnia country of C Yugoslavia under Hungarian Kingdom 66/2; Black Death 67/1; vassal state of Ottoman Empire 71/1

Bosnia-Herzegovina (*S. Cr.* Bosna i Hercegovina) under Ottoman rule 71/1; part of Austria-Hungary 108/1; after WW1 136/1; independence and civil war 171/2

Bosporan Kingdom S Russia 37/1

Botswana (*form.* Bechuanaland) S Africa independence 154/1

Bougainville one of Solomon Islands, W Pacific recaptured from Japanese 143/2

Bourbonnais (*a/c* Bourbon) region of C France annexed to France 82/1

Brandenburg region of E Germany under Bohemian rule 66/2; Black Death 67/1; Reformation 91/1; part of Prussia 116/2

Brazil discovered 78/1; early trade 81/1; Portuguese colony 87/1; 18C Atlantic economy 102/1; independent empire 113/1; economy and political development 159/1,2

Breitenfeld E Germany ✕93/3

Brest (*a/c* Brest-Litovsk *Pol.* Brześć nad Bugiem) W Russia WW1 133/1

Breton March NW France 52/1

Brigantes Britain early tribe 36/1

Brihuega C Spain ✕83/3

Britain invasion by Germanic tribes 54/1. See also England, United Kingdom

Britannia Inferior Roman province of N England 36/1

Britannia Superior Roman province of S England 36/1

British Bechuanaland S Africa 105/1

British Cameroons (*now part of* Cameroon)

British Central Africa (*later* Nyasaland) protectorate 111/1

British Columbia province of W Canada joins Confederation 120/2

British East Africa (*now* Kenya) colony 111/1

British Empire 119/2

British Guiana (*now* Guyana) S America colony 113/1

British Honduras (*now* Belize) C America colony 112/1

British North Borneo (*now* Sabah)

British Somaliland (*now part of* Somalia) E Africa protectorate 119/2

Brittany (*Fr.* Bretagne) NW France on borders of Frankish Empire 52/1; Black Death 67/1; annexed to France 82/1

Brunswick (*Ger.* Braunschweig) N Germany urban revolt 67/1; German state 116/2

Bukhara city and province of C Asia Mongol attack 60/1; Muslim conquest 51/1; in Tamerlane's empire 51/2; khanate 114/2

Bulgaria conversion to Christianity 45/2; Black Death 67/1; under Ottoman rule 71/1; Industrial Revolution 101/2; independence 125/2; Balkan alliances 124/1; WW1 133/1; conflict with Greece 136/1; WW2 141/2; Warsaw Pact and Comecon 146/1; end of Communist rule 169/1. See also Rumelia

Buna SE New Guinea recaptured by Allies 143/2

Bunce Island Sierra Leone British settlement 59/2

Bunker Hill NE USA ✕104/1

Burdigala (*mod.* Bordeaux) SW France Roman Empire 36/1

Burgundy (*Fr.* Bourgogne) region of E France annexed to France 82/1; province of France 83/2

Burkina (Faso) see Upper Volta

Burma Mongol invasion 61/1; spread of Buddhism 35/1; early state 89/2; tributary state of Chinese Empire 94/1; under British rule 97/3; Japanese support for independence movements 123/2; Japanese occupation 142/1; retaken by Allies 143/2; independence 155/1; political development 163/1

Bursa (*anc.* Prusa *later* Brusa) W Anatolia centre of Ottoman state 71/1

Burundi (*form.* Urundi) country of C Africa native state 59/2; independence 154/1; political development 161/1. See also Ruanda-Urundi

Buryatia (*form.* Buryat-Mongol ASSR) E Russia 169/2

Byblos (*mod.* Jubail) Syria Levantine city 22/3; early trade 31/2; Phoenician city 33/1

Byzantine Empire (*a/c* East Roman Empire) 48-9; conflict with Seljuks 50/1

Byzantium (*Eng.* Constantinople *mod.* Istanbul) E Thrace Greek colony 33/1; Peloponnesian War 33/2

Caesaraugusta (*mod.* Zaragoza *Eng.* Saragossa) N Spain Roman Empire 36/1

Caesarea C Palestine Byzantine Empire 36/1

Caesarea (*mod.* Cherchell) N Algeria Roman Empire 36/1

Caesarea (*a/c* Caesarea Cappadociae *mod.* Kayseri) C Anatolia Roman Empire 37/1; Byzantine Empire 49/1

Cairo (*Fr.* Le Caire *Ar.* Al Qahirah and Al Fustat – Old Cairo) Egypt Muslim conquest 51/1; Ottoman Empire 70/2

Calcutta E India British settlement 96/2; industry 97/3; centre of European trade 103/2

Calicut (*a/c* Kozhikode) SW India trade 81/1; industry 97/3

California state of SW USA ceded by Mexico 112/1; Depression 138/2

Callatis Bulgaria Greek colony 33/1

Camarina Sicily Greek colony 32/1

Cambodia (*known formally as* Democratic Kampuchea *earlier* Khmer Republic) temple kingdoms 65/1; invaded by Siam and Vietnam 89/2; French protectorate 119/2; independence 155/1; political development 163/1

Camden SE USA ✕104/1

Cameroon (*f/s* Cameroons, Cameroun *Ger.* Kamerun) country of W Africa German colony 119/2; independence 154/1

Canada Confederation 118/1; development 120/2; NATO 165/1; economy 174/1

Canton (*Chin.* Guangzhou) S China Mongol base 61/1; Ming provincial capital 69/1; treaty port 89/2; centre of European trade 103/2; captured by Japanese 123/2; economy 151/2

Cape Bojador NW Africa ✕59/2

Cape Coast Ghana centre of European trade 102-3

Cape Colony S Africa British colony 111/1

Cape of Good Hope S Africa Dutch settlement 59/2; first European voyage 78/1

Cape Province S Africa established by Dutch East India Co. 59/2

Cape Town South Africa Dutch settlement 59/2; centre of European trade 103/2

Cape Verde Islands W Africa Portuguese sovereignty 119/2; independence 154/1

Caporetto N Italy WW1✕133/1

Cappadocia (*Pers.* Katpatuka) county of E Anatolia Roman province 37/1; Byzantine province 49/1

Carales (*mod.* Cagliari) Sardinia Roman Empire 36/1

Carchemish (*Turk.* Karkamiş) E Anatolia 22/3

Caribbean colonial expansion 87/1; US involvement 159/1

Carinthia (*Ger.* Kärnten) province of S Austria medieval German Empire 53/2

Carniola (*Ger.* Krain) region of Austria/ Yugoslavia medieval Germany 55/2; acquired by Habsburgs 66/2

Caroline Islands C Pacific German sovereignty 119/2; captured by US from Japanese 143/2

Carpi N Italy ✕83/3

Carthage (*Lat.* Carthago) Tunisia Phoenician colony 27/1; Byzantine reconquest 48/1; Muslim conquest 50/1

Cassano N Italy ✕83/3

Castiglione N Italy ✕99/2

Castile region of Spain Habsburg Empire 93/1

Catalonia (*Sp.* Cataluña *Cat.* Catalunya) region of NE Spain under French rule 99/2; autonomous 136/1, 166/2

Caucasus development 1988-2000 170/3

Cawnpore (*n/s* Kanpur) N India Indian Mutiny 96/2

Central African Federation (Northern Rhodesia, Southern Rhodesia, Nyasaland)

Lemberg (Pol. Lwów now Russ. Lvov) N Austria-Hungary E Germany WW2 141/2

Lemnos island of the Aegaen ceded to Greece 125/2

Leningrad (form. and again from 1991 St. Petersburg Russ. Sankt-Peterburg between 1914 and 1923 Petrograd) NW Russia WW2 140-41

Lepanto (mod. Gr. Navpaktos) C Greece ✗70/2

Leptis Magna (a/s Lepcis Magna mod. Lebda) N Libya Stone Age site 27/2; Phoenician city 32/1; Roman Empire 37/1

Lesbos (mod. Gr. Lesvos a/c Mitylene) island of the Aegean Delian League 33/2

Lesotho (form. Basutoland) S Africa independence 154/1

Lexington NE USA ✗104/1

Leyte Gulf C Philippines WW2 naval battle 143/2

Liaoning province of NE China economy 1979-92 151/2

Liberia country of W Africa independent state 111/1, 119/2

Libya Arab conquest 50/2; under the Almohads 50/2; under Ottoman Empire 70/2; Italian colony 110/2, 119/2; independence 154/1; Islamic fundamentalism 157/3; political development 161/1; US base 165/1

Liegnitz (Pol. Legnica) W Poland Reformation 91/1

Ligny Belgium ✗99/2

Lincoln (anc. Lindum) E England Danish Viking base 54/1

Lindisfarne (a/c Holy Island) N England Viking attack 54/1

Lindsey early kingdom of E England 53/1

Lindum (mod. Lincoln) E England Roman Empire 36/1

Lisbon (Port. Lisboa anc. Olisipo) Portugal Muslim conquest 50/1; colonial trade 80-81; ✗99/2

Lithuania country of the Baltic conversion to Christianity 45/1; early expansion 66/2; Black Death 67/1; acquired by Russia 85/1; Reformation 91/1; independence 136/1; loses Memel territory to Germany 136/1; Soviet Socialist Republic 140/1; deportations 1941 149/2; independence 169/1

Livonia region of NW Russia conquered by Russia 85/1; Reformation 91/1

Locarno Switzerland 1925 Conference 136/1

Lodi N Italy Lombard League 55/2; ✗99/2

Lombardy region of N Italy Habsburg Empire 93/1; unification of Italy 117/1

Lonato N Italy ✗99/2

Londinium (mod. London) S England Roman Empire 36/1

London (anc. Londinium) S England Vikings 54/1; urban unrest 67/1; Industrial Revolution 100/1; WW1 133/1

Lorraine (Ger. Lothringen) region of NE France part of medieval German Empire 55/2; Habsburg Empire 93/1; German Empire 116/2

Louisiana state of S USA French rule 87/1; purchased by USA 105/2; Spanish rule 104/1; population 121/3; Depression 138/2

Lo-yang (als Luoyang) N China early civilization 21/1

Luanda Angola Portuguese settlement 59/2; early trade 81/1; centre of European trade 103/2

Luang Prabang SE Asia early political centre 65/1

Lucknow N India Indian Mutiny 96/2; industry 97/3

Lungchow SW China treaty port 95/2

Lusatia (Ger. Lausitz) region of E Germany Habsburg Empire 93/1

Lutetia (mod. Paris) N France Roman Empire 36/1

Lutter W Germany ✗93/3

Lützen C Germany ✗93/3, 99/2

Luxembourg (Ger. Luxemburg) NATO 147/4; EU 167/1

Luzon island of N Philippines Spanish control 89/1; US landings 143/2

Luzzara N Italy ✗83/3

Lycia country of SW Anatolia 33/1; Roman Empire 37/1

Lydia country of W Anatolia Byzantine Empire 49/1

Macao (Port. Macau) S China early Portuguese trade 89/1; Portuguese settlement 95/2; centre of European trade 103/2; Portuguese colony 118-9

Macassar (Indon. Makasar) East Indies Dutch settlement 89/1

Macedonia SE Europe 33/1; Roman province 37/1; Byzantine Empire 49/1; divided between Serbia, Greece and Bulgaria 125/2; Greek-Bulgarian conflict 136/1; Kosovo crisis 171/2

Madagascar (form. Malagasy Republic) Austronesian settlement 27/2; settlement from Africa 59/1; French penetration 111/1; French colony 119/2; independence 154/1; political development 161/1

Madeira island of E Atlantic Portuguese territory 119/2, 154/1

Madras (now Tamil Nadu) state and city, S India under British rule 96/2; trade and industry 97/3

Madrid C Spain captured by French 98/2; Industrial Revolution 100/2

Magenta N Italy ✗117/1

Maginot Line E France defence system 140/1

Magna Graecia the Greek colonies of S Italy 32/1

Maine state of NE USA British settlement 86/2; population 121/1; Depression 138/2

Malacca (Mal. Melaka) district of S Malaya early sultanate 64/2; European discovery 79/1; early trade 81/1; captured by Dutch 89/2; under Portuguese rule 89/2; centre of European trade 103/2; British possession 118/1

Málaga (anc. Malaca) S Spain ✗83/3

Malawi (form. Nyasaland) country of C Africa independence 154/1; political development 161/1; economy 174/1

Malaya spread of Islam 64/2; British control 119/2; occupied by Japanese 142/1. See also Malaysia

Malaysia (state formed by amalgamation of Malaya, Sarawak and Sabah) independence 155/1

Maldives islands of N Indian Ocean protectorate 119/2; independence 154/1

Mali (form. French Sudan) country of West Africa independence 154/1; political development 161/1

Mali Empire early state of W Africa 58/1

Malindi Kenya Muslim colony 59/1; early Portuguese trade 59/2

Malmédy E Belgium ceded by Germany 136/1

Maloyaroslavets W Russia ✗99/1

Malplaquet N France ✗83/3

Malta island of C Mediterranean British colony 119/2; WW2 141/2; independence 154/1

Mamelukes (a/s Mamluk) 58/1

Manchouli N China treaty town 95/2

Manchukuo (name given to Manchuria as Japanese puppet state)

Manchuria (called 1932-45 Manchukuo) region of NE China Manchu homeland 95/1; occupied by Russia 95/2; Russian and Japanese spheres of influence 123/2; Japanese puppet state 130/1; reoccupied by Russia 143/2

Manchus people of NE China, under the Ming 69/1; homeland expansion 94/1

Mandalay C Burma trade 89/2; terminus of Burma Road 123/2; occupied by Japanese 142/1; retaken 143/2

Manhao SW China treaty town 95/2

Manila C Philippines early trade 89/2; Spanish settlement 89/2; Spanish trade 103/2; captured by Japanese 142/1

Manitoba province of C Canada joins Confederation 120/2

Manus Island W Pacific Allied base 143/2

Manzikert E Anatolia ✗49/1, 50/2

Marcomanni early tribe of C Europe 37/1

Marengo N Italy ✗99/2

Mari people of C Russia 57/1, 85/1

Marianas (form. Ladrones) islands of W Pacific German colony 119/2; US occupation 143/2

Marienwerder (Pol. Kwidzyn) N Poland 1920 plebiscite 136/1

Maritime Provinces (Russ. Primorskiy Kray) Russ. Far East acquired from China 95/2

Mariy El W Russia republic of Russian Federation 169/2

Marne river NE France ✗132/2

Marquesas Islands S Pacific Polynesian dispersal centre 27/1; French colony 155/1 (inset)

Marseilles (Fr. Marseille anc. Massilia) S France galley port 83/2

Marshall Islands C Pacific German colony 119/2; occupied by US 143/2

Martinique island of W Indies French settlement 87/1; French territory 154/1 (inset)

Maryland state of E USA colony 86/2, 104/1; Depression 138/2

Massachusetts state of NE USA British colony 104/1; population 121/1; Depression 138/2

Massachusetts Bay NE USA British colony 86/2

Massawa N Ethiopia Ottoman settlement 59/2; Italian attack 111/1

Matsu island SE China Nationalist outpost 165/1

Mauritania country of NW Africa independence from France 154/1; political development 161/1

Mauritius (Fr. Maurice) island Indian Ocean British colony 119/2

Maya people and civilization of C America 24/1

Mecca (Ar. Al Makkah) W Arabia birth of Islam 51/1; Ottoman Empire 70/2

Mecklenburg unification of Germany 116/2

Media (a/c Mada) ancient country of NW Persia campaigns of Alexander 32/3

Medina (Ar. Al Madinah) W Arabia centre of Islam 51/1; Ottoman Empire 70/2

Mediolanum (mod. Milano Eng. Milan) N Italy Roman Empire 37/1

Mediterranean Sea Greek colonization 32-33; Phoenicians 32-33; Saracen invasions 54/1

Melanesia region of W Pacific early settlement 26/1

Melilla (anc. Rusaddir) N Morocco Habsburg Empire 93/1; acquired by Spain 98/2

Melitene (mod. Malatya) E Anatolia Roman Empire 37/1

Memel Territory (Ger. Memelgebiet or Memelland) region of SW Lithuania annexed by Germany 136/1

Memphis Lower Egypt city of Ancient Egypt 25/2; campaigns of Alexander 32/3; Roman Empire 37/1; Byzantine Empire 49/1

Mengtze (Fr. Mong-tseu) SW China treaty port 95/2

Mercia early kingdom of C England 53/1

Mengtze early kingdom of NE AFrica 27/2

Merv (since 1937 Mary anc. Alexandria) Russ. C Asia spread of Christianity 35/1; Muslim conquest 51/2

Mesoamerica classic period 24-25

Mesopotamia (mod. Iraq) early agriculture 19/1; centre of urban civilization 20/1; spread of Mithraism 34/1; Roman Empire 37/1; Muslim conquest 51/1

Mexico Mayas 24/2; Aztec Empire 72/2; imperial trade 81/1; political development 112/1; independence 118/1; US intervention 159/1; Zapatista revolt 159/1

Middle East (*a/c* Near East) Cold War 165/1

Midway island of C Pacific US base 165/1 (inset)

Milan (*It.* Milano *anc.* Mediolanum) N Italy Lombard League 55/2

Miletus W Anatolia Mycenaean city 31/2; Greek colony 33/1; Byzantine Empire 49/1

Mindanao island of S Philippines Japanese occupation 142/1; retaken by US 143/2

Ming Empire China 69/1

Min-yüeh region of S China 39/1

Mixtec States S Mexico 24/2

Mitanni ancient kingdom of Middle East 22/3

Mocha (*Ar.* Al Mukhā) S Yemen centre of European trade 103/2

Modena (*anc.* Mutina) N Italy Lombard League 55/2; unification of Italy 117/1

Moesia region of Balkans district of Byzantine Empire 49/1

Moesiae late Roman province of Greece 37/2

Moesia Inferior Roman province of the Balkans 37/1

Moesia Superior Roman province of the Balkans 37/1

Mogadishu (*n/s* Muqdisho *It.* Mogadiscio) Somalia Muslim colony 59/1; Italian occupation 110/1

Mohács Hungary ✗70/2

Moldavia (*Turk.* Boğdan *Rom.* Moldova) region of Romania/Russia Hungarian 66/2; under Ottoman control 71/1; part of Romania 125/2; independence (Moldova) 169/1

Moluccas (*Indon.* Maluku *Dut.* Molukken *form.* Spice Islands) islands of E Indies Muslim expansion 64/2; early Portuguese trade 81/1; Dutch control 89/2

Mondovi NW Italy ✗99/2

Monemvasia (*It.* Malvasia) S Greece Byzantine Empire 49/2; Ottoman conquest 70/2

Mongol Empire 60-61

Mongolia (*form.* Outer Mongolia) nomadic pastoralism 21/1; Mongol Empire 60-61; under Han Empire 41/1; Chinese incursions under Ming 69/1; Chinese protectorate 94/1; autonomy 95/2; Russian sphere of influence 119/2; limit of Japanese expansion 123/2

Montenegro (*S. Cr.* Crna Gora) region of S Yugoslavia under Ottoman rule 108/1; 19C alliances 124/1; independent state 125/2; WW1 133/1; forms part of Yugoslavia 136/1; WW2 141/2; Kosovo crisis 171/2

Montenotte N Italy ✗99/2

Montereau N France ✗99/2

Montmirail N France ✗99/2

Montreux Switzerland 1936 conference 136/1

Montserrat island West Indies British colony 155/1 (inset)

Moravia (*Czech.* Morava *Ger.* Mähren) region of C Czechoslovakia medieval German Empire 55/2; acquired by Bohemia 66/2; Hussite influence 67/1; Reformation 91/1; Habsburg Empire 93/1; forms part of Czechoslovakia 136/1

Mordovia W Russia republic of the Russian Federation 169/2

Morea (*a/c* Peloponnese) region of S Greece Byzantine Empire 49/2; conquered by Ottomans 71/1

Morocco (*Fr.* Maroc *Sp.* Marruecos) under Almohads 50/2; Sharifian dynasties 59/2; Spanish conquest 110/2; French and Spanish protectorates 111/1, 119/2; independence 154/1; conflict with Algeria 161/1; US bases 165/1

Morotai island N Moluccas, E Indies captured by Allies 143/2

Moscow (*Russ.* Moskva) W Russia early bishopric 45/2; city of Vladimir-Suzdal 57/1; captured by Napoleon 99/2; Industrial Revolution 101/2; industrial development 134/2; Bolshevik seizure of power 135/1

Mossi early states of W Africa 59/2

Mostar Herzegovina, Yugoslavia civil war 171/2

Mosul (*Ar.* Al Mawsil) Iraq Muslim conquest 51/1; Ottoman Empire 70/2; oilfield 157/2

Mozambique (*form.* Portuguese East Africa *Port.* Moçambique) early trade 81/1; Portuguese settlement 81/1; centre of European trade 103/2; Portuguese colony 119/2; independence 154/1; political development 161/1

Mughal Empire India 63/1

Mukden Manchuria capital of Manchuria 94/1; treaty town 95/2; Japanese occupation 123/2

Muscat and Oman (*now* Oman) SE Arabia British protectorate 119/2

Muscovy early principality of W Russia 85/1

Muslims minority in Bosnia and Serbia 171/2

Mwenemutapa early state of SE Africa 59/2

Mysia ancient country of W Anatolia 33/1

Muslims minority in Bosnia and Serbia 171/2

Mysore (*now* Karnataka) region of S India district of Mughal Empire 59/1; native state 96-97

Mytilene (*a/s* Mitylene) island of Aegean ceded to Greece 125/2

Nagasaki W Japan early European trade 81/1; Dutch trade 103/2; bombed by US 143/2

Nagorno-Karabakh Caucasus 169/1, 170/3

Nakhichevan region of SW Azerbaijan 170/3

Namibia (*form.* South West Africa *earlier* German South West Africa) German colony 111/1, 119/2; independence from South Africa 154/1, 161/1

Nanking (*n/s* Nanjing) N China Ming provincial capital 65/1; treaty port 89/2; occupied by Japan 117/2; economy 143/2

Nan-yüeh early kingdom of SW China 39/1

Nan-chao tribal kingdom of SW China 47/1

Nanning S China treaty port 95/2

Nantes NW France Scandinavian settlement 54/1

Naples, Kingdom of Black Death 67/1; to Austria 83/3; Habsburg Empire 93/1; satellite of France 99/2; unification of Italy 117/1

Narbonensis (*a/c* Gallia Narbonensis) Roman province of S France 36/1

Narbonne (*anc.* Narbo) S France Muslim conquest 50/1

Nations, Battle of the (Leipzig) E Germany ✗99/2

Naucratis Egypt Greek colony 33/1

Nauru island W Pacific independence 155/1 (inset)

Navarre (*Sp.* Navarra) region of N Spain/SW France acquired by France 83/2; Habsburg Empire 93/1

Navas de Tolosa S Spain ✗50/2

Neapolis (*mod.* Napoli *Eng.* Naples) S Italy Greek colony 33/1; Roman Empire 37/1

Nepal tributary state of Chinese Empire 94/1; 95/2

Nerchinsk, Treaty of 94/1

Netherlands (*a/c* Holland *form.* Dutch Republic United Provinces) Habsburg Empire 93/1; Industrial Revolution 100/2; trade with Africa and Asia 103/2; colonial power 119/2; NATO 147/4; EU 167/1. See also Belgium, Flanders, Holland

Netherlands, Austrian (*mod.* Belgium) revolt against Emperor 98/1

Netherlands East Indies (*now* Indonesia) occupied by Japanese 142/1. See also East Indies, Borneo, Java, Moluccas, Sumatra

Netherlands, Spanish (*later* Holland *or* United Provinces; *and* Belgium) Reformation 91/1; Dutch revolt 92/2

Neustria the Frankish lands of N France 52/1

Nevis island W Indies British colony 112/1; self-government with St. Christopher 155/1 (inset)

New Amsterdam (*earlier* Fort Amsterdam *now* New York city) colonized by Dutch 86/2

New Britain island Papua New Guinea early Melanesian settlement 27/1; retaken from Japanese 143/2; to New Guinea 155/1 (inset)

New Brunswick province of E Canada joins Confederation 1120/2

New Caledonia islands S Pacific early Melanesian settlement 26/1; French colony 119/2, 155/1; US base 142/1

Newchwang Manchuria treaty port 95/2

New England NE USA British settlement 86/2

Newfoundland province of E Canada rediscovered 78/1; British colony 86/2; British settlement 87/1; joins Dominion 120/2

New France French possessions in Canada 86/2

New Granada (*mod.* Colombia) Spanish colony 87/1; vice-royalty in rebellion against Spain 99/1; 18C Atlantic economy 102/1

New Guinea (*now part of* Papua New Guinea) early settlement 27/1; Dutch/German/British control 119/2; attacked by Japanese 142/1; retaken by Allies 143/2. See also West Irian

New Hampshire state of NE USA colony 104/1; population 121/1, Depression 138/2

New Hebrides (*Fr.* Nouvelles Hébrides *now* Vanuatu) islands S Pacific early Melanesian settlement 27/1; British/French condominium 119/2; US base 142/1; independence 155/1 (inset)

New Ireland island Papua New Guinea early Melanesian settlement 26/1; occupied by Japanese 142/1

New Jersey state of E USA colony 86/2, 104/1; population 115/3; Depression 131/2

New Mexico state of SW USA ceded by Mexico 107/1; population 121/1; Depression 138/2

New Orleans S USA French/Spanish occupation 87/1

New Sarai S Russia Mongol city 60/1

New South Wales state of SE Australia settlement and development 106/1; statehood 118/1

New Spain (*mod.* Mexico, C America and Caribbean) Spanish vice-royalty 78/1; early voyages of discovery 87/1; rebellion against Spain 99/1

New Territories S China acquired by Britain 95/2

New York City (1653-64 called New Amsterdam *earlier* Fort Amsterdam) 86/2; industry 121/1; population 121/3; economic growth 145/1

New Zealand early Polynesian settlement 27/1; settlement and development 107/2,3

Nicaea (*mod.* Iznik) W Anatolia Mithraic site 34/1; Byzantine Empire 49/2

Nicaragua country of C America early exploration 78/1; independence 112/1; Sandinista revolution 159/1

Nicobar Islands Indian Ocean territory of British India 119/2

Nicomedia (*mod.* Izmit) W Anatolia Christian centre 45/1; Byzantine Empire 49/1

Nicopolis W Greece Byzantine Empire 49/2

Niger country of W Africa French colony 111/1; independence 154/1; economy 174/1

Nigeria country of W Africa British colony 111/1, 119/2; independence 154/1; political development 161/1; economy 174/1

Nihavand (*anc.* Laodicea in Media) W Persia ✗51/1

Nineveh Mesopotamia early farming village 19/1; Assyrian Empire 22/3; Mitannian city 23/1

Ningpo (*n/s* Ningbo) E China treaty port 95/2

Port Arthur (*Chin.* Lushun *Jap.* Ryojun) Manchuria ceded to Russia and Japan 95/2, 119/2

Port Arthur (*now* Thunder Bay) C Canada growth 120/2

Port Moresby SE New Guinea Allied base WW2 142/1

Port Said N Egypt Egyptian-Israeli war 156/1

Portugal (*anc.* Lusitania) Muslim conquest 50/1; 18C Atlantic economy 102/1; trade with Africa and Asia 80-81, 103/2; colonial empire 119/2; WW1 130/1; NATO 147/4; US bases 165/1; EU 167/1

Portuguese East Africa (*now* Mozambique) 119/2

Portuguese Guinea (*now* Guinea-Bissau) W Africa Portuguese colony 119/2; independence 154/1

Portuguese Timor E Indies annexed by Indonesia 155/1

Posen (*Pol.* Poznań) W Poland unification of Germany 116/2; ceded by Germany 136/1

Posidonia (*later* Paestum *mod.* Pesto) S Italy Greek colony 32/1

Potidaea N Greece Greek colony 33/1

Prague (*Cz.* Praha) Czechoslovakia bishopric 45/2; Communist coup 169/1

Pressburg (*Cz.* Bratislava) C Czechoslovakia ✗54/1

Preveza C Greece ✗70/2

Prince Edward Island (*form.* St Jean) island of E Canada joins Dominion 120/2

Priština SW Yugoslavia Kosovo crisis 171/2

Prizren SW Yugoslavia Kosovo crisis 171/2

Provence region of S France Frankish Empire 53/2; medieval German Empire 55/2; province of France 83/2

Providence NE USA founded 86/2

Prusa (*mod.* Bursa) W Anatolia Byzantine Empire 49/2

Prussia (*Ger.* Preussen) region of E Germany Reformation 91/1; unification of Germany 116/2

Puerto Rico W Indies conquered by US 112/1

Pugachev uprising Russia 98/1

Punjab region of NW India Muslim expansion 51/1; state of British India 96/2, 97/1

Pusan (*Jap.* Fusan) S Korea 1950-3 war 153/1

Pylos (*a/s* Pilos *It.* Navarino) SW Greece Mycenaean palace site 31/2

Pyongyang (*Jap.* Heijo) N Korea 1950-53 war 153/1

Qadisiyal (*a/s* Al Qadisiyya) S Mesopotamia ✗51/1

Qarabagh region of Caucasus conquered by Ottomans 70/2

Qatar sheikhdom of Persian Gulf Gulf War 147/3; independence 154/1; Islamic fundamentalism 157/3

Qinghai (*f/s* Tsinghai) province of N China economy 1979-92 151/2

Quadi Germanic tribe 37/1

Quebec city, E Canada capital of New France 86/2; population 120/2

Quebec province, E Canada joins Confederation 120/2; economic development 120/2

Quelimane Mozambique Portuguese settlement 111/1

Quemoy island SE China Nationalist outpost 165/1

Quentovic (*a/s* Quentowic) N France Vikings 54/1

Qui Nhon S Vietnam war 162/3

Rabaul Papua New Guinea Japanese base in WW2 142/1

Ragusa (*now* Dubrovnik) W Yugoslavia Byzantine Empire 49/1; Ottoman vassal republic 70/2; Reformation 91/1

Rai (*anc.* Rhagae *Bibl.* Rages *Gr.* Europus) N Persia Mongol attack 61/1; Muslim conquest 51/1

Rajputana NW India region of native states 96/2, 97/3

Ramillies Belgium ✗88/3

Ramla Palestine ✗51/1

Rangoon (*anc.* Dagon) Burma early trade centre 89/2; occupied by Japanese 142/1; retaken by British 143/2

Rann of Kutch region of W India boundary disputes with Pakistan 163/1

Rapallo N Italy 1922 Conference 136/1

Ratisbon (*Ger.* Regensburg) S Germany ✗99/2

Reformation 91/1

Regensburg (*anc.* Castra Regina *obs. Eng.* Ratisbon) S Germany bishopric 45/2; Frankish royal residence 53/2

Reggio (*a/c* Reggio di Calabria *anc.* Rhegium) S Italy Ottoman siege 70/2

Réunion (*anc.* Bourbon) island Indian Ocean French colony 119/2

Rhaetia (*mod.* Switzerland) Roman province 37/1

Rhegium (*mod.* Reggio di Calabria) N Italy Greek colony 32/1, 33/2

Rheims (*Fr.* Reims *anc.* Durocortorun *later* Remi) N France archbishopric 52/2; ✗99/2

Rhine, Confederation of the Napoleonic creation 99/2

Rhineland (*Ger.* Rheinland) region of W Germany remilitarized 136/1, 137/2

Rhode Island state of NE USA colony 86/2; population 121/1; Depression 138/2

Rhodes (*mod. Gr.* Rodhos *Lat.* Rhodus *It.* Rodi) *island* SE Aegean Greek state 33/1; ✗51/1; Ottoman conquest 70/2. See also Dodecanese

Rhodesia (*form.* Southern Rhodesia *now* Zimbabwe) British colony 119/2; independence (UDI) 154/1

Rhodus (*mod. Gr.* Rodhos *Eng.* Rhodes) island SE Aegean Roman Empire 37/1

Riga Latvia, NW USSR WW2 141/2

Rio Barbate Spain ✗50/1

Rio Muni (*a/c* Spanish Guinea *now* Equatorial Guinea) W Africa Spanish colony 111/1

Rivoli N Italy ✗99/2

Riyadh (*Ar.* Ar Riyāḍ) C Saudi Arabia 157/3

Rocroi NE France ✗93/3

Romagna region of N Italy unification of Italy 117/1

Roman Empire 36-7

Romania Industrial Revolution 100/2; independence 108/1; inter-war alliances 124/1; on break-up of Ottoman Empire 125/2; WW1 133/1; acquisition of Transylvania 136/1; Warsaw Pact and Comecon 146/1; end of Communist rule 169/1. See also Moldavia, Wallachia

Rome (*anc.* Roma *It.* Roma) C Italy arrival of Christianity 34/1, 44/1; Roman Empire 36-7; sacked by Visigoths 40/1; Magyar raid 54/1; papal patrimony 55/2; under French rule 99/2; annexed by Italy 117/1; WW2 141/2

Roncesvalles N Spain ✗52/2

Rouen (*anc.* Rotomagus) N France archbishopric 52/2; Scandinavian settlement 54/1; urban revolt 67/1; *parlement* 83/2

Royale, Ile (*now* Cape Breton Island) E Canada French settlement 86/2

Ruhr region of NW Germany Industrial Revolution 95/2; occupied by French 128/1

Rum early sultanate of E Anatolia 50/2

Rupert's Land region of N Canada Hudson's Bay Company 86/2; British possession 87/1

Russia (in Europe) conversion to Christianity 45/2; Kievan Russia 56/1; Viking trade 56/1; Black Death 67/1; expansion 85/1; opposition to Napoleon 99/2; Industrial Revolution 100/2; serfdom 115/2; 1905 Revolution 115/3; 19C European alliances 124/1; world trade 1860-1913 127/1; foreign investment 1914 127/1; WW1 133/1; development 1926-40 134/2; Revolution 135/1; Allied intervention 135/1. See also USSR and Russian Federation

Russia (in Asia) expansion 84/2; acquisition of Maritime Province from China 95/2; 19C spheres of influence 1192

Russian Federation free elections 169/1; constituent republics 169/2

Ruthenia region of SW Ukraine acquired by Poland-Lithuania 66/2; incorporated into Czechoslovakia 136/1 occupied by Hungary 137/2

Rwanda (*form.* Ruanda) early state of C Africa 59/2; independence 154/1; political development 161/2

Ryazan C Russia town of Murom-Ryazan 57/1; acquired by Muscovy 85/1

Ryukyu Islands (*f/c* Loochoo Islands) E China Sea acquired by Japan 95/1

Saar (*Ger.* Saarland *Fr.* Sarre) district of W Germany League of Nations mandate and plebiscite 136/1

Sabrata (*a/c* Abrotonum) Libya Roman Empire 37/1

Sadowa (*a/c* Königgrätz) Bohemia ✗116/2

Safavid Empire Persia 63/1

Sahara region of N Africa trade routes 59/1

Sahel region of W Africa early settlement 27/2

Saigon (*n/c* Ho Chi Minh) S Vietnam early trade centre 89/2; Japanese base WW2 142/1; war 162/3

St. Christopher and Nevis W Indies British colony 112/1; 155/1 (inset)

Saint-Domingue (*now* Haiti) French colony 87/1

St. Petersburg (*1914-24* Petrograd *1925-91* Leningrad) W Russia founded 85/1; acquired by Muscovy 85/1; Industrial Revolution 101/2

Saipan island Marianas. C Pacific Japanese base in WW2 142-43

Sakhalin (*Jap.* Karafuto) island Russ. Far East north acquired by Russia 114/1; south acquired by Japan 123/2; south reoccupied by Russia 143/2; claimed by Japan 163/1

Sakha-Yakutiya (*form.* Yakut ASSR) Siberia republic of Russian Federation 169/2

Salamanca N Spain ✗98/2

Salamantica (*a/c* Helmantica *mod.* Salamanca) N Spain Roman Empire 37/1

Salamis (*later* Constantia) Cyprus Roman Empire 37/1

Salisbury (*n/c* Harare) S Rhodesia 111/1

Salonae (*a/s* Salona) Albania Roman Empire 37/1; Byzantine Empire 49/1

Salonika (*a/s* Salonica *a/c* Thessalonica *Gr.* Thessaloniki *Turk.* Selanik) N Greece bishopric 45/1; occupied by Ottomans 71/1; WW1 133/1

Samara (*1935-91* Kuybyshev) C Russia founded 85/1; on railway to east 114/1; Bolshevik seizure 135/1

Samarkand (*anc.* Maracanda) C Asia Mongol attack 61/1; Muslim conquest 51/1; Tamerlane's Empire 60/2

Samoa islands S Pacific early settlement 27/1; German colony 119/2 . See also Western Samoa

Samogitia (*Lith.* Žemaitija) region of NW Russia occupied by Lithuania 66/2

San Agostín (*now* St. Augustine) SE USA Spanish fort 86/2

Sandinista revolt Nicaragua 159/1

San Francisco (*form.* San Francisco de Asís) W USA Spanish settlement 87/1; economic growth 145/1

Santa Cruz (*n/c* Ndeni) Solomon Islands WW2 ✗143/2

Santa Fé de Bogotá (*n/c* Bogotá) Colombia Spanish capital of New Granada 87/1

Santo Domingo (*now* Dominican Republic) W Indies Spanish colony 87/1

Santuao E China treaty port 95/2

Picture credits

10 AKG Photo London; 12 Ancient Art & Architecture collection; 15 The Art Archive; 16 Chris Scarre; 18 The Art Archive; 21 Michael Holford; 23 The Art Archive; 25 Werner Forman Archive, National Museum of Anthropology, Mexico; 26 John Miles/Panos pictures; 29 Scala; 30 Ancient Art & Architecture Collection; 32 Scala; 34 Chris Scarre; 36 Scala; 38 Ancient Art & Architecture; 41 Michael Holford; 42 Werner Forman Archive; 45 AKG Photo London; 47 Werner Forman Archive, Christian Deydier, London; 48 The Art Archive; 51 The Art Archive; 52 The Art Archive; 54 Werner Forman Archive, Viking Ship Museum, Bygdoy; 57 AKG Photo London; 59 Robert Aberman; 60 Robert Harding Picture Library; 63 The Bridgeman Art Library; 65 Robert Harding Picture Library; 66 Werner Forman Archive; 69 National Palace Museum, Taiwan; 71 Sonia Halliday Photographs; 73 The Art Archive; 75 The Art Archive; 76 The Bridgeman Art Library; 79 The Art Archive; 81 South American Pictures; 82 Robert Harding Picture Library; 85 Michael Holford; 86 Thomas Gilrease Institute of American History and Art, Tulsa; 88 Tokyo National Museum; 90 AKG Photo London; 92 Beheer Collection, Gemeente Musea, Delft; 95 The Art Archive; 96 Popperfoto; 99 The Art Archive; 100 Science and Society Picture Library; 103 National Maritime Museum, Greenwich; 104 Corbis-Bettmann; 107 The Art Archive; 108 AKG Photo London; 110 The Art Archive; 112 The Art Archive; 115 Novosti (London); 116 Mary Evans Picture Library; 119 The Art Archive, Victoria and Albert Museum, Eileen Tweedy; 120 Corbis; 122 The Art Archive; 125 Jane's Information Group; 127 The Art Archive; 128 The Art Archive; 130 The Art Archive; 133 The Art Archive; 134 David King Collection; 136 Popperfoto; 139 Ullstein Bilderdienst; 142 The Art Archive; 144 Corbis; 147 Corbis; 148 Sygma; 150 Sygma; 152 Associated Press; 155 Hulton Getty; 156 Sygma; 158 Sygma; 160 Sygma; 162 Sygma; 164 Magnum; 165 Popperfoto; 168 Sygma; 171 AFP/Getty images; 173 Frank Spooner; 175 EWI; 176 Ashley Cooper/Corbis